Navy SEALs
Bug in Survival Guide

Miles Ruel

Table of contents

GET YOUR 3 BONUSES!

☐ SCAN HERE TO DOWNLOAD IT

Introduction

Why Bugging In Matters: The Navy SEALs Approach

In a world where uncertainty is the only certainty, being prepared is not just a choice—it's a necessity. As natural disasters, civil unrest, and global crises become more frequent and unpredictable, the ability to protect and sustain your home during an emergency is crucial. This guide is inspired by the tactics and strategies employed by Navy SEALs, the most elite special operations force in the world, known for their ability to adapt, survive, and thrive in the most challenging environments.

The idea of staying put during an emergency may seem counterintuitive at first. In many survival scenarios, the instinctive response is to evacuate—to leave the danger zone as quickly as possible. However, there are numerous situations where remaining in your home is not only safer but also more practical. Whether it's due to impassable roads, widespread chaos, or the inability to reach a safe destination, staying put could be your best, and sometimes only, option.

The Navy SEALs approach to this type of preparedness is rooted in the principles of preparation, fortification, and self-reliance. For a Navy SEAL, the ability to endure and overcome any obstacle is a matter of life and death. These same principles can be applied to ensure that your home becomes a fortress of safety, capable of withstanding any crisis.

In this guide, you will learn how to prepare your home for various emergencies, from natural disasters to long-term societal disruptions. The techniques and strategies presented here are drawn from the rigorous training and experience of Navy SEALs, adapted for civilian use. By the end of this book, you will be equipped with the knowledge and tools necessary to protect your loved ones and maintain your household's stability, no matter what challenges arise.

Overview of the Guide: What You Will Learn

This guide is structured to provide you with a comprehensive approach to staying put during emergencies, covering every critical aspect of survival and home security. Here's what you can expect to learn:

Mental and Physical Preparedness: We'll start by building the mindset and physical resilience necessary to handle any crisis. Just as Navy SEALs train to be mentally and physically prepared for the worst, you too will learn how to develop the toughness required to endure extended periods of uncertainty and stress.

Home Security and Fortification: The core of staying put is ensuring your home is a safe and secure place to hunker down. This section will guide you through assessing your home's vulnerabilities and implementing defensive measures to turn it into an impenetrable fortress.

Long-Term Food and Water Storage: Essential to surviving any prolonged crisis is having a reliable supply of food and water. You'll learn how to stockpile, store, and manage these resources to ensure you and your family remain nourished and hydrated throughout any emergency.

Off-Grid Energy Solutions: When the grid goes down, your home needs to stay powered. We'll explore various off-grid energy solutions, including solar power, generators, and energy conservation techniques, so you're never left in the dark.

Medical Preparedness: In an emergency, medical help may not be immediately available. This section covers how to build a comprehensive home pharmacy, manage medical conditions, and provide first aid during a crisis.

Crisis Communication and Networking: Staying informed and connected is crucial during an emergency. You'll learn about setting up reliable communication systems and establishing a network with neighbors and other trusted individuals.

Essential Survival Skills: Beyond just stockpiling resources, you'll need practical skills to survive. This section covers everything from self-defense tactics to fire-starting and navigation, ensuring you're prepared for any situation.

Financial and Legal Preparedness: Crises can disrupt financial systems and legal structures. We'll discuss how to safeguard your assets, plan for economic instability, and navigate the legal challenges that may arise during a prolonged emergency.

Advanced Fortification and Survival Projects: For those looking to take their preparedness to the next level, this section includes DIY projects for fortifying your home and creating concealed safe spaces that offer additional protection.

By the end of this guide, you will have a well-rounded understanding of how to effectively stay put, transforming your home into a sanctuary capable of withstanding even the most severe crises. Whether you are new to this concept or a seasoned prepper looking to refine your strategies, this book offers valuable insights and practical advice to enhance your preparedness.

Your journey to ultimate safety and resilience begins here.

Chapter 1: Understanding Bugging In

The Concept of Bugging In

Definition and Origins of Bugging In

The concept of staying put during a crisis is rooted in the fundamental human instinct for survival, a response to the ever-present threats posed by the environment and society. At its core, this strategy involves remaining in your home or a pre-established safe location during a crisis, rather than evacuating to an external shelter or unknown location. Unlike the more well-known "bugging out," which involves leaving your home to seek safety elsewhere, this approach takes advantage of the familiar, fortified space you've prepared in advance.

Historically, the practice of staying put can be traced back through countless civilizations and individuals who faced situations where leaving was not a viable option. In medieval times, for example, fortified castles and homes served as the primary defense against invading forces. People gathered within the sturdy walls, relying on stockpiled food, water, and other essential supplies to survive prolonged sieges. The strategy was simple: if your home could withstand external threats, it was often safer to stay where you were than to venture into unknown, potentially more dangerous territory.

In modern times, this idea has evolved significantly, especially as society has become more urbanized and interconnected. The 20th century, marked by events such as the Great Depression, World Wars, and the Cold War, saw the development of civil defense strategies encouraging people to shelter in place during air raids or nuclear threats. Bomb shelters and bunkers became symbols of security, representing safe locations designed to protect families from external dangers.

The psychological aspect of staying in your home during a crisis cannot be overstated. The decision to remain in a familiar space taps into the deep-seated need for control and comfort. Your home is more than just a physical structure; it's a place where you feel secure, where you know every corner, and where you've likely invested time preparing for emergencies. This familiarity can play a crucial role in maintaining morale and stability during stressful situations.

In recent years, the concept of staying put has gained renewed attention, particularly with the increase in natural disasters, civil unrest, and global pandemics. The COVID-19 pandemic, in particular, highlighted the necessity and effectiveness of sheltering in place, as governments around the world issued lockdown orders to curb the spread of the virus. This event served as a stark reminder that, in some cases, leaving your home is not only unnecessary but also ill-advised.

This approach offers several strategic advantages. First and foremost, it allows you to take full advantage of the resources you've meticulously prepared. From stockpiled food and water to medical supplies and defensive tools, your home becomes a well-equipped fortress, ready to sustain you and your loved ones for an extended period. By staying in place, you avoid the potential dangers of traveling during a crisis—such as roadblocks, traffic congestion, or exposure to hostile elements.

It's important to recognize that staying put is not a one-size-fits-all solution. The decision to remain in your home should be based on a thorough assessment of your specific situation, including the nature of the threat, the security of your location, and the availability of resources. While this strategy can be a powerful survival tool, it requires careful planning, preparation, and a deep understanding of the potential risks involved.

As we delve deeper into this guide, you will learn how to effectively implement this approach, transforming your home into a secure, self-sufficient haven capable of withstanding various crises. Whether you're facing a natural disaster, a pandemic, or civil unrest, the knowledge and strategies presented in this book will help you make informed decisions, ensuring the safety and well-being of your family.

By understanding the roots of this strategy and its relevance in today's world, you are already taking the first step toward becoming more prepared and resilient. In the following chapters, we will build upon this foundation, equipping you with the tools and techniques necessary to survive and thrive, no matter what challenges come your way.

The Psychology Behind Staying Put

The decision to stay in place during a crisis represents a significant psychological shift. Many people instinctively want to flee from danger, seeking safety by distancing themselves from perceived threats. However, staying put requires a different mindset—one that finds security within familiar surroundings. Understanding this shift is crucial, as it involves not only preparing your home but also preparing your mind for the challenges of confinement and isolation.

Historically, survival has often been linked to moving away from threats. Yet, in many modern crises, movement can introduce new dangers. Roads may be blocked, supplies may run out, and the act of fleeing can expose you to greater risks. A mental shift from flight to fortification allows you to view your home as a primary line of defense.

This change also involves redefining your sense of control. Evacuating requires reliance on unpredictable variables—roads, weather, and safe destinations—while staying in your home grants you greater control over resources and security. Your home becomes a managed environment where you can create stability.

Psychologically, staying put can be taxing due to isolation and confinement. Long-term stays in a single space can lead to restlessness and claustrophobia. Combatting these challenges requires setting up routines, engaging in physical and mental activities, and creating a space conducive to long-term habitation. Managing stress and anxiety through meditation, exercise, and hobbies is essential, as crises naturally amplify feelings of uncertainty.

Open communication and support within your household are key to maintaining morale, especially for children or those unaccustomed to isolation. Technology offers ways to stay connected, reducing feelings of isolation even when physical movement is restricted. By mentally preparing for these challenges, you increase both your resilience and your chances of success during a crisis.

When and Why to Choose Staying Put

Deciding whether to remain in your home or evacuate is one of the most critical choices during a crisis. While fleeing may seem like the safest option, it's not always the best decision. A thorough assessment of your situation is essential to determine the right course of action.

The nature of the threat is a key factor. For instance, in natural disasters like hurricanes, evacuation might be necessary if you live in a flood-prone area. But during pandemics or civil unrest, staying in your home may be safer. Your home's security, level of preparedness, and available resources all play a role. A fortified home with adequate supplies can serve as a refuge, while homes in vulnerable areas might require evacuation.

Consider the viability of bugging out—do you have a safe destination, and is the route accessible? Traveling may expose you to more risks than staying put. Timing is also crucial—waiting too long to leave may increase danger, but evacuating too early could deplete resources unnecessarily. Monitoring the situation and being ready to adapt is key to making the right choice.

In many cases, staying in place is preferable, especially when external threats can be mitigated by your home's security. This decision requires careful planning and a realistic understanding of your situation. It's not just about surviving but doing so in a way that minimizes risk and stress, ensuring you and your loved ones can endure the crisis safely.

Threat Analysis and Risk Assessment

In the realm of crisis preparedness, one of the most crucial steps you can take is conducting a thorough threat analysis and risk assessment. This process allows you to understand the specific dangers you might face and helps you formulate a strategy that maximizes your safety and the safety of those around you. By evaluating different types of threats and assessing their potential impact on your situation, you can make informed decisions about whether to remain in place or evacuate, and how to prepare your home and resources accordingly.

Understanding Different Types of Threats

The first step in threat analysis is recognizing the various kinds of crises that could prompt you to stay put. These threats can be broadly categorized into natural disasters, civil unrest, and pandemics, among others. Each of these threats presents unique challenges and requires different preparations.

Natural Disasters: These include events such as hurricanes, earthquakes, floods, wildfires, and tornadoes. Natural disasters can strike with little warning, and their impact can be immediate and devastating. The threat from natural disasters often includes the destruction of infrastructure, loss of utilities, and the need for immediate emergency response. Depending on your geographical location, some natural disasters may be more likely than others. For example, coastal areas are more prone to hurricanes, while regions along fault lines may be at greater risk for earthquakes. Understanding the specific natural threats in your area is essential for determining whether your home can withstand such events and whether remaining in place is a feasible option.

Civil Unrest: This type of threat can arise from political instability, economic collapse, or social tensions that escalate into widespread violence. Civil unrest can result in riots, looting, and clashes between groups, potentially making urban areas particularly dangerous. In such scenarios, the safety of remaining in your home largely depends on your ability to secure it and maintain a low profile. If your home is in a volatile neighborhood or close to areas where protests or riots are likely to occur, you must weigh the risks of staying put versus the dangers of trying to evacuate through potentially hostile environments.

Pandemics: The COVID-19 pandemic starkly reminded the world of the far-reaching effects a global health crisis can have. Pandemics disrupt daily life, overwhelm healthcare systems, and create widespread fear and uncertainty. The primary threat during a pandemic is exposure to the disease itself, which makes staying at home a particularly attractive option to minimize contact with others. The prolonged nature of pandemics requires sustained access to food, medical supplies, and other essentials, highlighting the importance of long-term planning and resource management.

Each of these threats requires a different approach, and understanding the nuances of each is crucial for effective preparation. Identifying potential threats is only the beginning. The next step is to conduct a comprehensive risk assessment to determine the best course of action for your specific situation.

Conducting a Risk Assessment

Risk assessment is the process of evaluating how likely each identified threat is to occur and the severity of its potential impact. This assessment helps you prioritize your preparations and decide whether bugging in is the most viable strategy.

To conduct an effective risk assessment, start by gathering information about the specific threats relevant to your area. This can include reviewing historical data, such as past occurrences of natural disasters, crime statistics, and public health records. Understanding patterns can help you anticipate future risks. For example, if your region experiences hurricanes frequently, it would be wise to prioritize preparations that fortify your home against high winds and flooding.

Next, evaluate the potential impact of each threat on your home and your ability to sustain your family. Consider factors such as the structural integrity of your home, the availability of supplies, and the reliability of local infrastructure. For instance, if you live in an earthquake-prone area, you'll want to assess whether your home is built to withstand seismic activity. If not, you might need to make structural improvements or identify safe areas within your home to shelter during a quake.

Another crucial element of risk assessment is considering your personal and family situation. This includes the health and mobility of household members, the presence of pets, and any special needs that might complicate evacuation or long-term confinement. For example, a household with elderly members or young children may face greater challenges during a prolonged bug-in scenario, necessitating additional preparations or alternative plans.

Once you've identified the most significant threats and assessed their potential impact, it's important to develop a plan that outlines your response to each scenario. This plan should include clear guidelines on when to bug in and under what circumstances bugging out might become necessary. Having predetermined criteria can help reduce uncertainty and anxiety during a crisis, allowing you to act decisively when the time comes.

Moreover, your risk assessment should be an ongoing process. Threats can evolve, and new information can emerge, altering the risk landscape. Regularly updating your assessment ensures that your preparations remain relevant and that you're ready to adapt to changing circumstances. This flexibility is key to successful crisis management, as it allows you to pivot quickly if conditions worsen or if a new threat emerges.

Understanding the types of threats you might face and conducting a thorough risk assessment are foundational steps in your bug-in strategy. By systematically evaluating the likelihood and impact of potential crises, you can make informed decisions that enhance your preparedness and increase your chances of staying safe. As you continue to refine your plans, keep in mind that preparation is not just about stockpiling supplies; it's about developing a deep understanding of the risks you face and being ready to respond effectively to whatever comes your way.

Preparing Your Home for Bugging In

Initial Home Assessment

When it comes to bugging in, your home is your fortress. It is the place where you will weather the storm, no matter what form that storm takes. Before you can confidently rely on your home as a safe haven, it's crucial to conduct an initial assessment to evaluate its readiness. This process involves scrutinizing every aspect of your home to identify both its strengths and vulnerabilities, ensuring that it is truly prepared to protect you and your loved ones during a crisis.

Evaluating Your Home's Current Readiness

The first step in your home assessment is to take a comprehensive look at its current state. This isn't just about a superficial inspection—it's about understanding how well your home can serve as a secure base during an emergency. Start by considering the basic infrastructure: the age and condition of your home, the materials used in its construction, and its overall design.

Older homes, while often built with sturdy materials, might have outdated systems that could fail under stress. For example, older electrical wiring, plumbing, and heating systems may not withstand the demands of a prolonged crisis, especially if these systems haven't been maintained or upgraded recently. Conversely, newer homes might have modern conveniences but could lack the solid construction techniques used in the past, particularly in regions where builders prioritize cost over durability.

Next, examine the essential systems that keep your home functional. This includes heating, cooling, water supply, and electricity. Consider how these systems would hold up if the grid went down or if they were subjected to severe weather conditions. Do you have alternative methods for heating and cooling your home? Is your water supply reliable, and do you have means of purification if the municipal system becomes contaminated? Evaluating these aspects will give you a clear picture of what areas need improvement.

Consider the layout of your home as well. Homes with multiple stories offer the advantage of increased security, as higher floors are less accessible to potential intruders. They can also pose challenges in terms of mobility, especially if you have family members who are elderly or have disabilities. Homes with open floor plans might lack natural choke points that could be used to defend against intrusions, while those with more segmented layouts might provide better opportunities to create secure zones.

Identifying Vulnerabilities and Strengths

Once you've evaluated the general condition of your home, it's time to identify specific vulnerabilities and strengths. Vulnerabilities are any weaknesses that could be exploited by external threats, whether natural or human-made. Strengths are the features of your home that enhance its ability to protect you during a crisis.

Start by focusing on entry points. Doors, windows, and other openings are the most obvious vulnerabilities in any home. Assess the condition of your doors and windows—are they sturdy and secure, or could they be easily breached? Consider the type of locks you have and whether they offer enough resistance against forced entry. Reinforcing doors with deadbolts and installing security bars on windows can significantly enhance your home's security.

Another potential vulnerability is your home's visibility from the street. Homes that are easily seen from the road or that have large windows facing public areas can be more tempting targets for looters during times of civil unrest. If your home is highly visible, consider ways to reduce its exposure, such as installing privacy fencing, using window coverings, or strategically placing landscaping elements like bushes or trees.

On the other hand, your home might have inherent strengths that can be leveraged during a crisis. For example, if your home is constructed with brick or stone, it naturally offers more protection than a home built with wood or vinyl siding. Similarly, homes with basements provide an excellent option for secure, below-ground shelter, which can be particularly useful in tornado-prone areas or during severe storms.

The roof is another critical area to assess. A well-maintained roof can protect your home from the elements, while a damaged or poorly constructed roof could lead to leaks, structural damage, and increased vulnerability during extreme weather events. Ensure that your roof is in good condition, with no loose shingles, leaks, or areas of weakness that could be exploited by heavy rain, wind, or even determined intruders.

It's also important to evaluate your home's surroundings. The immediate environment around your home can either be an asset or a liability. For instance, large trees near your house could pose a risk during storms, potentially falling and causing significant damage. The same trees can also provide cover and make it more difficult for anyone to observe your home from a distance. Similarly, if your property includes a large yard or land, it could be used for growing food or as a buffer zone to keep threats at a distance, but it also requires additional effort to secure.

After identifying these vulnerabilities and strengths, the next step is to prioritize the areas that need improvement. Focus first on addressing the most critical vulnerabilities—those that pose the greatest immediate risk. This might involve reinforcing entry points, upgrading your home's infrastructure, or installing security systems. At the same time, look for ways to enhance the strengths of your home, making the most of what you already have.

Conducting an initial home assessment is a vital step in your bug-in preparedness plan. By thoroughly evaluating your home's readiness and identifying both its weaknesses and strengths, you can take proactive measures to fortify your living space against the challenges of a crisis. This assessment not only helps ensure your physical safety but also provides peace of mind, knowing that you have done everything possible to make your home a true sanctuary in uncertain times.

Creating a Bug-In Plan

Creating a comprehensive bug-in plan is an essential step in ensuring that you and your family are prepared for any crisis that requires you to stay at home. A well-crafted plan not only provides a clear roadmap for action during an emergency but also helps to alleviate the uncertainty and stress that can accompany such situations. This chapter will guide you through the steps needed to develop a bug-in plan tailored to your specific needs, and emphasize the importance of involving your family in the process to create a unified, effective strategy.

Steps to Develop a Comprehensive Bug-In Plan

The foundation of a successful bug-in plan is a thorough understanding of your specific needs and circumstances. Every household is different, and your plan should reflect the unique challenges and resources that you have at your disposal.

Assess Your Specific Risks: Begin by identifying the potential threats you are most likely to face, based on your location and personal circumstances. These could include natural disasters, civil unrest, pandemics, or other emergencies. Understanding the specific risks allows you to tailor your plan to address the most likely scenarios effectively.

Evaluate Resources and Capabilities: Next, take stock of your home's resources and your family's capabilities. This includes not only physical supplies like food, water, and medical necessities but also skills and knowledge that could be crucial during an emergency. For instance, do you have someone in the household trained in first aid? Can you purify water or generate power off-grid if needed? Identifying these assets will help you to build a plan that maximizes your strengths.

Define Clear Objectives: A successful bug-in plan should have clear, achievable objectives. These might include maintaining a stable supply of food and water, securing your home against intruders, or ensuring reliable communication with the outside world. By setting specific goals, you can focus your efforts and measure your progress as you prepare.

Develop a Supply and Inventory System: One of the cornerstones of a bug-in plan is a well-organized inventory of essential supplies. This should include a detailed list of all necessary items—food, water, medications, fuel, and other essentials—along with their quantities and expiration dates. Establish a system for regularly checking and rotating your supplies to ensure nothing goes bad and that everything is readily accessible when needed.

Plan for Power and Communication: In a prolonged crisis, maintaining power and communication will be critical. Consider alternative power sources such as generators, solar panels, or battery systems, and ensure you have reliable means of communication, such as two-way radios, that do not rely on cellular networks. These preparations will help you stay informed and connected, even if the grid goes down.

Establish Security Measures: Your plan should include steps to secure your home from potential threats, both internal and external. This might involve reinforcing doors and windows, setting up surveillance systems, or creating safe zones within your home where your family can retreat in case of an intrusion. Security is not just about physical barriers—it's also about having a strategy in place for responding to different types of threats.

Create a Flexible Timeline: Emergencies are unpredictable, and your plan should be flexible enough to adapt to changing circumstances. Develop a timeline that outlines what actions need to be taken immediately, within the first few hours or days of a crisis, and over the longer term. Having a clear timeline helps ensure that critical tasks are completed promptly, reducing the risk of oversight during a stressful situation.

Involving Family Members and Creating a Unified Strategy

A bug-in plan is only as strong as the commitment and coordination of the people it's designed to protect. Involving your family in the planning process is not just beneficial—it's essential. When everyone understands the plan and their roles within it, the entire household becomes a cohesive unit capable of responding effectively to any crisis.

Open Communication: Start by having an open conversation with your family about the importance of preparedness and the need for a bug-in plan. Discuss the potential risks and why it's important to have a strategy in place. This dialogue should be ongoing, allowing family members to voice concerns, ask questions, and contribute ideas.

Assign Roles and Responsibilities: Each member of the household should have specific roles and responsibilities within the plan. For example, one person might be responsible for managing food and water supplies, while another handles communication or security. By assigning clear roles, you ensure that everyone knows what is expected of them and can act swiftly when needed.

Practice and Drills: To ensure that your plan works effectively under pressure, conduct regular practice drills with your family. These drills should simulate different emergency scenarios, allowing everyone to rehearse their roles and make adjustments as necessary. Practicing the plan helps to build confidence and ensures that everyone can execute their tasks even in stressful situations.

Educate and Train: Knowledge is power, and ensuring that your family is educated about emergency preparedness is key. This might involve teaching basic first aid, showing how to operate emergency equipment, or explaining the use of alternative communication devices. The more informed and trained each family member is, the better prepared they will be to handle unexpected challenges.

Regularly Review and Update the Plan: A bug-in plan is not a one-time effort. It should be reviewed and updated regularly to reflect changes in your household, new threats, or advancements in technology. Regular check-ins keep the plan fresh in everyone's mind and allow you to make necessary adjustments before a crisis occurs.

Creating a bug-in plan is about more than just stockpiling supplies—it's about developing a comprehensive strategy that addresses the unique needs of your household. By taking the time to carefully assess your situation, define clear objectives, and involve your family in the process, you can create a plan that not only ensures your survival but also strengthens the bonds within your household. Preparedness is a collective effort, and when everyone is on the same page, you are far more likely to weather any storm that comes your way.

Essential Bug-In Supplies

When preparing for a bug-in scenario, one of the most critical steps you can take is ensuring that you have the right supplies to sustain your household during a crisis. The goal is to create a stockpile that can support your family for an extended period, covering all basic needs while also addressing any specific requirements unique to your situation. This chapter will guide you through the essentials, providing a comprehensive checklist of supplies and offering strategies for how to prioritize and gather them effectively.

A Checklist of Basic Supplies Needed for a Successful Bug-In

Creating a well-rounded inventory of supplies is essential for weathering any crisis. While every household's needs may differ slightly, there are certain categories of supplies that are universally important:

Water: Water is arguably the most critical supply in any emergency. It's essential not just for drinking, but for cooking, hygiene, and potentially even medical purposes. The general rule of thumb is to store at least one gallon of water per person per day, with a minimum supply for two weeks. This ensures that you have enough water to sustain basic needs. Consider including water purification methods—such as filters, purification tablets, or a portable water purification system—in case your primary water supply is compromised.

Food: A well-thought-out food supply should consist of non-perishable items that are easy to store, require minimal preparation, and provide balanced nutrition. Canned goods, dried beans, rice, pasta, and dehydrated foods are excellent choices. Aim to store at least a two-week supply of food, but ideally, you should aim for one to three months, depending on storage space and the level of preparedness you desire. It's also important to include a variety of foods to prevent meal fatigue, ensuring that you have a mix of proteins, carbohydrates, and fats.

Medical Supplies and First Aid: Having a comprehensive first aid kit is essential. Your kit should include bandages, antiseptics, pain relievers, and any prescription medications that members of your household may require. Consider stocking up on over-the-counter medications for common ailments, such as cold and flu remedies, allergy medications, and anti-diarrheal treatments. Don't forget to include personal protective equipment like gloves, masks, and hand sanitizers, particularly in scenarios involving pandemics or other health crises.

Hygiene Products: Maintaining hygiene during a bug-in is crucial for preventing illness. Stockpile essential hygiene items such as soap, toothpaste, toilet paper, and feminine hygiene products. Baby wipes can be invaluable if water is in short supply, and bleach or other disinfectants can help keep your living space clean and sanitary.

Power and Lighting: In the event of a power outage, having alternative power sources and lighting options is vital. Batteries, solar chargers, and backup generators can provide electricity for essential devices. For lighting, consider battery-powered lanterns, flashlights, and candles. Solar-powered lights are also a reliable and sustainable option.

Communication Devices: Staying informed during a crisis is essential. Ensure you have a battery-powered or hand-crank radio to receive news and emergency broadcasts. Walkie-talkies can be useful for communication within your household or with neighbors if cell phone networks become unreliable.

Shelter and Warmth: If your home's heating system fails, you'll need alternative ways to stay warm. Stock up on extra blankets, sleeping bags, and warm clothing. If you live in a colder climate, consider having a portable heater that can operate without electricity, such as a propane or kerosene heater, but ensure you have proper ventilation and safety measures in place.

Tools and Supplies for Repairs: During a prolonged bug-in, you may need to make repairs to your home or gear. Having basic tools on hand—such as a hammer, screwdrivers, duct tape, and nails—can be invaluable. A good multi-tool and a sturdy knife are essential for a variety of tasks.

Entertainment and Mental Well-being: Prolonged confinement can take a toll on your mental health, so it's important to have items that can help alleviate boredom and stress. Books, puzzles, games, and other forms of entertainment can provide much-needed distraction. Consider also including items that promote relaxation, such as candles, essential oils, or even comfort foods.

How to Prioritize and Gather These Supplies Effectively

Gathering these supplies may seem overwhelming at first, but with a strategic approach, you can build a comprehensive bug-in stockpile without breaking the bank or running out of space.

Start with the Essentials: Begin by focusing on the most critical supplies—water, food, and medical necessities. These are your top priorities because they directly impact your ability to survive in the short term. Purchase items gradually, taking advantage of sales and bulk discounts when possible.

Assess and Allocate Space: Consider where you will store your supplies. Designate a specific area in your home that is cool, dry, and easily accessible. Use shelving units, storage bins, and vacuum-sealed bags to maximize space and keep items organized. Remember to store items in a way that allows you to rotate them regularly, ensuring that nothing goes to waste.

Budget Wisely: Preparedness doesn't have to be expensive. Create a budget that allows you to consistently add to your supplies over time. Prioritize purchases based on what you need most urgently and what gaps exist in your current stockpile. It's better to build your inventory steadily and sustainably than to overspend all at once.

Involve the Family: Engage your family in the process of gathering supplies. This not only distributes the workload but also ensures that everyone understands where supplies are stored and how to use them. Involving your family can lead to valuable discussions about specific needs and preferences, ensuring that the stockpile is tailored to your household.

Review and Adjust Regularly: Preparedness is an ongoing process. Periodically review your supplies to check for expired items, adjust for changing family needs, and replenish anything that has been used. Life circumstances, health conditions, and even personal tastes can evolve, so your bug-in plan and supplies should adapt accordingly.

Stay Informed and Adapt: The types of supplies you need can change depending on the specific threats you face. Stay informed about potential risks in your area, such as weather forecasts or civil disturbances, and adjust your stockpile as necessary. This proactive approach ensures that your supplies are always relevant and adequate.

Assembling a well-rounded stockpile of essential supplies is a crucial part of your bug-in strategy. By prioritizing critical needs, involving your family, and maintaining a consistent approach to gathering and managing supplies, you can ensure that your household is fully prepared for any emergency that requires you to stay put. The peace of mind that comes from being well-prepared is invaluable, allowing you to face the uncertainties of a crisis with confidence and resilience.

Common Mistakes and How to Avoid Them

Overconfidence and Complacency

In the realm of crisis preparedness, one of the most insidious threats is not an external danger, but an internal mindset: overconfidence and complacency. These attitudes can lull even the most prepared individuals into a false sense of security, undermining all the careful planning and effort that has gone into their bug-in strategy. Understanding the dangers of underestimating a situation and maintaining vigilance is crucial to ensuring that your preparations truly serve their purpose when the time comes.

The Dangers of Underestimating the Situation

Overconfidence often stems from the belief that because you've prepared, you're invincible. This mindset can manifest in various ways: you might believe that your stockpile is sufficient for any situation, that your home is impregnable, or that you've anticipated every possible scenario. Crises are by nature unpredictable. The unexpected can, and often does, happen, and those who are overly confident may find themselves caught off guard.

Underestimating the severity of a crisis can lead to a cascade of mistakes. For example, you might delay taking necessary actions because you believe the situation isn't as dire as it truly is. You might also overlook critical details, such as the need to rotate supplies, maintain equipment, or continue learning new skills. Overconfidence can lead to a dangerous relaxation of standards, where the initial rigor of your preparedness fades into complacency.

Moreover, every crisis is unique, and no amount of preparation can account for every variable. Natural disasters can escalate faster than predicted, civil unrest can spread to previously safe areas, and pandemics can evolve in ways that outstrip your current understanding. The reality is that no one can predict the full scope of a crisis, and underestimating the potential severity can have dire consequences. By assuming you've covered all your bases, you may neglect to take additional precautions that could make all the difference when the unexpected occurs.

Staying Vigilant and Prepared for the Unexpected

To combat overconfidence and complacency, it's essential to adopt a mindset of continuous vigilance and adaptability. Preparedness is not a one-time effort but an ongoing process that requires regular reassessment and adjustment. Staying vigilant means being aware of the changing dynamics of any crisis, as well as the evolving needs of your household.

One of the most effective ways to maintain vigilance is by regularly reviewing and updating your bug-in plan. This includes not only checking your supplies and equipment but also revisiting your risk assessments and staying informed about new threats. For instance, if you've prepared primarily for natural disasters, but civil unrest or a pandemic becomes a more immediate concern, your plans should be flexible enough to shift focus accordingly. This adaptability ensures that you remain prepared, no matter how circumstances change.

It's also important to practice humility in your approach to preparedness. Recognize that there are always gaps in your knowledge and areas where you can improve. Engage in continuous learning—whether it's acquiring new survival skills, staying updated on the latest emergency management techniques, or even participating in community preparedness groups where you can exchange knowledge and strategies with others. This commitment to growth helps prevent the stagnation that complacency breeds.

Another key to staying prepared is to conduct regular drills and simulations. These exercises allow you to test your plan in a controlled environment, exposing weaknesses and areas for improvement that might not be apparent during the planning stage. Drills also help ensure that all family members are familiar with their roles and responsibilities, reinforcing the importance of vigilance and readiness. By simulating different scenarios, you can better prepare for the unexpected and reduce the chances of being caught off guard.

Mental preparedness is equally important. In a crisis, the ability to stay calm, think clearly, and make informed decisions is crucial. Overconfidence can cloud judgment, leading to rash decisions that exacerbate the situation. By cultivating a mindset that acknowledges the seriousness of the threats you face while also remaining open to new information and perspectives, you can navigate crises more effectively. This mental resilience allows you to adapt as the situation unfolds, rather than being rigidly locked into a preconceived plan that may no longer be viable.

It's essential to remember that complacency doesn't just affect you—it can impact your entire household. If one person becomes complacent, it can set a tone that others might follow, weakening the overall preparedness of the group. Encourage open communication within your family about the importance of staying vigilant and emphasize that preparedness is a collective effort. Regularly discuss potential scenarios and how your plans might need to adapt, ensuring that everyone remains engaged and aware.

Overconfidence and complacency are silent threats that can undermine even the best-laid plans. By staying vigilant, continuously reassessing your preparations, and fostering a mindset of humility and adaptability, you can guard against these pitfalls. Preparedness is not just about having the right supplies or the best plan—it's about maintaining a proactive and flexible approach to whatever challenges arise. In doing so, you ensure that you and your family are truly ready to face the unexpected with confidence and resilience.

Failure to Communicate

Effective communication is a cornerstone of any successful bug-in plan. In times of crisis, the ability to share information, coordinate actions, and make informed decisions can mean the difference between safety and chaos. Despite its critical importance, communication is often overlooked or inadequately addressed in preparedness planning. The consequences of poor communication can be severe, leading to confusion, missed opportunities, and even putting lives at risk. This chapter explores the essential role of communication within the household and the importance of establishing external communication networks.

Importance of Communication Within the Household

In any emergency situation, clear and consistent communication within the household is vital. Every member of your family needs to be on the same page, understanding both the overall plan and their specific roles within it. Miscommunication or a lack of communication can lead to disorganization, increased stress, and potentially dangerous mistakes.

The first step in fostering effective communication is to ensure that everyone in the household understands the bug-in plan. This means not just knowing the basics, but also grasping the nuances of why certain decisions are made and how each person's role contributes to the overall safety and success of the group. Regular family meetings to discuss the plan, review procedures, and address any questions or concerns are essential. These meetings should be inclusive, allowing all members, regardless of age, to voice their thoughts and suggestions. Involving everyone in the planning process helps to ensure that each person feels invested in the plan and understands their responsibilities.

Another critical aspect of household communication is the establishment of clear protocols for different scenarios. For example, if an intruder were to breach your home, every member of the household should know exactly what to do—whether it's securing themselves in a safe room, gathering supplies, or signaling for help. Similarly, in the event of a medical emergency, there should be predefined steps for how to communicate the problem and respond effectively. These protocols help to minimize confusion and ensure that everyone can act swiftly and decisively when needed.

Besides planning for specific scenarios, it's important to maintain open lines of communication throughout the duration of any crisis. This includes regular check-ins to discuss how everyone is feeling, any concerns that have arisen, and whether adjustments to the plan are necessary. Stress and fear can lead to misunderstandings, so taking the time to ensure that everyone feels heard and understood is crucial. Moreover, these conversations help to maintain morale, reminding everyone that they are part of a team working together to get through the situation.

It's also worth considering how you will communicate if normal methods—like speaking directly—are compromised. This could happen in situations where noise needs to be minimized to avoid detection or where someone in the household becomes incapacitated. Developing non-verbal communication strategies, such as hand signals or written notes, can be an effective way to maintain communication under such circumstances.

Establishing External Communication Networks

While internal communication within your household is crucial, it's equally important to establish and maintain external communication networks. In a crisis, access to information from the outside world can provide valuable insights into what's happening beyond your immediate environment, helping you to make informed decisions about your next steps.

The first layer of external communication involves staying informed through news broadcasts, emergency alerts, and other official channels. A battery-powered or hand-crank radio is an indispensable tool in this regard, ensuring that you can receive updates even if the power is out or other communication methods fail. If internet access remains available, staying connected to trusted news websites or social media platforms can offer real-time updates and guidance.

Beyond passive information gathering, it's essential to establish proactive communication networks with trusted individuals outside your household. This might include neighbors, extended family members, or friends who are also preparing for emergencies. These networks serve multiple purposes: they provide a support system, allow for the exchange of information and resources, and offer a broader perspective on the unfolding situation. For example, if a neighbor spots potential danger—such as looters or a spreading fire—they can alert you quickly, giving you more time to respond.

To facilitate these external communications, consider using two-way radios, walkie-talkies, or other forms of short-range communication devices. These tools are particularly useful if cell towers become overloaded or go down altogether. Ensure that everyone in your communication network is familiar with the devices and knows the protocols for using them. Establishing a regular check-in schedule can help to maintain communication and ensure that everyone is safe and informed.

It's also important to have a plan for reaching out to emergency services if needed. While your primary goal is to be self-sufficient, there may be situations where outside help is necessary. Familiarize yourself with the procedures for contacting local authorities, emergency medical services, or other support agencies. Keep in mind that during a widespread crisis, these services may be overwhelmed, so having alternative plans in place is wise.

Consider the security of your communications. In certain scenarios, such as civil unrest or other high-stakes situations, it may be necessary to keep your communications discreet to avoid attracting unwanted attention. This could involve using coded language, avoiding certain topics over open channels, or even limiting communication to only essential messages. Being mindful of what you say and how you say it can help protect your household from external threats.

Communication is a critical component of any bug-in strategy, both within your household and with the outside world. By ensuring that everyone in your home is well-informed and involved in the plan, and by establishing reliable external communication networks, you significantly increase your ability to respond effectively to whatever challenges arise. Remember, a breakdown in communication can lead to confusion, missed opportunities, and increased danger. By prioritizing clear, consistent, and secure communication, you help to safeguard your household and enhance your overall preparedness.

Ignoring Maintenance and Upkeep

In the world of preparedness, planning and gathering supplies are just the beginning. To ensure your bug-in setup remains effective when you need it most, ongoing maintenance and regular updates are critical. Ignoring these aspects can turn even the best-prepared households into vulnerable ones when a crisis strikes. A well-maintained setup not only extends the longevity of your supplies and systems but also enhances your overall readiness by ensuring everything functions as intended. This chapter will delve into the importance of regular checks and how to keep your supplies and systems in working order.

Regular Checks and Updates to Your Bug-In Setup

Once you have established your bug-in plan and assembled your supplies, it's tempting to feel as though your work is done. Preparedness is a continuous process, not a one-time task. Regular checks and updates are essential to ensure that your setup remains viable over time. Just as you would regularly service your car to keep it running smoothly, your bug-in plan and supplies require periodic attention to stay in top condition.

Start by scheduling regular reviews of your entire bug-in setup. Depending on your circumstances, this might mean monthly, quarterly, or biannual checks. The goal is to identify any issues before they become critical. During these reviews, take a close look at each component of your plan. Are there any gaps in your supplies? Has any equipment become outdated or damaged? Are there new risks or changes in your environment that might necessitate adjustments to your strategy?

Updating your plan is equally important. As time passes, new information, technology, or life circumstances might necessitate changes. For example, if you've recently added new members to your household, you'll need to account for their needs in your stockpile. Similarly, if you've moved to a different location, your risk assessment may change, requiring a reevaluation of your bug-in strategy. Staying flexible and adapting to new developments ensures that your plan remains relevant and effective.

Another critical aspect of maintaining your bug-in setup is keeping an eye on expiration dates and the condition of your supplies. Food, water, medications, and other perishable items have a limited shelf life. Regularly rotating these supplies ensures that when the time comes to rely on them, they're still safe and effective. This practice also prevents waste, as you can use older items before they expire and replace them with fresh ones.

Keeping Supplies and Systems in Working Order

Beyond regularly checking your stockpile, it's crucial to keep all your equipment and systems in working order. This involves more than just making sure everything is in its place—it requires proactive maintenance to ensure that your tools and devices function properly when you need them.

Start with the basics: power sources and generators. If you have a backup generator, it's essential to run it periodically to ensure it's in good working condition. Check fuel levels, oil, and filters, and perform any necessary maintenance according to the manufacturer's recommendations. Similarly, if you rely on batteries for essential devices like flashlights, radios, or medical equipment, regularly test these devices and replace the batteries as needed. Rechargeable batteries should be cycled periodically to maintain their capacity.

Your water storage system is another critical area that requires ongoing maintenance. If you're storing water in containers, check them regularly for signs of contamination or leakage. It's also a good practice to refresh stored water every six months to a year, depending on the storage method and conditions. If you have a water filtration system, inspect it regularly, replace filters as needed, and ensure that it's ready to use at a moment's notice.

For those who have more complex systems in place, such as solar panels or home security systems, routine inspections and maintenance are even more critical. Solar panels should be cleaned regularly to maintain efficiency, and all connections should be checked for signs of wear or corrosion. Security systems, including cameras, motion detectors, and alarms, should be tested periodically to ensure they're functioning correctly. Any issues identified during these checks should be addressed immediately to prevent failures during a crisis.

Consider the condition of your home itself. The structural integrity of your home is foundational to your bug-in plan. Regularly inspect your home for potential vulnerabilities, such as cracks in the foundation, roof damage, or signs of water infiltration. These issues, if left unchecked, can compromise your home's ability to protect you during a crisis. Addressing them promptly can prevent minor problems from becoming major threats.

Keep an inventory of your tools and make sure they're in good condition. This includes everything from hand tools used for repairs to more specialized equipment like first aid kits or fire extinguishers. Tools should be stored in a dry, accessible location, and inspected regularly to ensure they're not rusted, broken, or otherwise unusable. Fire extinguishers, in particular, should be checked for pressure and replaced or serviced according to the manufacturer's guidelines.

In conclusion, ignoring maintenance and upkeep in your bug-in strategy is a recipe for failure. Regular checks, updates, and diligent maintenance ensure that your supplies and systems are ready to support you when you need them most. By staying proactive and committed to keeping everything in working order, you enhance your household's resilience and preparedness. This ongoing effort not only safeguards your investment in preparedness but also provides peace of mind, knowing that when a crisis does come, you are truly ready to face it.

Recap of Key Points

As we conclude this chapter, it's important to take a moment to reflect on the critical concepts we've covered, which lay the foundation for a robust bug-in strategy. These key points are not just guidelines—they are essential practices that ensure your preparedness efforts are effective and resilient in the face of any crisis.

First and foremost, we emphasized the importance of understanding the psychology behind bugging in. Recognizing the mental shift required to stay put rather than flee is crucial. This mindset is what will enable you to make sound decisions under pressure, ensuring that your home remains a place of safety rather than a potential liability. The mental preparedness to adapt to changing situations and maintain morale during long periods of confinement is just as vital as the physical preparations you make.

We also discussed the critical nature of assessing your home's readiness. This involves not only evaluating the physical structure of your home but also identifying potential vulnerabilities that could be exploited during a crisis. Whether it's ensuring that your windows and doors are secure or confirming that your roof can withstand severe weather, these assessments allow you to strengthen your defenses proactively. In doing so, you transform your home into a fortress capable of withstanding external threats, giving you peace of mind when the unexpected occurs.

Another significant point we explored is the development of a comprehensive bug-in plan. Such a plan must be tailored to your specific circumstances, taking into account the unique needs of your household and the potential risks you face. Involving your family in this process is not just beneficial—it's essential. By creating a unified strategy where everyone knows their role, you ensure that your household can operate as a cohesive unit during a crisis, reducing confusion and increasing efficiency.

We delved into the importance of gathering and maintaining essential supplies. Your stockpile is your lifeline during a bug-in scenario, and it's crucial that it's both comprehensive and well-organized. From water and food to medical supplies and power sources, having a well-rounded inventory ensures that you can meet your basic needs for an extended period. It's not just about gathering supplies—it's also about keeping them in good condition through regular maintenance and updates. This vigilance ensures that when you need these resources, they're ready to serve their purpose.

Furthermore, we addressed the dangers of overconfidence and complacency. It's easy to fall into the trap of believing that once you've made preparations, your work is done. Preparedness is an ongoing process that requires constant reassessment and adaptation. By staying vigilant, regularly reviewing your plans, and remaining open to new information, you guard against the risks that complacency brings, ensuring that your readiness remains sharp and effective.

Communication, both within your household and with the outside world, was another critical element we covered. Clear and consistent communication is the glue that holds your bug-in strategy together. Internally, it ensures that everyone in your household is aligned and aware of their responsibilities. Externally, establishing reliable communication networks allows you to stay informed and connected, which is vital for making informed decisions during a crisis.

We touched on the necessity of regular maintenance and upkeep. Ignoring these aspects can render your preparations ineffective just when you need them most. By committing to regular checks, updates, and repairs, you ensure that your home and supplies are always in peak condition, ready to support you through any emergency.

In summary, the key takeaways from this chapter are rooted in the principles of vigilance, adaptability, and proactive maintenance. Your bug-in strategy is only as strong as the weakest link, whether that's a neglected stockpile, a failure to communicate, or a complacent mindset. By internalizing these lessons and applying them consistently, you fortify not just your home, but your entire approach to preparedness. The effort you invest now will pay dividends when it matters most, allowing you to face any crisis with confidence, resilience, and a well-prepared home.

Moving Forward

With a solid understanding of the key concepts laid out in this chapter, the time has come to put these ideas into action. Preparedness is not just a theoretical exercise; it's about making tangible changes and taking concrete steps to ensure your home is ready for any crisis. Moving forward, the focus will shift from planning and assessing to implementing the strategies we've discussed, transforming your home into a resilient sanctuary.

How to Begin Implementing the Strategies Discussed

The first step in implementing these strategies is to take a detailed inventory of your current situation. Reflect on the assessments you've made regarding your home's structural integrity, your supply stockpile, and your communication plans. Identify the areas where you're already strong, and highlight those that need immediate attention. This might involve anything from reinforcing your home's entry points to enhancing your stockpile with critical supplies like water, food, and medical necessities.

Once you've identified these areas, prioritize your actions. Start with the most critical vulnerabilities—the issues that could pose the greatest risk in a crisis. This might mean investing in better security measures for your home, ensuring your emergency power systems are fully operational, or establishing more robust communication networks. The key is to approach these tasks methodically, making steady progress while avoiding the overwhelm that can come from trying to do everything at once.

It's also essential to involve your household in these preparations. As you begin to implement these strategies, engage your family in discussions and planning sessions. This not only helps to distribute the workload but also ensures that everyone is aligned with the overall plan. A collective effort strengthens the household's preparedness and builds a shared sense of responsibility.

As you implement these strategies, remember that this is a dynamic process. Your preparedness plan should be a living document, one that evolves with your circumstances. Regularly revisit your plan, adjust as needed, and stay informed about new developments in emergency management and survival tactics. This ongoing commitment will keep your readiness sharp and your household resilient.

Transitioning to the Next Chapter on Physical and Mental Preparedness

With the foundational strategies in place, it's time to turn your attention to the next crucial aspect of preparedness: physical and mental readiness. While having a well-stocked home and a solid plan are essential, your ability to weather a crisis also depends on the strength of your body and mind.

The next chapter will delve into the physical and mental preparations necessary to complement your bug-in strategy. You'll learn how to build the physical resilience needed to endure the stresses that come with long-term confinement and crisis situations. This includes not only maintaining your health and fitness but also understanding how to manage injuries, illnesses, and other physical challenges that might arise when professional medical help is not readily available.

Equally important is mental preparedness. The psychological impact of a crisis can be as debilitating as any physical threat. Developing mental toughness, coping mechanisms, and stress management techniques will be central to maintaining your well-being and that of your family. The next chapter will explore strategies for building mental resilience, helping you to stay focused, calm, and effective even in the most challenging circumstances.

As you move forward, remember that physical and mental preparedness are not separate from the strategies we've already discussed—they are integral components. A fortified home and a comprehensive plan are only as strong as the individuals who execute them. By preparing both your environment and yourself, you create a holistic defense against whatever challenges may come your way.

The journey you've started with this chapter is just the beginning. By taking deliberate steps to implement these strategies and transitioning smoothly into physical and mental preparedness, you are building a foundation of resilience that will serve you well in any crisis. As we move into the next phase, continue to approach each task with the same dedication and thoroughness, knowing that every effort you make now will significantly enhance your ability to protect and sustain your household in the future.

Video BONUS

Chapter 2: Mental and Physical Preparedness

Developing the Navy SEAL Mindset

Understanding the Navy SEAL Mentality

The Navy SEALs are widely recognized as one of the most elite military forces in the world. Their training is renowned not only for its physical intensity but also for the mental toughness it instills in those who endure it. To truly understand the Navy SEAL mentality is to grasp the essence of resilience, adaptability, and relentless determination—qualities that are not just relevant for the battlefield but also highly applicable to civilian life, especially in the context of crisis preparedness.

At the core of the Navy SEAL mindset are a few key principles that guide every action and decision. One of the most fundamental is the concept of **mission-first thinking**. SEALs are trained to prioritize the mission above all else, focusing entirely on the objective at hand. This principle fosters a sense of purpose and clarity, allowing them to push through pain, fear, and uncertainty. For civilians, adopting a mission-first mentality can be a powerful tool in emergency preparedness. By clearly defining your goals—whether it's ensuring your family's safety, securing your home, or maintaining your supplies—you create a focused mindset that helps eliminate distractions and reduce anxiety in high-pressure situations.

Another critical principle is **embracing the suck**—a phrase that embodies the acceptance of difficult and uncomfortable conditions. SEALs are trained to endure the harshest environments, both physically and mentally, by embracing the discomfort rather than resisting it. This mindset allows them to remain calm and composed, even in situations where others might falter. For civilians, this principle is particularly useful during prolonged crises where resources may be scarce, and the environment may be hostile. By mentally preparing yourself to face hardship with a sense of acceptance, you build resilience that can carry you through the most challenging circumstances.

Adaptability is another cornerstone of the Navy SEAL mentality. In the unpredictable world of special operations, plans often go awry. SEALs are trained to quickly adapt to changing situations, using creativity and resourcefulness to overcome obstacles. This ability to pivot and adjust is crucial in any emergency scenario, where conditions can change rapidly, and rigid plans may fail. For civilian preparedness, the lesson here is clear: flexibility in your plans and the ability to think on your feet can be the difference between success and failure. This might mean altering your bug-in strategy in response to new information or finding innovative solutions to problems as they arise.

Discipline is the glue that holds the Navy SEAL mentality together. It is not just about physical discipline, but mental and emotional discipline as well. SEALs are taught to control their emotions, maintain focus, and execute tasks with precision, even under extreme stress. This level of discipline is essential for maintaining a cool head during a crisis, where panic can lead to poor decisions and increased risk. For civilians, cultivating discipline means sticking to your preparedness routines, following through on your plans, and maintaining control over your emotions, no matter how dire the situation may seem.

One of the most empowering aspects of the Navy SEAL mindset is the belief in **self-reliance and accountability**. SEALs are trained to take full responsibility for their actions and outcomes. They understand that success or failure often hinges on individual performance and the choices they make. This principle is particularly relevant for those preparing for emergencies. In a crisis, you may not be able to rely on external help or resources. Being self-reliant—knowing that you are responsible for your own safety and that of your loved ones—fosters a mindset of empowerment and readiness. It pushes you to prepare thoroughly, learn new skills, and stay vigilant, knowing that your actions directly impact your survival.

Team cohesion is a vital component of the Navy SEAL mentality. SEALs operate in tightly knit teams where trust, communication, and mutual support are paramount. While civilian preparedness may seem like a solitary endeavor, the importance of community and family cannot be overstated. Just as SEALs rely on their teammates, you should foster strong relationships with those around you. Whether it's your immediate family, neighbors, or a broader community, building a network of trust and cooperation enhances your collective resilience in the face of a crisis.

The Navy SEAL mentality is a blend of resilience, adaptability, discipline, and teamwork—all of which are essential qualities for anyone preparing for emergencies. By adopting these principles, you can approach preparedness with a mindset that not only improves your chances of survival but also enhances your ability to thrive under pressure. The lessons from the SEALs teach us that while we cannot control the world around us, we can control how we respond to it. And it is this response, shaped by a well-prepared mind and spirit, that will determine our success in the face of any challenge.

Cultivating Mental Toughness

Mental toughness is not an innate trait reserved for the few—it's a skill that can be developed and refined over time. In the context of preparedness, cultivating mental resilience is just as important as physical readiness. It's the ability to stay calm under pressure, to push through adversity, and to make clear-headed decisions when the stakes are high. This chapter explores techniques for building mental toughness in everyday life and examines the critical role of discipline and focus in maintaining mental strength during crises.

Techniques for Building Mental Resilience in Everyday Life

Building mental resilience begins long before a crisis ever occurs. It's about conditioning your mind to handle stress, uncertainty, and adversity with grace and determination. One of the most effective ways to start cultivating this resilience is through **habitual exposure to discomfort**. This doesn't mean seeking out extreme hardships, but rather incorporating small challenges into your daily routine that push you out of your comfort zone.

For instance, taking cold showers, engaging in difficult physical exercises, or practicing intermittent fasting are all ways to introduce controlled discomfort into your life. These activities, while not inherently dangerous, force your mind to adapt to conditions that are less than ideal. Over time, this habitual exposure teaches you how to remain composed and focused when faced with more significant challenges.

Another powerful technique is **mindfulness meditation**. This practice involves sitting quietly and focusing on your breath, thoughts, and sensations in the present moment. While it may seem simple, mindfulness builds mental toughness by training you to observe your thoughts without reacting to them. In a crisis, the ability to maintain a calm and clear mind is invaluable. Mindfulness meditation helps you develop this capacity, allowing you to respond to stressful situations with deliberate thought rather than impulsive reactions.

Setting and achieving small, incremental goals is another effective way to build mental resilience. By consistently setting goals that challenge you just enough to stretch your limits, you reinforce the belief that you are capable of overcoming obstacles. Each small victory builds confidence, creating a positive feedback loop that strengthens your mental toughness over time. Whether it's learning a new skill, completing a difficult project, or improving your physical fitness, these small successes accumulate, preparing your mind for larger challenges.

Embracing failure as a learning tool is also crucial in building mental resilience. Too often, people shy away from failure, viewing it as a reflection of their worth. Those with strong mental toughness understand that failure is not an endpoint but a valuable part of the learning process. By reframing failures as opportunities for growth, you become more willing to take risks and face challenges head-on. This mindset not only enhances your ability to cope with setbacks but also prepares you to persevere in the face of adversity.

The Role of Discipline and Focus in Maintaining Mental Strength During Crises

When a crisis hits, mental toughness is put to the ultimate test. In these moments, discipline and focus become the pillars that support your mental strength. Discipline, in this context, is about maintaining a steady course of action despite the chaos around you. It's the ability to stick to your plan, follow through on necessary tasks, and avoid being derailed by fear or panic.

Discipline is cultivated through routine. In your everyday life, establishing routines that prioritize both mental and physical well-being strengthens your ability to maintain composure during a crisis. For example, a disciplined morning routine that includes exercise, healthy eating, and planning your day sets a positive tone that can carry you through stressful situations. When you're accustomed to following a routine, you're more likely to adhere to critical tasks during a crisis, even when emotions run high.

Focus, on the other hand, is the ability to concentrate on what matters most in the moment. In a crisis, distractions can be deadly—whether it's unnecessary tasks, panic-driven decisions, or external noise. Developing the skill of focus means training your mind to zero in on the essential elements of a situation, filtering out the noise, and making decisions based on clear priorities.

One way to enhance focus is through **visualization techniques**. Athletes often use visualization to mentally rehearse their performance, and this technique can be equally effective in preparing for crises. By visualizing yourself handling difficult situations calmly and effectively, you train your mind to follow that pattern in real life. This mental rehearsal can reduce anxiety and improve your ability to stay focused when real challenges arise.

Another key to maintaining focus during a crisis is **strategic compartmentalization**. This involves breaking down overwhelming situations into manageable parts and tackling them one at a time. By compartmentalizing tasks, you prevent yourself from becoming overwhelmed by the big picture and can maintain focus on immediate, actionable steps. This approach not only helps manage stress but also ensures that you remain productive and clear-headed, even in the midst of chaos.

Ultimately, the combination of discipline and focus forms a resilient mental framework that can withstand the pressures of any crisis. Discipline ensures that you remain grounded and consistent in your actions, while focus sharpens your ability to prioritize and execute those actions effectively. Together, they empower you to navigate crises with confidence, maintaining both mental and emotional stability when it matters most.

Cultivating mental toughness is an ongoing process that involves building resilience through daily habits, embracing challenges, and developing discipline and focus. These qualities are not just beneficial in times of peace—they are essential when facing the unexpected. By integrating these practices into your life, you prepare your mind to handle whatever crises may come, ensuring that you can protect yourself and those you care about with clarity, strength, and unwavering resolve.

Embracing Adaptability and Flexibility

In the world of crisis preparedness, one of the most vital qualities you can cultivate is adaptability. While meticulous planning is essential, the reality is that no plan survives contact with the unpredictable nature of emergencies. Adaptability allows you to pivot when circumstances change, making quick decisions that could be the difference between success and failure. Embracing flexibility in your mindset and strategies ensures that you can navigate through the uncertainties of a crisis with resilience and confidence.

Why Adaptability Is Crucial in Unpredictable Situations

Emergencies, by their very nature, are unpredictable. Whether it's a natural disaster, civil unrest, or a sudden personal crisis, the situation can evolve rapidly, rendering even the most well-laid plans obsolete. In such scenarios, adaptability becomes not just a useful trait but a critical survival skill. The ability to adjust your approach, revise your strategies, and respond to new information is essential for maintaining control and ensuring the safety of yourself and those around you.

One of the main reasons adaptability is so crucial is that it helps prevent paralysis in the face of change. When events unfold differently than expected, the rigid adherence to a plan can lead to indecision, delays, and missed opportunities. On the other hand, those who embrace adaptability can assess the new situation quickly, identify what needs to change, and implement a revised plan without hesitation. This dynamic approach is key to staying ahead of the curve in any crisis.

Adaptability also fosters a mindset of continuous learning. In a crisis, every moment offers lessons that can inform your next move. By staying flexible, you remain open to new information and perspectives, allowing you to adjust your tactics based on real-time developments. This willingness to learn and adapt is what enables you to turn setbacks into stepping stones, transforming challenges into opportunities for growth.

Furthermore, adaptability is closely linked to resilience. When you are adaptable, you are less likely to be thrown off course by unexpected events. Instead, you can absorb the shock, recalibrate, and continue moving forward. This resilience not only strengthens your ability to cope with the immediate crisis but also prepares you for future challenges, making each experience a building block for greater preparedness.

Strategies for Staying Flexible and Making Quick Decisions Under Pressure

Staying flexible in a crisis requires both a mindset shift and practical strategies. One of the first steps in cultivating adaptability is to **embrace uncertainty**. Accepting that not everything will go according to plan frees you from the need to control every aspect of a situation. This mindset allows you to remain calm and open to change, rather than resisting it. When you accept uncertainty as part of the process, you become more agile, ready to pivot as circumstances demand.

Another key strategy is to **practice decision-making in stressful situations**. This can be done through simulations, drills, or even real-life scenarios where you intentionally place yourself in unfamiliar or challenging environments. The more you expose yourself to pressure, the better you become at making quick, informed decisions when it counts. These experiences train your brain to process information rapidly and efficiently, reducing the likelihood of becoming overwhelmed when faced with the unexpected.

In addition, **prioritizing flexibility in your plans** from the outset is essential. This means building contingencies into your strategies—knowing what your backup options are and being prepared to shift gears when necessary. For example, if your primary evacuation route becomes impassable, have alternative routes mapped out. If a critical supply runs low, know where you can find substitutes. By planning for flexibility, you create a safety net that allows you to adapt without scrambling for solutions in the heat of the moment.

Another effective approach is to **stay informed and connected**. In a crisis, information is power. Keeping up with real-time updates and staying in touch with others can provide the insights you need to adapt your plans accordingly. Establish reliable communication channels, and be prepared to gather and assess new information quickly. This approach ensures that your decisions are based on the most current and relevant data, allowing you to make adjustments that are both timely and effective.

Delegation is another powerful tool in staying flexible. Recognize that you don't have to make every decision alone. Involving trusted family members or team members in the decision-making process not only shares the burden but also brings in different perspectives and ideas. This collaborative approach can lead to more innovative solutions and faster decision-making, as you can divide tasks and focus on the areas where you can be most effective.

Lastly, **maintaining emotional regulation** is crucial for adaptability. Stress can cloud judgment and lead to hasty or poorly considered decisions. By practicing techniques such as deep breathing, mindfulness, or even short breaks to reset your mind, you can keep your emotions in check and approach decisions with a clear head. This emotional resilience ensures that your adaptability is not compromised by panic or fear, allowing you to stay focused and composed under pressure.

Embracing adaptability and flexibility is essential for navigating the unpredictable nature of crises. By cultivating a mindset that welcomes change and equips you with practical strategies for quick decision-making, you position yourself to handle whatever comes your way with confidence and resilience. Remember, in a crisis, the ability to adapt is often what separates those who thrive from those who merely survive. By staying flexible and prepared to pivot, you ensure that you can not only meet challenges head-on but also emerge stronger and more capable on the other side.

Building Physical Resilience for Crisis Situations

Assessing Your Current Physical Condition

Physical fitness is a cornerstone of effective survival preparedness. In a crisis, your body becomes one of your most vital tools, capable of enduring stress, carrying out demanding tasks, and, if necessary, defending yourself and your loved ones. Assessing your current physical condition is the first step in ensuring that you are prepared to meet the physical challenges that any survival scenario might present. This chapter will guide you through the process of evaluating your fitness, identifying areas for improvement, and understanding the critical role that physical fitness plays in survival situations.

How to Evaluate Your Physical Fitness and Identify Areas for Improvement

Before you can improve your physical fitness, you need to have a clear understanding of where you currently stand. A thorough self-assessment allows you to identify strengths and weaknesses, setting the foundation for a targeted fitness regimen that enhances your preparedness.

Begin by taking an honest inventory of your physical capabilities. This includes assessing your **cardiovascular endurance**, **muscular strength**, **flexibility**, and **overall stamina**. Cardiovascular endurance refers to your body's ability to sustain prolonged physical activity, such as running, hiking, or even brisk walking. To evaluate this, consider how long you can perform such activities without feeling excessively fatigued. If climbing a flight of stairs leaves you winded, this could indicate a need for improvement in your cardiovascular health.

Muscular strength, on the other hand, is about the power and endurance of your muscles—how much weight you can lift, how many repetitions you can perform, and how well your body handles resistance. Simple tests, such as how many push-ups or squats you can do in a minute, can give you a good indication of your strength levels. If you struggle to perform these exercises, it may highlight areas where you need to focus on building muscle.

Flexibility is another critical component, often overlooked in survival preparedness. Being flexible reduces the risk of injury and allows you to perform a wider range of physical tasks. To assess your flexibility, see how easily you can touch your toes, rotate your torso, or perform a deep squat. Tight muscles or limited range of motion are signs that you might need to incorporate stretching or mobility exercises into your routine.

Overall stamina is perhaps the most telling indicator of your physical readiness. Stamina is not just about how long you can exert yourself, but how well your body recovers after physical exertion. Pay attention to how you feel after a workout or physically demanding activity. Do you bounce back quickly, or do you need an extended period to recover? If it's the latter, this could signal a need for endurance training.

Beyond these physical assessments, it's also important to consider any **underlying health conditions** that might affect your physical fitness. Conditions such as asthma, diabetes, or arthritis can influence your ability to perform certain tasks or sustain prolonged physical activity. Understanding these limitations is crucial, as it allows you to tailor your fitness plan in a way that accommodates your specific needs without exacerbating any health issues.

Once you've identified the areas where you excel and those where improvement is needed, you can begin to create a fitness plan that targets these weaknesses while maintaining your strengths. The goal is to build a balanced physical profile that enhances your overall preparedness, making you more resilient and capable in the face of physical demands during a crisis.

The Importance of Fitness in Survival Scenarios

In survival situations, physical fitness is not a luxury—it's a necessity. When disaster strikes, the demands on your body can increase dramatically, and your physical condition can be the deciding factor in your ability to navigate the crisis successfully.

Consider scenarios where you might need to evacuate quickly, carrying heavy supplies, or traverse difficult terrain to reach safety. In these situations, cardiovascular endurance and muscular strength are not just beneficial—they're essential. If your body isn't conditioned to handle these demands, you may find yourself unable to move as quickly or efficiently as necessary, putting yourself and others at risk.

Beyond the immediate physical demands, fitness also plays a crucial role in **reducing the risk of injury**. A strong, flexible body is less prone to sprains, strains, and other injuries that could incapacitate you during a critical moment. This is particularly important in survival scenarios where medical help may not be readily available, and a minor injury could have serious consequences.

Moreover, physical fitness is closely tied to **mental resilience**. When you know your body is capable and strong, it boosts your confidence and reduces stress. This mental edge is invaluable in a crisis, where staying calm and focused can make all the difference. The physical challenges of a survival situation are often matched by mental ones, and having a fit body contributes to a fit mind, helping you think clearly and make better decisions under pressure.

Being physically fit allows you to be more **self-reliant**. In a crisis, the ability to take care of yourself and others without relying on outside help is crucial. Whether it's lifting heavy debris, moving supplies, or defending your home, a strong and capable body enables you to meet these challenges head-on, without waiting for assistance that might never arrive.

Assessing your current physical condition and understanding the importance of fitness in survival scenarios are critical steps in your preparedness journey. By taking the time to evaluate your fitness honestly and identifying areas for improvement, you can build a stronger, more resilient body that's ready to face whatever challenges may come. Physical fitness is not just about looking good—it's about being ready, capable, and confident when it matters most. As you continue to develop your preparedness plan, make physical fitness a priority, knowing that it's one of the most important tools in your survival arsenal.

Developing a Functional Fitness Routine

Physical preparedness is not just about hitting the gym or running long distances; it's about developing a fitness routine that is functional—designed specifically to help you navigate the physical demands of a crisis situation. Whether it's lifting heavy objects, climbing over obstacles, or simply maintaining the stamina to keep going under stress, a well-rounded fitness plan that builds strength, endurance, and agility is essential. This chapter will guide you through creating a functional fitness routine tailored to meet the unique challenges you may face in a survival scenario.

Exercises and Routines That Build Strength, Endurance, and Agility

To develop a functional fitness routine, it's crucial to focus on exercises that mirror the movements and tasks you might need to perform during a crisis. This approach ensures that your workouts are not just about gaining muscle or losing weight but about preparing your body to perform efficiently and effectively when it matters most.

Strength Training is the foundation of any functional fitness routine. Strong muscles are essential for tasks such as lifting and carrying heavy objects, climbing, or even defending yourself if necessary. Incorporating compound exercises that work multiple muscle groups simultaneously is particularly effective. Exercises like **deadlifts**, **squats**, and **push-ups** are excellent for building overall body strength. These movements mimic real-life activities, such as lifting supplies or moving through challenging environments, making them directly applicable to survival situations.

For example, squats build lower body strength, crucial for maintaining stability and balance, while deadlifts strengthen your back and core, essential for lifting and carrying heavy loads. Push-ups, on the other hand, not only build upper body strength but also enhance your core stability, which is vital for almost any physical task.

Endurance Training is equally important, as it ensures that you can sustain physical activity over extended periods. This is particularly critical in scenarios where you might need to travel long distances on foot, engage in prolonged manual labor, or simply endure a high level of physical stress over time. Incorporating cardiovascular exercises like **running, cycling,** or **swimming** into your routine is key to building this endurance. These activities improve your cardiovascular health, increase lung capacity, and enhance your overall stamina.

To make your endurance training even more functional, consider adding interval training or high-intensity interval training (HIIT) to your regimen. HIIT workouts involve short bursts of intense activity followed by brief rest periods, mimicking the stop-and-go nature of many survival situations. For instance, sprinting for 30 seconds, followed by a minute of walking, replicates the energy expenditure of running to safety and then recovering while still on the move.

Agility and Flexibility are often overlooked in traditional fitness routines, but they are vital in a survival context. Agility allows you to move quickly and efficiently through complex environments, whether that's navigating debris, climbing obstacles, or dodging hazards. Exercises like **box jumps**, **ladder drills**, and **agility cones** are excellent for improving your ability to change direction quickly and maintain balance. These drills train your body to react swiftly and effectively, which could be crucial in an emergency.

Flexibility, meanwhile, reduces the risk of injury and improves your range of motion, making it easier to perform a variety of tasks under stress. Incorporating regular stretching routines or practices like **yoga** can significantly enhance your flexibility. Stretching exercises that focus on the hamstrings, shoulders, and lower back can help ensure that your body remains limber and capable of handling unexpected physical demands.

How to Tailor Your Fitness Plan to Meet the Demands of Crisis Situations

Developing a functional fitness routine is not just about choosing the right exercises—it's also about tailoring those exercises to meet the specific demands you might face in a crisis. To do this effectively, start by considering the most likely scenarios you could encounter. Are you preparing for a natural disaster that might require evacuation on foot? Or perhaps you're focused on defending your home during a period of civil unrest. Each scenario places different demands on your body, and your fitness routine should reflect those needs.

For example, if you anticipate needing to carry heavy loads, such as a bug-out bag or emergency supplies, prioritize exercises that build your ability to lift and carry. **Farmer's walks**—where you walk while holding heavy weights in each hand—are excellent for this, as they simulate carrying heavy items over a distance. Similarly, if your plan involves a lot of running or moving quickly, place a greater emphasis on cardiovascular conditioning and agility drills.

Besides tailoring your routine to the physical demands of potential crises, it's also important to ensure that your fitness plan is **sustainable and realistic**. This means setting goals that are challenging yet achievable and creating a schedule that fits into your daily life. Consistency is key to building and maintaining functional fitness, so it's better to have a modest, regular routine that you stick with than an overly ambitious plan that you abandon after a few weeks.

It's also crucial to periodically **reevaluate and adjust** your fitness routine. As your physical condition improves, or as your understanding of the potential crises you might face evolves, your routine should adapt accordingly. This could involve increasing the intensity of your workouts, adding new exercises, or shifting your focus to different areas of fitness as needed.

Remember that functional fitness is about more than just physical capabilities—it's also about mental preparedness. Incorporate exercises that challenge your mental toughness, such as pushing through fatigue or completing a workout under time constraints. This not only builds physical endurance but also trains your mind to stay focused and determined under pressure, a critical asset in any survival scenario.

Developing a functional fitness routine tailored to survival situations is an essential part of your preparedness plan. By focusing on exercises that build strength, endurance, and agility, and by tailoring your routine to meet the specific demands of potential crises, you can ensure that your body is ready to perform when it matters most. Functional fitness is about preparing for the real-world challenges you might face, equipping you with the physical and mental resilience needed to protect yourself and your loved ones in any situation.

Maintaining Health and Nutrition During a Crisis

In the midst of a crisis, when the world around you is in turmoil, your physical health and resilience become paramount. The ability to sustain your body's strength, energy, and overall well-being directly impacts your capacity to navigate the challenges at hand. Proper nutrition plays a critical role in maintaining physical resilience, while strategic approaches to health and fitness ensure that you remain strong even when access to resources is limited. This chapter explores how to maintain your health and nutrition during a crisis, providing practical tips to keep your body and mind in peak condition when it matters most.

The Role of Proper Nutrition in Sustaining Physical Resilience

Nutrition is the fuel that powers your body, and during a crisis, it becomes even more crucial. The physical demands of a survival situation—whether it's enduring long periods of stress, performing manual labor, or making quick, strategic decisions—require a steady supply of energy and essential nutrients. Proper nutrition supports not only your physical endurance and strength but also your cognitive function, immune system, and overall ability to recover from exertion and stress.

In a crisis, your body may be pushed to its limits, and without the right nutrients, it can quickly become depleted. Carbohydrates, proteins, and fats are the macronutrients that provide energy, repair tissues, and regulate bodily functions. Carbohydrates are the body's primary energy source, especially during intense physical activity. Complex carbohydrates, such as those found in whole grains, legumes, and certain vegetables, release energy slowly, providing a sustained fuel source that helps maintain your stamina over time.

Proteins, found in foods like meats, beans, and nuts, are essential for repairing and building muscle tissue. In a survival situation, where your muscles may be working harder than usual, adequate protein intake is crucial for maintaining strength and preventing muscle breakdown. Fats, particularly healthy fats like those in nuts, seeds, and avocados, provide a dense source of energy and are vital for brain function and the absorption of fat-soluble vitamins.

Besides macronutrients, micronutrients—vitamins and minerals—play a significant role in maintaining your physical resilience. Vitamins such as C, D, and E, along with minerals like zinc and magnesium, are critical for immune function, energy production, and overall health. During a crisis, when your body may be under increased physical and psychological stress, ensuring that you have a balanced intake of these nutrients can help ward off illness, boost your energy levels, and keep your mind sharp.

Tips for Maintaining Fitness and Health When Access to Resources Is Limited

One of the biggest challenges during a crisis is maintaining your health and fitness when access to food, water, and medical supplies may be restricted. With the right strategies, you can make the most of limited resources and keep your body functioning at its best.

First, prioritize **nutrient-dense foods** in your stockpile. When space and resources are limited, every calorie counts. Focus on storing foods that provide a high nutritional value per serving. Canned fish, dried beans, whole grains, nuts, and seeds are all excellent choices because they are packed with essential nutrients and have a long shelf life. These foods not only keep you full but also supply the vitamins, minerals, and macronutrients necessary to sustain your physical health over time.

Water is another critical resource that can be scarce during a crisis. Staying **hydrated** is essential for maintaining physical performance, cognitive function, and overall health. Dehydration can lead to fatigue, confusion, and even severe health complications. To ensure you have enough water, store as much as possible before a crisis hits and have multiple methods for water purification on hand, such as filtration systems, purification tablets, or boiling. This way, you can make sure that any water you do have access to is safe to drink.

When it comes to fitness, maintaining a regular **exercise routine** is crucial, even when resources are limited. You may not have access to a gym or your usual equipment, but that doesn't mean you can't stay active. Bodyweight exercises—such as push-ups, squats, lunges, and planks—require no equipment and can be done in small spaces. These exercises are effective at building and maintaining strength, endurance, and flexibility, all of which are important for handling the physical demands of a crisis.

Incorporating **functional movements** into your routine is also key. These are exercises that mimic real-life actions, such as lifting, carrying, and climbing. For example, practicing carrying heavy objects or performing exercises that involve lifting your own body weight prepares your muscles for the types of tasks you might need to perform in a survival scenario. By focusing on these functional movements, you ensure that your fitness routine is directly applicable to the challenges you may face.

Rest and recovery are equally important components of maintaining health and fitness. During a crisis, stress levels can be high, and your body may be working harder than usual. Ensuring that you get enough rest, sleep, and downtime allows your body to recover, repair tissues, and maintain resilience. If sleep is disrupted by the situation, short naps and relaxation techniques like deep breathing or meditation can help you recharge.

Mental health is a critical aspect of overall well-being, especially during prolonged crises. High levels of stress and anxiety can take a toll on your physical health, weakening your immune system and sapping your energy. Incorporating stress management techniques—such as mindfulness, breathing exercises, or even simple hobbies that bring you joy—can help mitigate the effects of stress and keep your mind and body strong.

Maintaining health and nutrition during a crisis requires thoughtful planning, adaptability, and a focus on maximizing the resources at your disposal. By prioritizing nutrient-dense foods, staying hydrated, maintaining a functional fitness routine, and managing stress, you can sustain your physical resilience even in challenging conditions. Your health is your most valuable asset in any survival scenario, and by taking proactive steps to protect it, you enhance your ability to withstand the pressures of a crisis and emerge stronger on the other side.

Stress Management and Psychological Fortitude

Recognizing and Managing Stress

Stress is an inevitable part of any crisis situation. The uncertainty, fear, and physical demands of an emergency can place immense pressure on both the body and mind. Recognizing the signs of stress, both in yourself and others, is the first step in managing it effectively. When left unchecked, stress can lead to impaired judgment, decreased physical performance, and even long-term health problems. This chapter explores how to identify the signs of stress and offers practical techniques for managing it in high-pressure situations.

Identifying the Signs of Stress in Yourself and Others

Stress manifests in various ways, and its effects can differ from person to person. The ability to recognize these signs early can prevent stress from escalating into more serious issues. Physically, stress often presents as increased heart rate, shallow or rapid breathing, muscle tension, and headaches. You might also notice changes in appetite, sleep disturbances, or gastrointestinal problems. These physical symptoms are the body's way of responding to a perceived threat, activating the "fight or flight" response that can be helpful in short bursts but harmful if prolonged.

Emotionally, stress can lead to feelings of anxiety, irritability, or overwhelming worry. You might find yourself more prone to frustration or anger, or perhaps feeling unusually withdrawn or detached from those around you. Mentally, stress can impair concentration, make decision-making more difficult, and lead to negative thinking patterns. If you notice yourself becoming easily overwhelmed, fixating on worst-case scenarios, or struggling to focus on tasks, these could be signs that stress is taking a toll on your mental state.

It's equally important to recognize these signs in others, especially if you're responsible for a group during a crisis. Changes in behavior, such as increased agitation, uncharacteristic silence, or a decline in performance, can indicate that someone is struggling with stress. By being attentive to these cues, you can offer support or intervene before the stress becomes debilitating.

Techniques for Managing Stress in High-Pressure Situations

Once you've identified stress, the next step is to manage it effectively. One of the most powerful tools for stress management is **controlled breathing**. Deep, slow breaths can help calm the nervous system, reducing the physical symptoms of stress. A simple technique is the "4-7-8" method: inhale deeply through your nose for a count of four, hold the breath for seven seconds, and then exhale slowly through your mouth for a count of eight. This practice not only slows your heart rate but also helps clear your mind, making it easier to stay calm and focused.

Another effective strategy is **progressive muscle relaxation (PMR)**. This technique involves tensing and then slowly releasing each muscle group in your body, starting from your toes and working your way up to your head. By focusing on the physical sensation of releasing tension, you can reduce the overall level of stress in your body. This method is particularly useful in moments of acute stress, where physical relaxation can help break the cycle of escalating tension.

Mindfulness and meditation are also powerful tools for managing stress. These practices involve bringing your attention to the present moment, acknowledging your thoughts and feelings without judgment, and then gently redirecting your focus to something calming, like your breath or a particular sensation. Regular mindfulness practice can increase your resilience to stress, helping you maintain a calm and centered mind even in chaotic situations.

Besides these techniques, it's important to maintain **regular physical activity**, even during a crisis. Exercise is a natural stress reliever, releasing endorphins that boost your mood and energy levels. Even simple activities like stretching, walking, or doing bodyweight exercises can help alleviate stress and improve your mental outlook.

Social support is another crucial element in managing stress. Sharing your concerns with a trusted friend, family member, or colleague can provide emotional relief and a fresh perspective on the situation. Sometimes, just knowing that someone else understands what you're going through can make a significant difference in how you handle stress.

Maintaining a **positive mindset** can greatly influence how you experience and manage stress. This doesn't mean ignoring the reality of the situation but rather focusing on what you can control and finding small victories or positives even in challenging circumstances. This shift in perspective can help mitigate the effects of stress and keep you motivated to push through difficult times.

Building Psychological Fortitude

While managing stress is essential, the ultimate goal is to build psychological fortitude—the mental toughness that allows you to not only withstand pressure but to thrive in the face of adversity. Psychological fortitude is what separates those who crumble under stress from those who rise to meet the challenge with determination and resilience.

Building psychological fortitude begins with **self-awareness**. Understanding your strengths, weaknesses, triggers, and typical reactions to stress allows you to anticipate challenges and develop strategies to overcome them. This self-knowledge acts as a foundation for all other aspects of mental toughness.

Setting realistic goals is another key component of psychological fortitude. In a crisis, it's easy to become overwhelmed by the enormity of the situation. Breaking down challenges into manageable tasks and setting clear, achievable goals helps maintain focus and momentum. Each small success builds confidence and reinforces the belief that you can handle the situation, no matter how daunting it may seem.

Emotional regulation is also critical. This involves acknowledging your emotions without allowing them to dictate your actions. Techniques such as mindfulness, deep breathing, or even journaling can help you process emotions constructively, preventing them from undermining your resolve. By mastering your emotions, you retain the clarity needed to make sound decisions, even under pressure.

Another important aspect is cultivating **resilience through adversity**. Psychological fortitude grows stronger with each challenge you overcome. Rather than shying away from difficult situations, see them as opportunities to test and build your mental strength. Reflecting on past challenges and how you overcame them can also reinforce your belief in your ability to handle future crises.

Adaptability plays a significant role in building psychological fortitude. The ability to pivot and adjust to changing circumstances without becoming discouraged is vital. Life is unpredictable, and those who are mentally flexible are better equipped to handle whatever comes their way. This adaptability is closely linked to maintaining a growth mindset—believing that you can learn, grow, and improve through each experience, no matter how difficult.

Lastly, cultivating a sense of **purpose** can greatly enhance psychological fortitude. When you have a clear sense of why you are enduring hardship—whether it's protecting your family, achieving a personal goal, or simply surviving—it provides the motivation to keep going when the going gets tough. This purpose acts as a guiding light, helping you navigate through the darkest times with determination and resolve.

Building psychological fortitude is about more than just surviving stress—it's about thriving in adversity. By developing self-awareness, setting realistic goals, mastering emotional regulation, embracing challenges, staying adaptable, and holding onto a sense of purpose, you can cultivate the mental toughness needed to face any crisis with confidence. This fortitude not only helps you manage the immediate pressures of a crisis but also prepares you to emerge from it stronger and more resilient, ready to take on whatever life may throw your way.

Maintaining Morale and Motivation

In the midst of long-term emergencies, maintaining morale and motivation is as crucial as securing food, water, and shelter. The psychological toll of prolonged crises can erode your mental resilience, making it difficult to stay focused, productive, and hopeful. High morale and sustained motivation are not luxuries but necessities for enduring hardship and emerging stronger on the other side. This chapter explores strategies for keeping morale high during extended emergencies and underscores the importance of community, family support, and self-care in maintaining psychological health.

Strategies for Keeping Morale High During Long-Term Emergencies

Long-term emergencies test endurance, both physically and mentally. When faced with an extended crisis, it's easy to fall into despair or lose the drive to push forward. Maintaining high morale can make a significant difference in your ability to cope with ongoing challenges.

One effective strategy is to **create a routine**. In times of uncertainty, a routine provides a sense of normalcy and control. It structures your day, giving you a clear framework within which to operate. Even simple routines, like set meal times, daily exercise, or designated work periods, can help maintain a sense of purpose and direction. This structure not only keeps you active but also helps prevent the aimlessness that can lead to demoralization.

Setting **short-term, achievable goals** is another powerful way to keep morale high. In a prolonged emergency, the big picture can often feel overwhelming. Breaking down tasks into smaller, manageable goals allows you to focus on what can be accomplished in the immediate future. Each goal you achieve, no matter how small, provides a psychological boost, reinforcing your sense of progress and capability.

Staying informed while avoiding information overload is also crucial. In a crisis, it's important to stay aware of the situation, but constant exposure to negative news can increase anxiety and reduce morale. Limit your intake of news to specific times of the day and choose reliable sources to avoid the stress of misinformation or speculation. Balancing awareness with peace of mind helps you remain focused and optimistic.

Engaging in meaningful activities is another way to boost morale. Whether it's a hobby, a creative project, or a skill you've wanted to develop, engaging in activities that bring you joy and satisfaction can provide a much-needed break from the stress of the crisis. These activities not only distract from negative thoughts but also help you maintain a positive outlook by focusing on personal growth and creativity.

It's also important to **acknowledge and celebrate small victories**. In the midst of an ongoing emergency, it can be easy to overlook progress. Whether it's successfully completing a task, overcoming a challenge, or simply making it through another day, recognizing these achievements reinforces a positive mindset and helps build momentum. Celebrating these small wins, even with something as simple as a shared meal or a moment of reflection, strengthens morale and fosters a sense of accomplishment.

The Importance of Community, Family Support, and Self-Care in Maintaining Psychological Health

While individual strategies are essential, maintaining morale and motivation over the long term is deeply rooted in community and family support, as well as self-care. Humans are inherently social beings, and in times of crisis, the support of others can provide the emotional sustenance needed to persevere.

Community and family support are critical pillars of psychological health during a crisis. Strong connections with those around you create a support network that can provide comfort, encouragement, and practical assistance. In a family setting, open communication is key. Regularly discussing feelings, challenges, and successes helps keep everyone on the same page and reinforces the sense of being in this together. Sharing responsibilities and decisions not only lightens the burden on any one person but also fosters unity and collective resilience.

In a broader community context, connecting with neighbors or like-minded individuals can provide additional support. Whether it's sharing resources, exchanging information, or simply offering a kind word, these interactions remind you that you're not alone. Community support can also lead to collaborative problem-solving, where multiple perspectives and ideas come together to find solutions to common challenges.

Self-care is another crucial aspect of maintaining psychological health during prolonged emergencies. While it might seem secondary to more immediate survival needs, self-care is essential for sustaining the energy and mental clarity needed to endure a crisis. This includes basic practices like getting enough sleep, eating nutritious food, and staying physically active, all of which directly impact your mood and cognitive function.

Equally important is **emotional self-care**. This involves recognizing when you're feeling overwhelmed and taking steps to address it. Whether through mindfulness, meditation, journaling, or simply taking a break, these practices help manage stress and prevent burnout. Remember that self-care is not selfish—it's a necessary investment in your ability to care for others and face the challenges ahead with resilience.

Maintaining a sense of **hope and purpose** is vital. This can be nurtured through faith, a commitment to a cause, or simply the desire to protect and support your loved ones. Hope provides the motivation to keep going, even when the situation seems bleak. It's the belief that, no matter how difficult the present may be, there is something worth striving for—a brighter future, a stronger self, or the well-being of those you care about.

Maintaining morale and motivation during long-term emergencies requires a combination of practical strategies, community and family support, and self-care. By creating routines, setting achievable goals, staying informed, engaging in meaningful activities, and celebrating small victories, you can keep your spirits high and your focus sharp. Coupled with the support of loved ones and a commitment to self-care, these practices form a resilient foundation that allows you to endure hardship with strength and resolve. Ultimately, it's not just about surviving the crisis—it's about maintaining the psychological health and motivation needed to emerge from it stronger and more united than before.

Video BONUS

Chapter 3: Home Security and Fortification

Assessing and Strengthening Home Security

Conducting a Home Security Audit

Securing your home effectively begins with a thorough understanding of its current strengths and weaknesses. A home security audit is the foundation upon which all your fortification efforts should be built. This process involves a detailed evaluation of your existing security measures and the identification of any vulnerabilities that could be exploited in a crisis or by potential intruders. By taking a systematic approach to assessing your home's security, you can develop a comprehensive plan that addresses both obvious and subtle risks, ensuring that your home is as secure as possible.

How to Evaluate Current Security Measures and Identify Vulnerabilities

The first step in conducting a home security audit is to take an objective look at the current state of your security systems and practices. This involves walking through every part of your property—inside and out—with a critical eye. Start from the exterior and work your way inward, just as a potential intruder might.

Begin by assessing the **perimeter** of your property. This includes fences, gates, and any barriers that mark the boundary of your home. A secure perimeter is your first line of defense, deterring unauthorized access before anyone gets close to the house itself. Examine the condition of your fences—are they tall enough to deter climbing? Are there gaps or weak points that could be easily breached? Gates should be solid, lockable, and in good repair. Consider the visibility of your home from the street; if your property is too visible, it may attract unwanted attention, but if it's too secluded, it might provide cover for potential intruders.

Next, move on to the **entry points** of your home. Doors and windows are the most common points of entry for burglars and intruders, making their security paramount. Check the strength and integrity of all doors, especially exterior doors. Are they made of solid wood or metal, or are they hollow and easily kicked in? What kind of locks do you have? Deadbolts are essential, but even these can vary in quality. Ensure that locks are high-grade and properly installed, with long screws securing the strike plates into the doorframe.

Windows should also be examined closely. Are they secured with locks that are easy to manipulate from the outside? Consider installing window locks, bars, or security film that makes the glass more resistant to breaking. Pay particular attention to basement windows, which are often overlooked but can be a weak spot in your home's defenses.

Another critical aspect of your security audit is to evaluate your **lighting**. Proper lighting is a powerful deterrent against intruders who prefer to operate under the cover of darkness. Assess whether your property is adequately lit at night, particularly around entry points and potential hiding spots like large shrubs or the corners of your house. Motion-activated lights are particularly effective, as they startle intruders and draw attention to unusual activity.

After the physical barriers and deterrents, turn your attention to any **surveillance systems** you may have in place. If you already have security cameras, assess their placement and coverage. Are they positioned to monitor all vulnerable areas, such as doors, windows, and the garage? Can they record footage clearly in both daylight and nighttime conditions? Ensure that your cameras are not easily tampered with and that they provide a clear view of critical areas. If you don't have cameras, now is the time to consider where they would be most effective.

Tools and Techniques for Assessing Your Home's Security Needs

To conduct a thorough home security audit, it's essential to use a combination of observation, technology, and a structured approach. Start by creating a checklist of all the areas and elements you need to inspect. This helps ensure that you don't overlook any part of your property during the audit.

Consider using **security assessment tools** like smartphone apps designed for home security checks. These can guide you through the process and provide recommendations based on your inputs. Some apps allow you to simulate different scenarios, such as a power outage or a forced entry, helping you understand where your home's weaknesses might lie.

Additionally, **professional security consultation** can be invaluable, especially if you're serious about fortifying your home. Security experts can provide insights that you might not consider, such as advanced lock systems, alarm setups, or the latest in home security technology. They can also perform a vulnerability assessment, where they actively attempt to find and exploit weaknesses in your current setup, giving you a clear picture of what needs to be improved.

One technique to consider is performing a **threat analysis** based on your home's location and history. For example, homes in certain neighborhoods might be more prone to specific types of crimes, such as burglaries or vandalism. Understanding the common threats in your area allows you to tailor your security measures more effectively. You can gather this information from local law enforcement agencies, community watch programs, or by researching crime statistics online.

Another effective method is to **simulate intruder scenarios**. Walk through your home as if you were a potential burglar—how would you attempt to break in? What areas would you target? This exercise can reveal vulnerabilities that you might not notice during a standard walkthrough. For instance, you might discover that a side door is out of view of neighbors or that a particular window is shielded by bushes, making it an appealing entry point.

Finally, don't forget to assess **internal security measures**. This includes ensuring that sensitive information, valuables, and important documents are stored securely, such as in a safe or a hidden, locked drawer. Evaluate your ability to detect and respond to an intruder inside the home. Do you have an alarm system that will alert you to movement inside the house? Are your family members trained on what to do in case of a breach?

Conducting a comprehensive home security audit is a critical step in protecting your home and loved ones. By thoroughly evaluating your current security measures and identifying vulnerabilities, you can take proactive steps to strengthen your defenses. Whether through improving physical barriers, enhancing surveillance, or implementing smarter security practices, the insights gained from your audit will guide your efforts to create a safer, more secure home environment. The next steps involve addressing the identified weaknesses and reinforcing your home's security, transforming it into a well-protected haven against potential threats.

Understanding Common Security Threats

In today's world, the nature of threats to your home's security is diverse and ever-evolving. From the typical burglary to more complex scenarios like home invasions or civil unrest, each type of threat requires a different approach in order to effectively protect your property and loved ones. Understanding these common security threats and their implications is the first step in crafting a security strategy that is robust and adaptable. By tailoring your approach to address specific risks, you can ensure that your home remains a safe haven, even in the most challenging circumstances.

Types of Security Threats and Their Implications

The most common security threat that homeowners face is **burglary**. Burglars typically look for easy targets—homes that appear unoccupied, poorly lit, or have minimal visible security measures. The primary goal of a burglar is usually to enter quickly, grab valuables, and exit before being detected. The implications of a burglary can range from financial loss to emotional trauma, as the invasion of one's personal space often leaves a lasting psychological impact.

To understand how to mitigate this threat, consider the typical behaviors of burglars. They often scout neighborhoods to identify vulnerable homes, looking for signs such as piled-up mail, uncut grass, or open windows. Burglars may also knock on doors to see if anyone is home before attempting a break-in. Knowing these tactics allows you to implement preventative measures, such as maintaining your property's appearance, installing visible security cameras, and ensuring that your home appears occupied even when you're away.

Another more dangerous threat is the **home invasion**. Unlike a burglary, where the intruder seeks to avoid contact with residents, a home invasion involves forcibly entering a home with the intention of confronting the occupants. This could be for theft, kidnapping, or even more malicious purposes. Home invasions are particularly alarming because they involve a direct threat to personal safety, not just property. The implications are severe, potentially leading to violence or trauma for anyone inside the home.

Home invasions often occur with little warning, and the intruders may use deception or brute force to gain entry. For example, they might pose as delivery personnel or service workers to gain your trust, or they could force their way in through a front door or window. Understanding this threat emphasizes the importance of having strong physical barriers, such as reinforced doors and windows, and being cautious about whom you open your door to. Having a quick and accessible plan for retreating to a safe room or panic room can be a life-saving measure in the event of such an attack.

Civil unrest represents a broader, more unpredictable threat. Unlike targeted crimes like burglary or home invasion, civil unrest involves widespread disruption that can affect entire neighborhoods or cities. This might include riots, protests, or looting, often sparked by political, economic, or social tensions. The implications of civil unrest are far-reaching, as law enforcement and emergency services may be overwhelmed, leaving you and your community to fend for yourselves.

During civil unrest, homes can become targets for looters or vandals, especially if they are perceived as wealthy or poorly defended. The chaos of such events makes it difficult to predict when or where violence might occur, which means your security strategy must be versatile and comprehensive. For instance, fortifying your home's perimeter and having a robust surveillance system can deter opportunistic criminals who are looking for easy targets amidst the chaos. Being prepared to shelter in place, with sufficient supplies and a clear plan for defending your home, is crucial when outside help may not be available.

Tailoring Your Security Strategy to Address Specific Threats

Given the diversity of potential security threats, it's clear that a one-size-fits-all approach to home security is insufficient. Tailoring your security strategy to address specific threats is essential for creating a layered defense that can adapt to various scenarios.

For **burglary prevention**, focus on deterrence and making your home less attractive to would-be intruders. This includes implementing visible security measures, such as cameras, alarms, and motion-activated lighting, which can make your home a less appealing target. Reinforcing entry points—doors, windows, and garage doors—can slow down or prevent access, buying you time to alert authorities or activate other security measures.

In preparing for a **home invasion**, the emphasis should be on early detection and rapid response. A well-designed security system that includes door and window sensors, panic buttons, and intercoms can alert you to an attempted breach before it occurs. Reinforced doors, shatterproof windows, and a secure perimeter are critical in preventing or delaying forced entry. It's also important to have a well-rehearsed plan for retreating to a safe room, where you can secure yourself and your family until help arrives.

When addressing the threat of **civil unrest**, your strategy should be comprehensive, covering both physical security and logistical preparedness. Strengthen your home's defenses with robust barriers, secure storage for essential supplies, and an emergency power source to keep your security systems operational during a blackout. Establish a communication plan with neighbors to share information and coordinate efforts in the event of widespread disruption. In some cases, you may need to consider alternative evacuation routes or have a bug-out plan ready if the situation becomes too dangerous to stay.

Understanding the various security threats that your home might face is crucial for developing an effective defense strategy. By recognizing the specific risks associated with burglary, home invasion, and civil unrest, you can tailor your security measures to address these threats directly. This targeted approach not only enhances your home's security but also provides peace of mind, knowing that you are prepared for whatever challenges may come your way. As you continue to build and refine your security strategy, remember that the goal is to create a layered defense that adapts to different scenarios, ensuring that your home remains a safe haven in an unpredictable world.

Enhancing Entry Point Security

When it comes to fortifying your home against potential threats, the security of your entry points—doors, windows, and other access points—is paramount. These are the most vulnerable areas of any property, and if not properly secured, they can provide easy access for intruders. Strengthening these points not only deters criminals but also significantly increases the time and effort required to breach your home, giving you precious moments to respond or for authorities to arrive. In this chapter, we will explore effective strategies for securing these critical areas, along with advanced locking systems and reinforcements that can maximize your home's security.

Strategies for Securing Doors, Windows, and Other Entry Points

Doors are the primary entry point for most homes, and as such, they require the most attention when it comes to security. The front door is often the first target for burglars, so ensuring it is both strong and secure is essential. Start by evaluating the material of your doors. Solid wood or metal doors are the best choices for exterior security, as they are more resistant to forced entry compared to hollow-core or glass doors. If your door is not already made from these materials, consider replacing it or reinforcing it with a security door.

The **door frame** is just as important as the door itself. No matter how strong the door is, a weak frame can be easily broken with force. Reinforcing the frame with a metal strike plate and longer screws (at least 3 inches) ensures that the door is more securely anchored to the wall, making it harder to kick in. Installing a door reinforcement bar or a door jamb reinforcement kit can add another layer of security by distributing the force across the frame, reducing the likelihood of it breaking under pressure.

Windows are another common target for intruders, especially those that are easily accessible from the ground. Standard glass windows can be shattered with minimal effort, so it's crucial to consider ways to strengthen them. One effective method is to apply **security film** to the glass. This film is a thin, transparent layer that makes the glass more resistant to breaking. If the window is struck, the film holds the shards together, preventing easy access even if the glass is shattered.

For added protection, consider installing **window locks** that secure the sash from being lifted or forced open. These locks come in various styles, including keyed locks, sliding window locks, and wedge locks, each providing a different level of security. In areas where crime rates are particularly high, **window bars** or grilles may be a worthwhile investment. These metal barriers are installed over the window and provide a physical obstacle that is extremely difficult to bypass without tools, further deterring potential intruders.

Sliding doors and windows require special attention because they are inherently less secure than hinged doors and standard windows. These doors are often made of glass and can be lifted off their tracks if not properly secured. To enhance the security of sliding doors, install **blocking bars** or **door braces** that prevent the door from being opened, even if the lock is compromised. You can also reinforce the door's track by installing a security pin that prevents the door from being lifted out of its frame.

Garage doors are another potential weak spot, particularly those that can be manually opened or that use outdated automatic openers. Securing your garage starts with ensuring that the door is strong and in good repair. For automatic doors, consider upgrading to a model with rolling code technology, which changes the access code every time the door is used, making it more difficult for criminals to use code-grabbing devices. Securing the emergency release lever with a zip tie or installing a garage door lock can prevent the door from being opened manually.

Advanced Locking Systems and Reinforcements for Maximum Security

While traditional locks provide a basic level of security, advanced locking systems can significantly enhance the protection of your home's entry points. **Deadbolts** are the first line of defense and are far superior to standard spring-latch locks. When choosing a deadbolt, opt for one that extends at least one inch into the door frame when locked. This provides a stronger hold and makes it more resistant to forced entry. **Grade 1 deadbolts** are the highest quality and offer the best security. These are designed to withstand a greater amount of force and are recommended for exterior doors.

For an added layer of security, consider installing **smart locks**. These devices use digital technology to control access to your home. Smart locks can be operated via a smartphone app, which allows you to lock or unlock your door remotely, monitor who is entering and exiting your home, and receive alerts if the lock is tampered with. Some smart locks also have integrated alarm systems that sound when someone tries to break in. The convenience of smart locks lies in their ability to offer keyless entry while also providing robust security features that are difficult to bypass.

In addition to advanced locking systems, **door and window reinforcements** can make a significant difference in the security of your home. **Reinforced strike plates** are an essential upgrade for any door. These plates are installed on the door frame where the lock's bolt enters, and they help to distribute the force of a kick or other impact across a wider area. This reinforcement reduces the likelihood of the door frame splitting and the door being forced open.

For windows, **security bars** and **grilles** are highly effective in preventing unauthorized access. These can be custom-made to fit the aesthetics of your home while still providing a strong physical barrier. **Window sensors** that trigger an alarm if the window is opened or broken are an excellent way to add an extra layer of protection. These sensors are often integrated into a larger home security system, ensuring that you are immediately alerted to any potential breach.

Consider the installation of **reinforced doors** or **security doors** for the most vulnerable entry points. Security doors are designed with heavy-duty materials such as steel and are often equipped with multiple locking points to prevent forced entry. They can be installed over your existing door or as a replacement and are available in designs that maintain the aesthetic appeal of your home while providing maximum security.

Enhancing the security of your home's entry points is a critical component of overall home fortification. By implementing strategies to secure doors, windows, and other access points, and by investing in advanced locking systems and reinforcements, you can significantly reduce the risk of unauthorized entry. These measures not only protect your property but also provide peace of mind, knowing that your home is well-defended against potential threats. As you continue to strengthen your home's security, remember that each layer of protection you add makes it that much more difficult for intruders to breach, ensuring that your home remains a safe and secure refuge.

Implementing Surveillance and Monitoring Systems

Surveillance and monitoring systems are essential components of a comprehensive home security strategy. They act as both a deterrent to potential intruders and a vital tool for detecting and responding to threats. By providing real-time visibility of your property, these systems enhance your ability to protect your home and loved ones. In this chapter, we will explore the critical role that surveillance plays in home security and provide detailed guidance on choosing and setting up cameras, motion detectors, and alarm systems.

The Role of Surveillance in Home Security

Surveillance serves multiple functions in a home security setup. Primarily, it acts as a deterrent. The presence of visible cameras can discourage potential intruders from targeting your home, as they are less likely to attempt a break-in if they know their actions are being recorded. This psychological barrier is powerful—knowing that there is a higher risk of being caught or identified can make criminals think twice before engaging in illegal activities.

Beyond deterrence, surveillance systems provide crucial real-time information. In the event of a security breach, cameras and sensors allow you to quickly assess the situation, determine the nature and extent of the threat, and respond accordingly. Whether it's a suspicious person approaching your property, an attempted break-in, or even a package theft, having eyes on the scene enables you to take swift action—whether that means alerting the authorities, activating an alarm, or securing your home.

Moreover, surveillance systems offer valuable evidence in the aftermath of an incident. Recorded footage can be used to identify perpetrators, support police investigations, and serve as evidence in legal proceedings. In cases of disputes or insurance claims, having clear, time-stamped video recordings can be indispensable.

Another important aspect of surveillance is the peace of mind it offers. Knowing that your home is constantly monitored, whether you are present or away, can significantly reduce anxiety about potential security threats. With modern systems, remote access features allow you to check in on your property from anywhere in the world via smartphone or computer, ensuring that you are always connected to what matters most.

Choosing and Setting Up Cameras, Motion Detectors, and Alarm Systems

When selecting and installing surveillance equipment, it's essential to choose systems that are both effective and suited to your specific needs. The market offers a wide variety of options, from basic setups to sophisticated systems with advanced features. Understanding the capabilities of different components and how they can work together is key to creating a robust security network.

Cameras are the backbone of any surveillance system. When choosing cameras, consider the coverage you need. Exterior cameras should be positioned to monitor all entry points, including doors, windows, garages, and driveways. Wide-angle lenses are useful for covering large areas, while pan-tilt-zoom (PTZ) cameras offer the flexibility to adjust the field of view remotely, allowing you to focus on specific areas when necessary.

For optimal security, opt for cameras with **high-definition (HD) resolution**. HD cameras capture clear, detailed images, making it easier to identify faces, license plates, and other important details. Night vision capability is another crucial feature, as many break-ins occur under the cover of darkness. Infrared (IR) cameras provide clear images in low-light conditions, ensuring that your surveillance remains effective around the clock.

Placement of cameras is as important as the cameras themselves. Position exterior cameras at a height that is out of reach but still allows for a clear view of entry points. Angles should be adjusted to minimize blind spots, and it's wise to overlap coverage areas to ensure continuous monitoring. Consider placing cameras in less obvious locations as well, such as above second-story windows or near side entrances, to catch intruders who might try to avoid the more conspicuous cameras.

Motion detectors complement your camera system by triggering recordings or alerts whenever movement is detected within a specified area. These sensors are particularly useful in areas that don't require constant monitoring but where activity should be flagged, such as backyards, garages, or side alleys. Motion detectors can be set to different sensitivity levels to avoid false alarms triggered by small animals or weather conditions. When integrated with your camera system, motion detectors ensure that you are notified of activity as it happens, allowing you to view the live feed and assess the situation immediately.

Besides cameras and motion detectors, **alarm systems** are a critical component of home security. An alarm system provides an immediate response to a potential threat, often scaring off intruders and alerting you and your neighbors to the situation. When choosing an alarm system, look for one that offers multiple layers of protection, such as door and window sensors, glass break detectors, and panic buttons.

Door and window sensors alert you whenever these entry points are opened, while glass break detectors are designed to recognize the specific sound frequency of breaking glass, triggering the alarm if a window is smashed. Panic buttons, typically located in easily accessible areas like bedrooms or living rooms, allow you to activate the alarm manually in case of an emergency.

Modern alarm systems often come with **smart home integration**, allowing you to control and monitor the system through your smartphone or other devices. This capability is particularly useful when you are away from home, as you can receive instant alerts and remotely arm or disarm the system as needed. Many alarm systems offer the option of professional monitoring services, where a security company is notified immediately if the alarm is triggered, and they can contact emergency services on your behalf.

For the most effective surveillance and monitoring setup, **integration** is key. Ensure that your cameras, motion detectors, and alarm systems are interconnected, either through a centralized control panel or a smart home platform. This integration allows for seamless operation, where an event detected by one component triggers a coordinated response across the entire system. For example, motion detected in the backyard could activate the cameras, turn on exterior lights, and sound the alarm simultaneously, creating a multi-layered defense against potential intrusions.

Implementing a comprehensive surveillance and monitoring system is an essential step in securing your home. By carefully selecting and strategically positioning cameras, motion detectors, and alarm systems, you can create a robust security network that not only deters intruders but also provides real-time alerts and valuable evidence in the event of a security breach. As you build out your system, keep in mind that the goal is to create a seamless, integrated setup that covers all potential entry points and provides peace of mind, knowing that your home is under constant watch. With the right combination of surveillance tools and thoughtful placement, your home will be well-protected against any threats that may arise.

Building an Impenetrable Fortress: Step-by-Step

Fortifying the Perimeter

Your home's perimeter is the first line of defense against potential intruders. A well-fortified perimeter not only delays or prevents unauthorized access but also acts as a powerful deterrent, making your property a less appealing target for criminals. By establishing physical barriers and creating strategic deterrents, you can significantly enhance your home's security long before any threat reaches your front door. This chapter explores effective methods for fortifying your perimeter, focusing on the use of fences, gates, landscaping, and other physical deterrents.

Establishing Physical Barriers: Fences, Gates, and Landscaping

The first step in fortifying your perimeter is to establish strong physical barriers that define the boundaries of your property and restrict access. **Fences** are the most common and effective way to achieve this. When selecting a fence, consider both its height and the materials used. A fence should be tall enough to prevent easy climbing—typically at least six to eight feet high—and constructed from durable materials such as wood, vinyl, or metal. Chain-link fences, while common, offer less privacy and are easier to climb, so they may need additional features like barbed wire or anti-climb spikes to enhance security.

For a more robust barrier, consider installing a **solid privacy fence**. These fences, made from materials like wood or composite panels, not only block physical access but also limit visibility into your property, reducing the chances of your home being targeted by opportunistic criminals. Privacy fences can be reinforced with metal brackets and concrete footings to make them more resistant to tampering or forced entry.

Besides fences, **gates** play a crucial role in securing your perimeter. Gates should be constructed from the same sturdy materials as your fence and equipped with reliable locking mechanisms. For maximum security, consider installing **automatic gates** that can be controlled remotely, allowing you to manage access without leaving the safety of your home. These gates can also be integrated with your surveillance system, enabling you to monitor and control who enters your property in real time.

Landscaping is another powerful tool in fortifying your perimeter. Strategic landscaping can both enhance your home's security and improve its aesthetic appeal. **Natural barriers** such as thorny bushes or dense hedges can be planted along the perimeter to deter intruders. These plants create a physical obstacle that is difficult and painful to navigate, making it less likely that someone will attempt to breach your property. Popular choices include plants like hawthorn, rose bushes, and pyracantha, all of which have sharp thorns and grow densely enough to form an effective barrier.

Besides using plants as barriers, landscaping can also be designed to improve visibility around your property. Keep shrubs and trees trimmed back, especially near windows and entry points, to eliminate potential hiding spots for intruders. This open visibility ensures that any suspicious activity is more likely to be noticed by you, your neighbors, or even passing security patrols.

Creating Deterrents: Preventing Unwanted Entry Before Threats Reach the Home

While physical barriers are essential, they are most effective when combined with deterrents that discourage potential intruders from even attempting to approach your home. These deterrents send a clear message that your property is well-protected and that any attempt to breach it will be met with significant resistance.

Lighting is one of the most effective deterrents you can implement. Well-lit properties are far less attractive to criminals, who prefer to operate under the cover of darkness. Install **motion-activated lights** around the perimeter of your home, particularly near entry points and pathways. These lights should be positioned high enough to prevent tampering and adjusted to cover all vulnerable areas. The sudden activation of bright lights can startle intruders and draw attention to their presence, often causing them to abandon their plans altogether.

Another powerful deterrent is **signage**. Clearly visible signs that indicate the presence of security measures— such as alarms, surveillance cameras, or guard dogs—can make a significant impact on a criminal's decision-making process. Even if you do not have a dog, a sign warning of a "beware of dog" can be enough to make an intruder think twice. Similarly, signs that warn of video surveillance or that the property is under 24-hour monitoring can enhance the perceived risk of being caught.

Security cameras themselves also serve as a strong deterrent, especially when they are clearly visible. Place cameras at key points along the perimeter, such as at gates, driveways, and the main entrance. Even dummy cameras, when strategically placed, can be effective in deterring potential intruders by creating the impression that the entire property is under constant surveillance.

Another layer of deterrence can be added through the use of **alarm systems**. Perimeter alarms that are triggered by movement or tampering with gates and fences can provide an early warning of a potential breach. These alarms can be linked to a central security system that alerts you or a monitoring service immediately, allowing for a rapid response.

Noise deterrents such as gravel paths or driveways can also be effective. The sound of crunching gravel underfoot makes it difficult for someone to approach your home silently, increasing the likelihood that they will be detected before they can reach the house. This simple, yet effective, measure adds another layer of security to your perimeter.

For those looking to take perimeter security a step further, **electronic security systems** such as electric fences or laser-based motion detectors can be installed. While these systems are more complex and expensive, they offer a high level of security by detecting and deterring intruders before they can even touch your property. Electric fences deliver a non-lethal shock that acts as a powerful deterrent, while laser motion detectors can trigger alarms or lights when someone crosses a protected boundary.

Fortifying your home's perimeter is a critical step in creating a secure environment that protects your property and loved ones. By establishing strong physical barriers such as fences, gates, and strategic landscaping, and by implementing effective deterrents, you can significantly reduce the likelihood of unauthorized access to your home. These measures, when combined, create a layered defense that not only delays potential intruders but also discourages them from attempting to breach your property in the first place. As you continue to enhance your home's security, remember that the goal is to create a perimeter that is both impenetrable and intimidating, ensuring that your home remains a safe and secure refuge.

Reinforcing Walls and Structural Elements

When it comes to home security, the strength of your walls, doors, and windows plays a crucial role in defending against forced entry. While most people focus on locks and alarms, the structural integrity of your home is equally important in preventing intruders from gaining access. By reinforcing these elements, you can make your home far more resilient to attacks, turning it into a fortress that deters and withstands even the most determined intruders. This chapter will delve into techniques for strengthening your home's structural elements and explore the materials and methods that can fortify your residence against potential threats.

Techniques for Strengthening Walls, Doors, and Windows Against Forced Entry

The walls of your home are its first line of defense, and reinforcing them can make a significant difference in your overall security. Standard residential walls, typically made of wood framing with drywall, offer minimal resistance to forced entry or impact. To enhance their strength, consider **reinforcing the studs and sheathing**. One method is to add a layer of plywood or oriented strand board (OSB) behind the drywall, which adds rigidity and makes it more difficult for someone to break through. This additional layer can be secured with long screws or bolts that anchor it to the wall studs, creating a much more durable barrier.

For an even stronger solution, **reinforced concrete** or **masonry walls** can be used, particularly in critical areas like safe rooms or exterior walls that are more vulnerable to attack. Concrete walls, either solid or filled with reinforcing steel (rebar), provide exceptional resistance to both impact and forced entry. If rebuilding or major renovations are not feasible, you can still reinforce existing walls by applying **high-impact resistant wall coverings**, such as Kevlar sheets or ballistic fiberglass panels. These materials are designed to withstand significant force and can stop bullets, adding a layer of ballistic protection to your home.

Doors, as primary entry points, require robust reinforcement to prevent them from being easily breached. The strength of a door is determined not just by the door itself but also by the door frame and the hardware used. **Solid core doors**, made from wood or metal, are much more resistant to forced entry than hollow-core doors, which can be easily kicked in or smashed. If your doors are not already solid core, upgrading them should be a top priority.

Besides using solid core doors, reinforce the **door frame** by installing **heavy-duty strike plates** and long screws that penetrate deep into the wall studs. The strike plate is the metal plate that the door latch or deadbolt slides into, and reinforcing it helps distribute the force of a kick or impact over a larger area, making it harder for the door to be forced open. **Deadbolt locks** should also be used on all exterior doors, with a minimum of a 1-inch bolt throw to ensure a secure lock.

Security hinges are another critical component in reinforcing doors. Standard hinges can be a weak point, as they are often exposed on the exterior side of the door, making them susceptible to tampering. Security hinges with non-removable pins or concealed hinges prevent intruders from easily removing the door from its frame. Additionally, **door reinforcement kits** that include door armor, hinge shields, and jamb reinforcements can further fortify your door against forced entry.

Windows are often the most vulnerable part of a home's exterior, and they require special attention to ensure they cannot be easily breached. **Security film** is an effective way to reinforce windows without compromising visibility. This clear, adhesive film bonds with the glass, making it shatter-resistant. If an intruder attempts to break the window, the film holds the shards together, preventing easy access. For even greater protection, consider installing **laminated security glass**, which is composed of multiple layers of glass and plastic. Laminated glass is much harder to break through and provides additional time to respond to a threat.

In areas where windows are particularly vulnerable, such as ground floors or basements, installing **window bars** or **grilles** offers a strong physical barrier. These can be custom-fitted to your windows and designed to match the aesthetics of your home while providing significant resistance to forced entry. For a less obtrusive option, **security shutters** can be installed. These shutters, which can be manually or automatically operated, roll down over the window to protect it from impact and forced entry while also providing privacy and insulation.

Exploring Materials and Methods for Making Your Home More Resilient to Attacks

To ensure that your home is as resilient as possible, it's important to choose the right materials and methods for reinforcing its structural elements. **Steel** and **reinforced concrete** are among the most durable materials available for home construction and retrofitting. Steel, used in door frames, security doors, and window grilles, offers exceptional strength and durability. Reinforced concrete walls, particularly those with embedded rebar, provide a solid barrier that is highly resistant to impact, fire, and weather-related damage.

For those looking to add ballistic protection, materials like **Kevlar** and **ballistic fiberglass** are highly effective. Kevlar, known for its use in bulletproof vests, can be installed within walls to provide a layer of bullet resistance. Ballistic fiberglass panels, often used in safe rooms or panic rooms, are lightweight yet extremely strong, capable of stopping bullets and absorbing impact from forced entry attempts.

In addition to these materials, **polycarbonate** and **acrylic** are excellent options for reinforcing windows. These materials are much stronger than traditional glass and are often used in environments where high impact resistance is required, such as banks or government buildings. Polycarbonate windows, for instance, can withstand repeated blows without breaking, making them ideal for securing your home's most vulnerable entry points.

Retrofitting your home's existing structure with these materials can significantly increase its resilience to attacks. For example, applying ballistic panels to interior walls or reinforcing the roof and attic spaces with steel can create safe zones within your home where you can retreat in the event of an intruder. Similarly, reinforcing the connection points between walls, floors, and ceilings with steel brackets and anchors can prevent these areas from being easily breached or compromised during an attack.

For an even more comprehensive approach, consider **integrating security design** into any home renovations or new construction projects. This might involve constructing walls with concrete or masonry from the outset, installing steel-reinforced door frames, or incorporating laminated glass windows as a standard feature. By thinking about security at the design stage, you can ensure that your home is built to withstand a wide range of potential threats.

Reinforcing the structural elements of your home is an essential step in creating a secure environment that can withstand forced entry and other forms of attack. By strengthening walls, doors, and windows with the right materials and techniques, you can significantly enhance your home's ability to resist intruders and protect your family. Whether you are retrofitting an existing home or planning new construction, investing in these reinforcements is a crucial part of building a resilient and secure sanctuary. As you continue to fortify your home, remember that each improvement not only increases physical security but also provides peace of mind, knowing that your home is prepared to withstand any challenge.

Installing Defensive Systems

Creating a secure home environment goes beyond simple locks and alarms. To truly fortify your home against potential threats, it's essential to integrate advanced defensive systems that provide both active and passive protection. This involves the installation of reinforced doors, bullet-resistant materials, and safe rooms, as well as a thoughtful consideration of how to balance active defense mechanisms with passive ones. By combining these elements, you can create a comprehensive defense strategy that ensures your home remains a safe haven in any situation.

Integrating Defensive Features: Reinforced Doors, Bullet-Resistant Materials, and Safe Rooms

One of the most effective ways to bolster your home's security is by installing **reinforced doors**. Unlike standard doors, which can often be breached with relative ease, reinforced doors are designed to withstand significant force, making them a critical component of any defensive system. These doors are typically constructed from materials such as steel or solid wood and are reinforced with internal metal frames, heavy-duty hinges, and multi-point locking systems that secure the door at multiple points along the frame. This makes them extremely difficult to force open, even with tools or brute strength.

Reinforced doors are particularly important at entry points like the front and back doors, but they are also invaluable for interior spaces, such as safe rooms. A **safe room** is a fortified space within your home designed to protect you and your family during an emergency. The walls of a safe room are typically reinforced with materials like concrete or steel, and the door is a high-security, reinforced model that can resist both physical and ballistic attacks.

The integration of **bullet-resistant materials** into your home's structure provides an additional layer of defense, particularly in areas where you or your family might need to take refuge during a violent incident. Bullet-resistant materials, such as Kevlar panels, ballistic fiberglass, and polycarbonate windows, can be installed in walls, doors, and windows to prevent bullets from penetrating and causing harm. These materials are often used in conjunction with other defensive systems, such as reinforced doors and safe rooms, to create a secure environment that can withstand even the most determined attacks.

Besides protecting against gunfire, bullet-resistant materials can also serve as a deterrent. If an intruder knows that your home is fortified with these advanced materials, they may be less likely to attempt an attack in the first place. The psychological impact of knowing that a home is well-defended cannot be underestimated, as it increases the perceived risk for the intruder.

Safe rooms are a crucial element in a well-rounded defensive strategy. These rooms should be strategically located in your home—ideally in a place that is easily accessible from key living areas but not obvious to outsiders. A safe room should be equipped with communication devices, such as a landline phone or a dedicated cellular phone, so you can contact emergency services even if your primary communication systems are compromised. Safe rooms should have adequate ventilation, water, food supplies, and first-aid kits to ensure you can remain safe and comfortable for an extended period if necessary.

Considerations for Active and Passive Defense Mechanisms in Your Home

When installing defensive systems, it's important to consider the balance between **active** and **passive** defense mechanisms. Both play crucial roles in a comprehensive home security plan, but they serve different purposes and require different levels of involvement from the homeowner.

Active defense mechanisms are those that require real-time action or response. Examples include alarm systems, surveillance cameras, and motion detectors. These systems are designed to detect and respond to intrusions as they happen, often by alerting you or law enforcement to the presence of a threat. Active systems are highly effective in deterring intruders and responding to breaches, but they depend on being noticed and acted upon quickly. This means that you or a monitoring service must be prepared to respond immediately when an alarm is triggered.

One of the key considerations for active defense systems is ensuring they are well-integrated and provide comprehensive coverage of your property. For instance, surveillance cameras should be placed to monitor all entry points and vulnerable areas, and they should be connected to a central monitoring system that allows you to view footage in real time. Alarm systems should be configured to cover all potential entry points, including doors, windows, and even less obvious access points like basement windows or attic entrances.

In contrast, **passive defense mechanisms** are designed to provide protection without requiring active intervention. These include reinforced doors, bullet-resistant materials, and safe rooms—features that are always in place, providing constant security without the need for immediate action. Passive systems are particularly valuable because they work regardless of whether you are aware of the threat. For example, a reinforced door provides resistance against forced entry whether or not you are at home, and bullet-resistant windows offer protection even in the absence of an active defense.

One important consideration when installing passive defense systems is ensuring that they are discreet yet effective. While it's important for these systems to be robust, they should also blend seamlessly into your home's design to avoid drawing unnecessary attention. For instance, bullet-resistant windows can be installed in place of regular windows without altering the appearance of your home, while reinforced doors can be designed to look like any other door in your house.

Another key factor is the **redundancy** of both active and passive systems. For example, having multiple layers of defense—such as a reinforced door with an advanced locking system, combined with an alarm that is triggered by forced entry—ensures that even if one system fails, another is in place to provide protection. Similarly, a safe room with both passive defenses (such as bullet-resistant walls) and active defenses (like a monitored communication system) provides comprehensive security in a crisis.

Installing defensive systems that integrate both active and passive mechanisms is essential for creating a secure home environment. Reinforced doors, bullet-resistant materials, and safe rooms form the backbone of a passive defense strategy that provides constant protection, while active systems like alarms and surveillance cameras offer real-time monitoring and response capabilities. By thoughtfully balancing these elements, you can ensure that your home is well-protected against a wide range of potential threats, providing both physical security and peace of mind for you and your family. As you continue to enhance your home's defenses, remember that a layered approach—where each system complements and reinforces the others—will always be the most effective strategy for keeping your home safe.

Securing Utilities and Critical Infrastructure

In the realm of home security, it's easy to focus on physical barriers and surveillance systems while overlooking the critical role that utilities and infrastructure play in maintaining a secure environment. Power, water, and communication lines are the lifeblood of your home's functionality, and any disruption to these services can severely compromise your ability to protect your property and your family. Securing these essential systems against tampering or disruption is a vital component of a comprehensive security strategy. This chapter explores how to protect these critical infrastructures and offers strategies for safeguarding the services that support your home's security.

Protecting Power, Water, and Communication Lines from Tampering or Disruption

The uninterrupted flow of electricity is crucial for maintaining the operation of security systems, lighting, and essential household functions. Unfortunately, power lines are vulnerable to both accidental disruptions and intentional tampering. To safeguard your home's power supply, it's important to take both preventative and reactive measures.

Start by **securing access to your electrical infrastructure**. This includes ensuring that your electrical panel and any external power supply boxes are locked and located in areas that are not easily accessible to outsiders. You may also consider installing security cameras near these utilities to monitor for any suspicious activity. In areas prone to natural disasters or where sabotage is a concern, investing in a **backup generator** is essential. A generator can keep critical systems running in the event of a power outage, ensuring that your security systems, lights, and essential appliances remain operational. It's advisable to choose a generator that can power your entire home, or at least the most critical circuits, and ensure it's fueled and ready for use at all times.

Water supply is another critical utility that requires protection. An uninterrupted water supply is necessary not only for basic survival but also for maintaining hygiene, sanitation, and certain security systems, such as sprinkler systems. To protect your water supply, ensure that your water main and any external piping are secured and out of easy reach. Locking mechanisms on water valves can prevent tampering, and installing **water sensors** in critical areas can alert you to leaks or unauthorized use, allowing for immediate response.

In areas where water supplies are at risk of contamination, either through environmental hazards or deliberate acts, it's prudent to install **water purification systems** that can ensure your water remains safe to use. These systems can range from simple filters to more advanced setups that can remove a wide range of contaminants. Maintaining a stockpile of bottled water or water storage tanks is crucial for situations where the regular supply is disrupted.

Communication lines are another vital aspect of home security. The ability to communicate with emergency services, neighbors, and family members is essential during a crisis. Communication lines—whether landline, internet, or cellular—are susceptible to both physical damage and technological disruptions. To safeguard your communication infrastructure, first ensure that any external phone or internet lines are well-protected. This might involve placing them underground or encasing them in protective conduit that makes them less vulnerable to tampering or environmental damage.

For redundancy, consider having multiple forms of communication available. For instance, maintaining a landline phone in addition to your mobile phone provides a backup in case one service is disrupted. Satellite phones and two-way radios can offer reliable communication options when conventional networks are down, particularly in remote areas or during widespread outages. It's also wise to have a **backup internet connection**—such as a mobile hotspot or satellite internet—if your primary service is disrupted.

Strategies for Safeguarding Essential Services That Support Your Home's Security

Once you've secured the physical aspects of your utilities, it's important to focus on the broader strategies that ensure these services remain reliable and secure in the long term. This involves both proactive measures to prevent disruptions and contingency plans for when issues do arise.

Redundancy is a key principle in safeguarding essential services. By having multiple systems in place, you create layers of security that ensure continuity even if one system fails. For power, this might mean having both a generator and battery backups for critical devices like security systems and communication equipment. For water, it could involve having both municipal supply and stored water reserves. And for communication, it might mean having a combination of landline, mobile, and radio systems to ensure you can always reach out for help.

Maintenance is another critical aspect of securing utilities. Regularly inspecting and servicing your electrical, water, and communication systems can prevent many problems before they occur. This includes checking for wear and tear on cables and pipes, ensuring backup generators and batteries are fully charged and operational, and updating software or hardware on communication devices to protect against hacking or obsolescence. Preventative maintenance is particularly important for backup systems that are not used regularly—when you need them, they must work flawlessly.

Another strategy is to **harden your infrastructure** against environmental threats. This can include measures like surge protectors and lightning arrestors for electrical systems, which protect against power spikes and lightning strikes. Similarly, insulating or burying water pipes can prevent them from freezing in cold weather, and securing external communication lines can protect them from high winds or other physical damage. For those in areas prone to earthquakes, flooding, or other natural disasters, additional reinforcements may be necessary to ensure that your infrastructure can withstand these challenges.

Cybersecurity is increasingly important as more home systems, including security and communication networks, become internet-connected. Protecting these systems from cyberattacks is essential. Ensure that all devices connected to the internet—such as smart security cameras, thermostats, and even appliances—are secured with strong, unique passwords and updated regularly to protect against vulnerabilities. Consider using a dedicated, secure network for your home security systems, separate from your regular internet usage, to reduce the risk of hacking. Implementing a firewall and encryption for your home network adds an extra layer of protection against unauthorized access.

Emergency planning is crucial for dealing with utility disruptions. This involves having a clear plan in place for how to respond if power, water, or communication systems fail. Know where your shutoffs are for utilities and how to operate them, ensure that all family members are familiar with the emergency plan, and practice drills regularly so everyone knows what to do in case of a failure. Having a well-stocked emergency kit that includes flashlights, batteries, water, and a means of communication is also essential.

Securing your home's utilities and critical infrastructure is a fundamental aspect of comprehensive home security. By protecting power, water, and communication lines from tampering or disruption, and by implementing strategies to safeguard these essential services, you ensure that your home remains functional and secure even in the face of adversity. The key to success lies in redundancy, maintenance, infrastructure hardening, cybersecurity, and thorough emergency planning. These measures not only protect the physical infrastructure of your home but also provide the peace of mind that comes from knowing you are prepared for any eventuality.

Creating Safe Rooms and Panic Rooms

Designing a Safe Room

In an unpredictable world, the importance of having a secure, fortified space within your home cannot be overstated. A well-designed safe room serves as a refuge during emergencies, providing protection from intruders, natural disasters, or other life-threatening situations. To ensure that your safe room is both effective and accessible when needed, careful planning and thoughtful design are essential. This chapter delves into the key considerations for selecting the location, design, and accessibility of your safe room, as well as the critical features it must include to offer true safety and security.

Key Considerations for Safe Room Location, Design, and Accessibility

The location of your safe room is one of the most crucial decisions in the design process. Ideally, the safe room should be easily accessible from the main living areas of your home, ensuring that you can reach it quickly in an emergency. For this reason, many homeowners choose to place their safe room on the ground floor, near or within central rooms like the master bedroom or family room. This proximity allows for rapid entry, which is especially important during events such as home invasions or severe weather, when every second counts.

When choosing a location, consider the structural strength of the area. Rooms that are naturally enclosed by reinforced walls—such as basements or internal rooms without windows—are ideal candidates for conversion into safe rooms. Basements, in particular, offer excellent protection against both intruders and natural disasters like tornadoes or hurricanes due to their underground location and solid construction. If a basement is not feasible, an interior room with few or no windows is the next best option. These rooms are less vulnerable to external threats and can be more easily fortified.

The design of the safe room itself should prioritize both security and comfort, as you may need to stay there for an extended period. Start by reinforcing the walls, floor, and ceiling with materials that can withstand various forms of attack. Concrete and steel are commonly used for their strength and durability. Walls can be further reinforced with ballistic panels or Kevlar sheets to provide additional protection against bullets or shrapnel. The door to the safe room is another critical element—choose a high-security door made from solid steel, equipped with heavy-duty locks and deadbolts. This door should be able to resist both physical force and attempts at bypassing the lock.

Accessibility is another key consideration. The entrance to the safe room should be discreet yet easily reachable. Consider camouflaging the door to blend in with the surrounding walls or integrating it into a closet or cabinetry. In some cases, the entrance may be concealed behind a piece of furniture or a hidden panel, making it harder for intruders to locate. Inside the room, ensure that the layout is simple and that all necessary supplies and communication tools are within easy reach. The room should be large enough to accommodate all household members comfortably, with enough space to move around, lie down, and store essential items.

Essential Features for a Safe Room: Ventilation, Communication, and Supplies

Beyond structural security, a well-designed safe room must include several essential features to ensure that it functions effectively during an emergency. Chief among these are ventilation, communication, and adequate supplies.

Ventilation is critical to maintaining a safe and habitable environment, especially if you may need to remain in the room for an extended period. A safe room should be equipped with an independent ventilation system that can provide fresh air while preventing contaminants from entering. In many cases, a filtered air supply system is ideal, as it can protect against smoke, gas, and other airborne hazards. This system should have a manual override so that you can control airflow in the event of a power outage or other issues. Consider also adding a carbon dioxide detector and an air quality monitor to ensure that the air remains breathable.

Communication is another essential feature. In an emergency, the ability to contact the outside world can be a matter of life and death. Your safe room should be equipped with a reliable means of communication, such as a dedicated landline phone, a cellular phone with a strong signal, or a satellite phone. It's also advisable to include a two-way radio, which can be invaluable if other forms of communication fail. All communication devices should be kept fully charged and connected to backup power sources, such as a generator or battery pack, to ensure they remain operational during a prolonged emergency.

Besides communication tools, consider installing a closed-circuit television (CCTV) system that allows you to monitor the situation outside the safe room. Cameras placed around your home's exterior and in key interior areas can feed live video to a monitor in the safe room, providing you with real-time information about the situation and helping you make informed decisions about when it's safe to leave.

Supplies are the final critical component of a safe room. The room should be stocked with enough food, water, and medical supplies to last for at least 72 hours, although a longer supply is preferable in the event of extended emergencies. Non-perishable foods such as canned goods, protein bars, and freeze-dried meals are ideal for this purpose. Water is even more important—store enough bottled water to provide at least one gallon per person per day. Consider including a water filtration system or purification tablets as a backup in case your stored water supply runs low.

Medical supplies are also essential. Your safe room should contain a well-stocked first aid kit, including basic medical supplies like bandages, antiseptics, pain relievers, and any necessary prescription medications. If possible, include advanced medical supplies like a tourniquet, burn treatments, and splints, along with a first aid manual that provides instructions for handling more serious injuries. A small fire extinguisher and a flashlight with extra batteries are also crucial for dealing with potential hazards inside the room.

Comfort items should not be overlooked, especially if you have young children or elderly family members who may be more vulnerable to stress during an emergency. Blankets, pillows, and basic hygiene items like wet wipes, toilet paper, and hand sanitizer can make a significant difference in maintaining morale and well-being. Consider including entertainment options like books, puzzles, or a battery-operated radio to help pass the time.

Designing a safe room requires careful consideration of location, structural integrity, accessibility, and essential features like ventilation, communication, and supplies. By taking these factors into account, you can create a secure and comfortable refuge that will protect you and your family during even the most severe emergencies. A well-designed safe room is more than just a secure space—it is a critical component of your overall home security strategy, providing peace of mind and a reliable sanctuary in times of crisis. As you plan and build your safe room, remember that attention to detail and thorough preparation are key to ensuring that it serves its purpose effectively when you need it most.

Constructing a Panic Room

In the realm of home security, a panic room represents the ultimate refuge during a crisis, offering a fortified space where you and your loved ones can retreat to stay safe from immediate threats. While often confused with safe rooms, panic rooms are designed with more advanced security features, focusing specifically on withstanding active threats like home invasions. Understanding the differences between these two types of rooms and knowing when to choose each is crucial in ensuring your home is prepared for any scenario. This chapter will guide you through the distinctions between safe rooms and panic rooms, and provide a detailed, step-by-step process for constructing a panic room with the highest level of security.

Differences Between Safe Rooms and Panic Rooms and When to Choose Each

At first glance, safe rooms and panic rooms might seem interchangeable, as both provide secure spaces designed to protect occupants during emergencies. Their purposes and features can differ significantly, depending on the threats they are designed to mitigate.

Safe rooms are generally multi-purpose spaces intended to offer protection during a variety of emergencies, such as natural disasters, home invasions, or chemical spills. These rooms are typically designed to withstand external forces, like high winds or earthquakes, and are often equipped with basic survival supplies, communication devices, and ventilation systems. Safe rooms can be used for longer-term shelter, making them ideal for situations where you may need to stay protected for several hours or even days.

Panic rooms, on the other hand, are specifically designed for short-term protection during immediate, high-threat situations, such as a home invasion or active shooter scenario. The primary function of a panic room is to provide a secure, impenetrable space where you can quickly retreat and remain safe until help arrives. Panic rooms are built to withstand direct attacks, with reinforced walls, doors, and security systems that prevent unauthorized entry. They typically feature advanced security technologies, such as ballistic protection, surveillance systems, and communication links to emergency services.

When deciding between a safe room and a panic room, consider the specific threats you are most likely to face. If your primary concern is protection from natural disasters or long-term emergencies, a safe room may be more appropriate. If you live in an area with higher crime rates or have concerns about targeted attacks, a panic room offers the heightened security necessary to protect you during a violent encounter.

Step-by-Step Guide to Building a Panic Room with Advanced Security Features

Constructing a panic room requires careful planning and execution to ensure that it offers the level of protection needed in life-threatening situations. Below is a step-by-step guide to building a panic room, with an emphasis on integrating advanced security features.

1. Selecting the Location

The first step in constructing a panic room is choosing an appropriate location within your home. The room should be easily accessible from the main living areas but discreet enough that it's not immediately obvious to intruders. Ideal locations include walk-in closets, basements, or rooms that can be concealed behind false walls or bookshelves. The location should allow for quick entry and secure lockdown, minimizing the time you are exposed to danger.

2. Reinforcing the Structure

Once the location is chosen, the next step is reinforcing the room's structure to withstand forced entry and other threats. Start by reinforcing the walls with materials like **ballistic fiberglass**, **Kevlar panels**, or **reinforced concrete**. These materials are designed to absorb and deflect bullets, impact forces, and even blasts. The ceiling and floor should also be reinforced, particularly if the room is on an upper level, to prevent access from above or below.

3. Installing a High-Security Door

The door to your panic room is the most critical element in its security. A high-security door should be made of solid steel or another ballistic-resistant material and should be equipped with multiple locking mechanisms. Consider a door with a **multi-point locking system** that secures the door at several points along the frame, making it nearly impossible to force open. The door frame itself should be reinforced with steel, and the hinges should be tamper-proof, either by using non-removable pins or concealed hinges.

4. Ensuring Ventilation and Air Filtration

Proper ventilation is essential, especially if you may need to remain in the panic room for an extended period. The room should be equipped with a dedicated ventilation system that can operate independently of the rest of the house. This system should include **HEPA filters** to remove airborne contaminants and, ideally, a **gas mask** or **oxygen supply** in case of chemical or smoke exposure. Ensure that the ventilation system is designed to prevent tampering from the outside, with ducts that are protected by steel grilles or mesh.

5. Integrating Communication Systems

A panic room must have reliable communication systems to alert authorities and stay informed during an emergency. Install a **landline phone** or **dedicated cellular phone** with an external antenna to ensure a strong signal, even if the main phone lines are cut. It's also advisable to include a **two-way radio** as a backup communication method, especially in areas where cellular service may be unreliable. For continuous monitoring, consider installing a **closed-circuit television (CCTV) system** that provides live video feeds from around your home directly to the panic room, allowing you to assess the situation outside the room in real-time.

6. Providing Power and Backup Systems

Reliable power is crucial for maintaining security systems and communication devices in a panic room. The room should be connected to the home's main power supply, but also have **backup power sources** such as a **battery bank** or **generator** to ensure that critical systems remain operational during a power outage. The backup system should be capable of powering lights, communication devices, and ventilation for several hours.

7. Stocking Essential Supplies

While panic rooms are typically designed for short-term use, it's important to stock them with essential supplies in case you need to stay inside longer than anticipated. This includes **non-perishable food** and **water** for at least 24-72 hours, **first aid supplies**, **medications**, and **personal hygiene items**. Consider including items like **fire extinguishers**, **flashlights**, and **tools** that could be useful in an emergency. Comfort items, such as blankets and seating, can also help make the room more bearable during extended stays.

8. Testing and Drills

Once your panic room is constructed and equipped, it's vital to regularly test all systems and conduct drills with your family to ensure everyone knows how to access the room quickly and operate its features. Regular maintenance checks should be performed on all equipment, especially backup power systems and communication devices, to ensure they are always in working order. Drills should cover various scenarios, such as home invasions, fire, or natural disasters, and should include practicing lockdown procedures and communication with emergency services.

Constructing a panic room involves careful consideration of location, structural integrity, and advanced security features to create a space that offers maximum protection in the most dangerous situations. By following the steps outlined above, you can build a panic room that not only provides a secure refuge but also integrates the necessary tools and systems to ensure your safety and survival during a crisis. A well-designed panic room is an investment in your family's security, offering peace of mind and a reliable plan of action when every second counts.

Stocking and Equipping Your Safe/Panic Room

A well-designed safe or panic room is only as effective as the supplies and tools it contains. In the event of an emergency, this secure space becomes your refuge, possibly for hours or even days, so it must be adequately stocked to sustain you and your family. Properly equipping your safe or panic room involves careful planning to ensure that you have all the necessary items for survival, communication, and comfort. This chapter will guide you through the essential supplies to keep in your safe room for long-term sustainability and the tools and communication devices you'll need for emergency situations.

Essential Items and Supplies for Long-Term Sustainability

When preparing your safe or panic room, consider the types of emergencies you might face and how long you could realistically be confined. The goal is to create a self-sufficient environment where you can survive comfortably without outside assistance for at least 72 hours, though longer preparations are ideal.

Water is the most critical resource. Each person in the room will need at least one gallon of water per day for drinking and basic hygiene. For a family of four, that means storing at least 12 gallons of water for three days, with more if you anticipate needing to stay longer. Water should be stored in sealed, durable containers, and it's wise to have a water purification method on hand, such as a portable filter or purification tablets, in case your supply runs low or becomes contaminated.

Food is the next priority. Choose non-perishable, high-energy foods that require little or no preparation. Examples include canned goods, protein bars, dried fruits, nuts, and freeze-dried meals. Ensure you have a manual can opener if your food supply includes canned items. While the primary focus is on sustenance, consider including some comfort foods or snacks, especially if you have children, to help maintain morale during a stressful situation.

Medical supplies are essential for dealing with injuries or illnesses that might occur while you're in the room. Your safe room should be equipped with a comprehensive first aid kit that includes bandages, antiseptics, pain relievers, and any prescription medications your family members might need. It's also prudent to include more advanced medical supplies such as splints, burn treatments, and tourniquets, along with a first aid manual that provides instructions for treating serious injuries.

Sanitation and hygiene supplies are critical for maintaining health in a confined space. Stock your safe room with items like wet wipes, hand sanitizer, toilet paper, and trash bags. A portable toilet or bucket with a seat lid can be invaluable for waste management, especially if you're in the room for an extended period. Including feminine hygiene products and diapers if needed is also essential.

Lighting and power are important for both comfort and security. Battery-powered lanterns, flashlights, and plenty of extra batteries should be on hand. Consider including a hand-crank or solar-powered light as a backup. A small portable power bank or generator can be used to keep essential devices charged, especially if you need to maintain communication or monitor external cameras.

Comfort items can make a significant difference in how bearable your time in the safe room is. Blankets, pillows, and sleeping bags provide warmth and rest, while basic items like a change of clothes, socks, and personal hygiene products (toothbrushes, toothpaste, etc.) contribute to a sense of normalcy. Including entertainment items like books, games, or a battery-operated radio can help alleviate boredom and reduce stress.

Tools and Communication Devices for Emergency Situations

Equipping your safe room with the right tools and communication devices is crucial for both survival and staying informed during an emergency. These items ensure that you can maintain contact with the outside world, monitor the situation, and respond appropriately to changing circumstances.

Communication devices are your lifeline in a crisis. A dedicated landline phone connected directly to the phone line (not a cordless model) ensures communication even if the power is out. A cellular phone with a strong signal is also vital, preferably with a backup battery or charger. Consider investing in a satellite phone, which operates independently of local networks and can function during widespread outages.

A **two-way radio** is another critical tool, especially if you are coordinating with others outside the room or if other forms of communication fail. These radios are reliable, easy to use, and can provide a direct line to family members, neighbors, or emergency responders.

For **situational awareness**, install a **closed-circuit television (CCTV) system** that allows you to monitor your home's exterior and key interior areas from inside the safe room. This system provides real-time video feeds, helping you assess the situation and decide when it's safe to leave. A battery-operated or solar-powered radio is also invaluable for receiving updates on weather conditions, news, and emergency broadcasts.

Tools for emergency repairs or self-defense should be included as well. A multi-tool or Swiss Army knife can handle a variety of small tasks, from opening cans to cutting materials. A crowbar, hammer, or sturdy wrench can be useful for both construction and defense, particularly if you need to break through debris or reinforce barricades. If you are trained and legally permitted to do so, keeping a firearm with appropriate ammunition in the safe room can provide a means of self-defense; this decision should be carefully considered and weighed against the risks.

Fire safety equipment is another must-have. A small fire extinguisher can help you deal with minor fires that might break out due to electrical issues or other hazards within the room. Smoke detectors and carbon monoxide detectors should be installed to alert you to these dangers, especially if your safe room is in a basement or other enclosed area.

Escape tools should also be considered. While the purpose of a panic room is to stay put until it's safe to leave, having tools that allow you to escape if the room is compromised is essential. This might include a rope ladder for upper-level rooms, a pry bar for removing obstacles, or an emergency window punch for breaking glass.

Stocking and equipping your safe or panic room involves more than just storing food and water. It requires a comprehensive approach that includes essential supplies for long-term sustainability, as well as the tools and communication devices necessary to navigate an emergency effectively. By carefully selecting and organizing these items, you can ensure that your safe room provides not only physical protection but also the resources needed to survive and maintain contact with the outside world. Proper preparation transforms a safe room from a simple shelter into a fully equipped, secure environment where you can confidently face any crisis.

Training and Drills for Using Safe Rooms

A well-equipped safe room is only effective if you and your family know how to use it properly during an emergency. Training and conducting regular drills are essential to ensure that everyone in your household can quickly and efficiently access the safe room, operate its features, and remain calm under pressure. This chapter explores how to practice using your safe room effectively and how to develop and rehearse emergency plans with your family, ensuring that you are fully prepared for any situation.

How to Practice Using Your Safe Room Effectively

Familiarity with your safe room's layout, equipment, and procedures is crucial in a high-stress situation. The first step in effective training is ensuring that every family member knows the exact location of the safe room and how to access it quickly. Start by walking through the process of getting to the safe room from various points in your home. Identify potential obstacles, such as locked doors or furniture that may block the path, and address these issues to create a clear, unobstructed route.

Next, familiarize everyone with the safe room's features and equipment. This includes teaching family members how to operate locks, communication devices, and any surveillance systems installed within the room. For example, practice locking and unlocking the safe room door from the inside, using communication tools like radios or phones to contact emergency services, and monitoring live video feeds from external cameras. Repeated practice ensures that these actions become second nature, reducing the likelihood of mistakes during a real emergency.

Another important aspect of training is learning how to manage stress and remain calm while in the safe room. High-stress situations can lead to panic, which impairs judgment and decision-making. To counter this, incorporate stress management techniques into your drills, such as deep breathing exercises or focusing on specific tasks to maintain a sense of control. Encourage family members to communicate calmly and clearly during drills, reinforcing the importance of staying composed under pressure.

Timing is also critical in an emergency, so practice getting to the safe room as quickly as possible. Conduct timed drills where family members move from various locations in the house to the safe room, aiming to reduce the time it takes with each practice. Remember, the goal is not just speed but also efficiency and safety—ensure that everyone moves quickly but without unnecessary risk.

Finally, practice using the safe room in different scenarios. For instance, simulate a home invasion by practicing at night or when family members are in separate rooms. Conduct drills during different times of the day and under various conditions, such as when the power is out or when a family member is incapacitated. These variations help prepare your family for a range of possible situations, ensuring that you are ready to respond no matter the circumstances.

Developing and Rehearsing Emergency Plans with Family Members

Creating a comprehensive emergency plan is an essential component of safe room preparedness. This plan should outline specific actions to take during various emergencies, such as home invasions, natural disasters, or fires, and clearly define each family member's role.

Start by discussing potential threats and scenarios with your family. This conversation should cover the types of emergencies you are most likely to face, the safest responses to each, and the importance of following the plan. Encourage input from all family members to ensure that everyone understands their role and feels confident in their ability to execute the plan.

Once the basic plan is established, write it down in a clear, concise format. Include key details such as:

1. **Emergency triggers**: Define the specific events or signals that indicate it's time to move to the safe room. This might include the sound of an alarm, a power outage, or a specific code word agreed upon by the family.

2. **Assigned roles**: Assign specific tasks to each family member based on their abilities and the nature of the emergency. For example, one person might be responsible for securing the door, while another contacts emergency services or monitors the surveillance system.

3. **Communication protocols**: Outline how you will communicate with each other during an emergency, both inside and outside the safe room. This includes using phones, radios, or intercom systems and knowing what information needs to be conveyed to authorities.

4. **Contingency plans**: Consider potential complications, such as a family member being unable to reach the safe room or the power going out. Develop backup plans for these scenarios, ensuring that there are alternative strategies in place.

With the plan in place, rehearse it regularly through family drills. Begin with simple, straightforward drills that focus on specific parts of the plan, such as reaching the safe room or locking the door. As your family becomes more comfortable with these tasks, increase the complexity by combining multiple elements of the plan or adding unexpected challenges, such as simulating a power outage or a blocked path.

During each drill, take the time to debrief and discuss what went well and where improvements can be made. Encourage open communication and constructive feedback, allowing each family member to express any concerns or suggestions. Use this feedback to refine the emergency plan and drills, ensuring that they remain effective and relevant.

It's also important to refresh your training and drills periodically. As children grow older or new family members join the household, roles and responsibilities may need to be adjusted. Any changes to the safe room's layout or equipment should be incorporated into the training sessions. Regular practice helps keep the plan fresh in everyone's mind and reinforces the skills needed to respond effectively in an emergency.

Training and conducting drills for using your safe room are vital steps in ensuring that your family can respond quickly and efficiently in a crisis. By practicing regularly, familiarizing yourselves with the room's features, and developing a clear, actionable emergency plan, you create a strong foundation of preparedness. This not only enhances your physical safety but also provides the peace of mind that comes from knowing you are ready to protect your loved ones when it matters most.

Video BONUS

Chapter 4: Long-Term Food Storage

Principles of Effective Food Stockpiling

Assessing Your Family's Nutritional Needs

When preparing for long-term food storage, understanding your family's nutritional needs is the cornerstone of an effective stockpile. This knowledge ensures that during an emergency, you can maintain not only sustenance but also health and well-being. Proper nutrition goes beyond simply having enough calories; it involves ensuring that your family receives the right balance of macronutrients—carbohydrates, proteins, and fats—as well as essential vitamins and minerals.

Understanding Daily Caloric and Nutritional Requirements

Every person's caloric needs vary depending on factors such as age, gender, activity level, and overall health. On average, an adult requires between 2,000 to 2,500 calories per day, though this can vary significantly. Children typically need fewer calories, with requirements increasing as they grow. In a high-stress situation or one requiring more physical exertion, caloric needs may increase, making it important to factor in a buffer when planning your stockpile.

Macronutrients are the building blocks of your diet. Carbohydrates, which include grains, legumes, and starchy vegetables, should make up about 45-65% of your daily intake, as they are your body's primary source of energy. Proteins, necessary for muscle repair and immune function, should comprise 10-35% of your diet. These can be found in beans, nuts, seeds, and stored meats or meat alternatives. Fats, although often consumed in smaller quantities, are crucial for energy storage and cell function. They should account for 20-35% of your daily calories and can be sourced from oils, nuts, and shelf-stable dairy products.

Beyond macronutrients, ensuring adequate intake of **vitamins and minerals** is essential to avoid deficiencies that can impair health. Stockpiling a variety of foods rich in vitamins A, C, D, and B-complex, as well as minerals like calcium, magnesium, and iron, is key. Dried fruits, vegetables, fortified cereals, and supplements can help fill these nutritional gaps, especially during extended periods where fresh produce is unavailable.

Tailoring Your Stockpile to Meet Specific Dietary Needs and Preferences

Every family is unique, and your stockpile should reflect the specific dietary needs and preferences of its members. For instance, if someone in your household is gluten-intolerant, it's essential to include gluten-free grains like rice, quinoa, and gluten-free pasta. Similarly, if there are vegetarians or vegans in the family, your stockpile should include a variety of plant-based protein sources, such as beans, lentils, tofu, and nuts.

For those with specific health conditions, such as diabetes or hypertension, it's important to focus on foods that help manage these conditions. Diabetics, for example, will need low-glycemic index foods that don't cause rapid spikes in blood sugar, such as whole grains, legumes, and non-starchy vegetables. For those managing hypertension, low-sodium options should be prioritized, and it may be beneficial to include herbs and spices for seasoning rather than relying on high-sodium alternatives.

In addition to medical needs, consider food preferences to ensure that your family is willing to eat the stockpiled food during an emergency. Stocking familiar foods that your family already enjoys can provide comfort and a sense of normalcy during stressful times. It's also wise to introduce some of these shelf-stable items into your regular diet before an emergency occurs, so everyone becomes accustomed to them, reducing resistance when the time comes to rely on your stockpile.

Consider the **cultural or religious dietary practices** that may be important to your family. If certain foods are prohibited or specific preparation methods are required, make sure your stockpile respects these traditions. By carefully assessing your family's nutritional needs and tailoring your food reserves accordingly, you create a stockpile that not only sustains but also nurtures your loved ones in challenging times.

Determining the Quantity of Food to Store

After understanding your family's nutritional needs, the next step is determining how much food to store. This process involves careful calculations to ensure that you have enough food to last through the emergency, whether it's a short-term disruption or a prolonged crisis.

Calculating the Amount of Food Needed Based on the Number of People and Duration of Storage

To calculate the amount of food required, start by establishing the duration for which you want your stockpile to last. Common timeframes include 72 hours, two weeks, one month, or even longer, depending on the level of preparedness you aim for. Multiply the number of days by the daily caloric requirement for each person in your household. For example, for a family of four with an average requirement of 2,000 calories per person per day, a one-month supply would need to provide approximately 240,000 calories in total.

Break this down further into food groups to ensure a balanced diet. You might decide, for instance, that 50% of these calories should come from carbohydrates, 30% from proteins, and 20% from fats. This means allocating 120,000 calories to carbohydrate-rich foods, 72,000 calories to protein sources, and 48,000 calories to fats. Converting these caloric needs into actual food quantities involves understanding the caloric content of various foods. For example, a pound of rice contains roughly 1,600 calories, so to meet your carbohydrate needs, you would need around 75 pounds of rice or equivalent alternatives.

It's also important to consider **serving sizes** and packaging. Foods that are dense in calories and nutrients, such as grains, beans, and oils, are generally easier to store in large quantities compared to fresh produce, which has a shorter shelf life and takes up more space. For each food category, calculate the number of servings you'll need, then multiply by the recommended serving size to determine the total quantity. For instance, if one serving of rice is half a cup (about 100 grams), and each person will consume two servings a day, a family of four would need roughly 24 pounds of rice for a two-week period.

Factors to Consider, Such as Emergency Scenarios and Storage Space

When determining how much food to store, consider the various emergency scenarios you might face. Short-term events, like natural disasters, may only require a few days' worth of food, while longer-term disruptions, such as pandemics or economic instability, could necessitate a much larger stockpile. If you live in an area prone to natural disasters, such as hurricanes or earthquakes, you may also need to account for the possibility of being cut off from supplies for extended periods.

Storage space is another critical factor. Ensure that your stockpile fits within your available space without compromising safety or accessibility. Foods should be stored in a cool, dry, and dark place, free from pests and humidity, which can lead to spoilage. If you're limited on space, focus on foods that are calorie-dense and nutrient-rich, such as grains, legumes, and dehydrated or freeze-dried options that take up less room but provide substantial nutrition.

Consider also the **rotation of your stockpile**. Food should be organized so that older items are used first, reducing waste and ensuring that your supplies remain fresh. This is where regular monitoring and rotation come into play, as it's important to keep your stockpile not only full but also usable. You can achieve this by integrating your stockpile into your daily meals, regularly replenishing items as they are consumed.

Determining the quantity of food to store requires careful calculation and planning. By considering the number of people, the duration of potential emergencies, and the available storage space, you can build a food reserve that ensures your family is well-fed and healthy during any crisis. Tailoring your stockpile to meet specific needs and preferences further enhances its effectiveness, providing both sustenance and comfort when it's needed most.

Selecting the Right Storage Containers and Methods

Effective long-term food storage hinges on the selection of appropriate containers and methods to preserve food quality and prevent spoilage. Even the most carefully planned stockpile can be compromised if not stored correctly, leading to waste and potentially leaving you without essential supplies when they are most needed. This chapter will explore the best practices for choosing storage containers and the techniques you can use to seal and store food, ensuring that your reserves remain fresh and safe over extended periods.

Choosing Containers That Preserve Food Quality and Prevent Spoilage

The containers you choose for food storage are a critical element in maintaining the quality and longevity of your supplies. Different foods require different types of containers, and the right choice can significantly extend the shelf life of your stockpile.

Food-grade plastic buckets are a popular option for bulk storage of dry goods like grains, rice, and beans. These containers are durable, resistant to moisture, and can hold large quantities of food, making them ideal for long-term storage. When selecting plastic buckets, ensure they are labeled as food-grade, which means they are made from materials safe for storing food without leaching harmful chemicals. These buckets should be paired with airtight lids to protect the contents from air, moisture, and pests.

For smaller quantities or more sensitive items, **mason jars** or **glass containers** with tight-sealing lids are an excellent choice. Glass is impermeable, meaning it doesn't absorb flavors, odors, or colors, and it's resistant to both moisture and pests. Mason jars are particularly useful for storing dehydrated foods, herbs, spices, and canned goods. Their transparent nature also allows you to easily monitor the contents without opening the jar, reducing the risk of contamination.

Vacuum-sealed bags are another effective method for preserving a variety of foods. These bags remove air before sealing, which slows down the oxidation process that can cause food to spoil. They are ideal for storing smaller portions of dried foods, such as nuts, grains, and dried fruits, as well as for sealing meats and cheeses that you plan to freeze. The vacuum seal keeps out air and moisture, which are the primary culprits of spoilage.

Mylar bags combined with oxygen absorbers are widely regarded as one of the best options for long-term food storage, especially for items like grains, beans, and dried foods. Mylar is a metallic, food-grade material that provides a strong barrier against light, moisture, and oxygen. When sealed properly, these bags can preserve food for decades. Oxygen absorbers placed inside the bags remove any remaining oxygen, creating an environment that significantly extends the shelf life of the contents.

For liquid storage, **glass bottles** or **stainless steel containers** are preferred. These materials do not react with acidic foods or beverages, making them ideal for storing oils, vinegar, or water. Stainless steel containers are particularly durable and resistant to corrosion, making them suitable for storing liquids in various conditions.

Regardless of the type of container, it's crucial to ensure that all storage vessels are **airtight**. Exposure to air can lead to oxidation, which degrades food quality and accelerates spoilage. Airtight containers help keep out moisture, pests, and contaminants, all of which can compromise the integrity of your stockpile.

Techniques for Sealing and Storing Food to Extend Shelf Life

Proper sealing and storage techniques are just as important as the choice of container. These methods help protect your food from environmental factors that can reduce its shelf life.

One of the most effective methods is **vacuum sealing**, which removes air from the packaging before sealing it. This process is particularly useful for preventing the oxidation of foods that are sensitive to air, such as nuts, seeds, and dried fruits. Vacuum-sealed bags are compact, allowing for efficient storage, and they can be used for both pantry storage and freezing. For foods that you plan to freeze, vacuum sealing can also prevent freezer burn, which occurs when food is exposed to air in the freezer.

For dry goods like grains, rice, and beans, **using oxygen absorbers** in conjunction with Mylar bags is a highly effective technique. Oxygen absorbers are small packets that contain iron powder, which reacts with oxygen to form iron oxide, effectively removing oxygen from the surrounding environment. This process creates a near-oxygen-free environment inside the sealed bag, preventing the growth of aerobic bacteria, mold, and insects. Once sealed, Mylar bags with oxygen absorbers can keep food fresh for 10 to 30 years, depending on the type of food and storage conditions.

Canning is another valuable technique, especially for preserving fruits, vegetables, and meats. The canning process involves placing food in jars and heating them to a temperature that destroys harmful microorganisms. The heat also causes the air to be expelled from the jar, creating a vacuum seal as it cools. This method not only preserves the food but also enhances its flavor over time. Pressure canning is recommended for low-acid foods like meats and vegetables, while water bath canning is suitable for high-acid foods like fruits and pickles.

Freezing is a common method for preserving a wide range of foods, from meats and vegetables to prepared meals. To maximize the shelf life of frozen foods, ensure they are properly wrapped or placed in airtight containers to prevent freezer burn. Vacuum sealing is particularly effective for frozen storage, as it removes air that can cause ice crystals to form. Keep in mind that while freezing preserves food quality for an extended period, it's important to maintain a consistent, cold temperature to prevent thawing and refreezing, which can degrade food quality.

For foods stored at room temperature, **temperature control** is essential. Store your food in a cool, dark, and dry environment, ideally between 50°F and 70°F. Heat and light can accelerate the degradation of food, causing it to lose nutritional value and flavor. If possible, avoid storing food in areas that experience temperature fluctuations, such as garages or attics, as these can cause condensation inside containers, leading to spoilage.

Rotation is another key strategy in managing long-term food storage. The first-in, first-out (FIFO) method is a simple but effective way to ensure that older items are used before newer ones, keeping your stockpile fresh. Label each container with the date of storage and regularly check expiration dates, making sure to rotate your supplies to prevent waste.

Selecting the right storage containers and applying proper sealing and storage techniques are critical to extending the shelf life of your food reserves. By carefully choosing containers that protect against spoilage and employing methods like vacuum sealing, canning, and the use of oxygen absorbers, you can ensure that your stockpile remains fresh and safe for long-term use. Effective storage not only preserves the nutritional value and flavor of your food but also provides the peace of mind that comes from knowing your family will be well-nourished in any situation.

Best Foods for Long-Term Storage and Nutrition

Staple Foods for Sustenance and Energy

In any long-term food storage plan, staple foods serve as the foundation of your stockpile. These are the foods that provide the bulk of the calories and nutrients needed to sustain energy levels and overall health during an extended period. Identifying the right staples and ensuring a diverse selection is crucial for maintaining a balanced diet over time.

Identifying Essential Staples Like Grains, Legumes, and Proteins

Grains are the cornerstone of any emergency food reserve. They are calorie-dense, versatile, and have a long shelf life, making them ideal for long-term storage. Common grains such as rice, wheat, oats, and corn provide essential carbohydrates, which are the body's primary energy source. Brown rice and whole wheat offer added nutritional benefits, such as higher fiber content and additional vitamins and minerals compared to their refined counterparts. Quinoa is another excellent choice due to its high protein content and complete amino acid profile, making it a valuable addition to any stockpile.

Legumes are another critical component of a well-rounded food reserve. They are rich in protein, fiber, and essential nutrients like iron and potassium. Beans (such as black beans, pinto beans, and kidney beans), lentils, and chickpeas are among the most popular choices. These foods not only provide sustenance but also help maintain muscle mass and support immune function, which is crucial during stressful times. Legumes also pair well with grains, creating a complete protein source when combined, such as in rice and beans.

Proteins are essential for maintaining muscle, repairing tissues, and supporting overall body functions. While grains and legumes provide some protein, it's important to include other sources in your stockpile. Canned meats, such as chicken, beef, or tuna, are convenient and have a long shelf life. Dried meats, like jerky, and freeze-dried options are also excellent for long-term storage. For those following a vegetarian or vegan diet, consider adding plant-based protein sources like tofu, tempeh, and nuts, as well as protein powders made from soy, pea, or hemp.

How to Diversify Your Stockpile to Ensure a Balanced Diet

A balanced diet is key to maintaining health and energy levels during a crisis. While grains, legumes, and proteins form the basis of your food reserve, diversifying your stockpile with a variety of foods ensures that you're not only getting the necessary macronutrients but also the essential vitamins and minerals required for overall well-being.

Diversification can be achieved by including a range of grains, such as combining rice, wheat, oats, and quinoa. This variety not only prevents meal fatigue but also ensures a broader spectrum of nutrients. Similarly, a mix of different legumes, like black beans, lentils, and chickpeas, can keep meals interesting while providing different textures and flavors.

To further diversify your protein sources, consider stocking up on nuts and seeds, which are not only rich in protein but also provide healthy fats and essential micronutrients like magnesium and vitamin E. Nut butters, such as peanut butter or almond butter, are also excellent for storage and can be used in a variety of ways.

Including a variety of cooking oils in your stockpile is important for both nutrition and food preparation. Oils like olive oil, coconut oil, and vegetable oil provide essential fats that are necessary for absorbing fat-soluble vitamins and maintaining energy levels. They also add flavor and richness to meals, making them more satisfying.

Another way to diversify your stockpile is by incorporating dried fruits and vegetables, which can be used in cooking or eaten as snacks. These foods retain most of their nutritional value and add vital vitamins and minerals that are often lacking in a diet based solely on dry goods.

In summary, building a diverse stockpile that includes a variety of grains, legumes, proteins, and other essential foods is crucial for maintaining a balanced diet during an emergency. This diversity ensures that you and your family will have the energy and nutrients needed to stay healthy and resilient, no matter how long the crisis lasts.

Nutrient-Dense Foods for Health and Wellbeing

While staple foods provide the bulk of your calories, it's essential to include nutrient-dense foods in your stockpile to ensure that you're also getting the vitamins and minerals necessary for long-term health. These nutrients play a critical role in maintaining immune function, mental clarity, and overall well-being, particularly during stressful times.

Incorporating Vitamins and Minerals Through Dried Fruits, Vegetables, and Supplements

Dried fruits are a convenient and long-lasting source of vitamins, particularly vitamin C, which is crucial for immune health, and dietary fiber, which supports digestion. Fruits like raisins, apricots, apples, and cranberries retain much of their nutritional value when dried and are easy to store. These can be eaten as snacks, added to cereals, or used in baking, providing both nutrition and variety to your meals.

Dried vegetables are equally important, offering essential vitamins and minerals that might be missing from a diet based primarily on grains and legumes. Vegetables like spinach, kale, carrots, and bell peppers can be dried and stored for long periods. They are rich in vitamins A, C, and K, as well as minerals like potassium and magnesium. Adding dried vegetables to soups, stews, or rice dishes is a simple way to boost the nutritional content of your meals.

In addition to dried fruits and vegetables, consider incorporating **supplements** into your stockpile to cover any potential gaps in your diet. Multivitamins can provide a broad spectrum of essential nutrients, while specific supplements like vitamin D, calcium, or omega-3 fatty acids can address particular needs. Supplements should not replace whole foods but rather complement your diet to ensure you're getting all the necessary nutrients.

Selecting Foods That Provide Essential Nutrients During Extended Periods

When selecting nutrient-dense foods for long-term storage, focus on those that offer multiple health benefits and can be stored easily. **Canned fruits and vegetables** are a good option, as they retain much of their nutritional value and have a long shelf life. Look for options with no added sugars or preservatives to keep your diet as healthy as possible.

Whole grains like brown rice, quinoa, and oats are not only staples but also excellent sources of essential vitamins and minerals, including B vitamins, iron, and magnesium. These nutrients are crucial for energy production, immune function, and maintaining healthy blood levels.

Nuts and seeds are another category of nutrient-dense foods that should be part of your stockpile. They are rich in healthy fats, protein, and important minerals like zinc and selenium. Almonds, walnuts, chia seeds, and flaxseeds, for example, offer a concentrated source of nutrients and can be stored for long periods without spoiling.

For those who may have limited access to fresh foods, **freeze-dried fruits and vegetables** provide an alternative that retains almost all of the original nutrients. These products are lightweight, easy to store, and can be rehydrated for use in cooking or eaten as-is for a nutritious snack.

Fortified foods can also play a role in ensuring adequate nutrient intake. Products like fortified cereals, rice, and pasta are enriched with vitamins and minerals that might otherwise be lacking in a long-term storage diet. These foods can help fill nutritional gaps, especially in the absence of fresh produce.

Incorporating nutrient-dense foods into your long-term food storage is essential for maintaining health and wellbeing during extended periods of reliance on your stockpile. By including a variety of dried fruits, vegetables, whole grains, nuts, seeds, and supplements, you can ensure that your family receives the necessary vitamins and minerals to stay healthy and resilient, no matter the duration of the crisis.

Long-Lasting Prepared and Packaged Foods

In the realm of long-term food storage, commercially prepared and packaged foods offer a convenient and reliable solution. These products are specifically designed to endure extended periods of storage while still providing the nutrition and energy needed during emergencies. Relying solely on pre-packaged emergency rations has its pros and cons. In this chapter, we will explore the types of commercially prepared foods available, their benefits, and the potential drawbacks to consider when integrating them into your overall food storage plan.

Exploring Commercially Prepared and Packaged Foods Designed for Long-Term Storage

Commercially prepared and packaged foods come in a variety of forms, each designed to meet specific storage and nutritional needs. These products are often created with shelf stability in mind, ensuring they can last for years without spoiling, even under less-than-ideal storage conditions.

One of the most popular categories is **freeze-dried meals**, which are lightweight, easy to prepare, and highly durable. Freeze-drying removes the moisture from food while retaining its nutritional content, flavor, and texture. These meals often come in vacuum-sealed pouches, which help prevent spoilage and extend shelf life. To prepare, you simply add hot water, and the meal rehydrates in minutes, making them an excellent option for quick, no-fuss meals during an emergency.

MREs (Meals Ready-to-Eat) are another widely recognized option. Originally developed for military use, MREs are complete, self-contained meals that require no additional preparation or cooking. They typically include an entrée, side dish, snack, dessert, and a beverage, all packed in a durable, airtight pouch. Some MREs even come with a flameless heater, allowing you to warm the meal without needing an external heat source. MREs are designed to be nutritionally balanced and are engineered to have a long shelf life, making them ideal for emergency scenarios where cooking facilities are unavailable.

Canned foods also play a significant role in long-term food storage. While not as lightweight as freeze-dried options, canned foods are widely available and can be stored for several years. Items such as canned meats, fruits, vegetables, and soups provide essential nutrients and variety to your diet. The canning process preserves food by sealing it in an airtight container and heating it to a temperature that kills bacteria and other pathogens. This method not only extends the shelf life of the food but also retains much of its original flavor and nutritional value.

Dehydrated foods are another viable option. Similar to freeze-drying, dehydration removes moisture from food, significantly extending its shelf life. Dehydrated foods are usually less expensive than freeze-dried ones and can be rehydrated by soaking in water or adding them directly to soups and stews. Commonly dehydrated items include fruits, vegetables, and grains, which can be stored in airtight containers or vacuum-sealed bags to protect them from moisture and pests.

Powdered and concentrated foods such as powdered milk, eggs, and protein powders are also essential components of a long-term food storage plan. These products are easy to store and can be reconstituted with water when needed, providing valuable nutrients that might otherwise be difficult to obtain during an emergency.

Benefits and Drawbacks of Relying on Pre-Packaged Emergency Rations

While pre-packaged emergency rations offer convenience and long shelf life, there are both benefits and drawbacks to relying on them exclusively for your long-term food storage.

Benefits:

1. **Convenience**: Pre-packaged foods are designed for quick and easy preparation. Most require minimal cooking or preparation, which is crucial during an emergency when time, resources, and cooking facilities may be limited. The simplicity of these meals reduces stress and allows you to focus on other critical tasks.

2. **Long Shelf Life**: These foods are specifically formulated to last for several years, sometimes even decades, making them a reliable option for long-term storage. Properly stored, they can provide peace of mind, knowing that you have a stable food supply that will not spoil.

3. **Portability**: Many pre-packaged foods, particularly freeze-dried meals and MREs, are lightweight and compact, making them easy to transport if you need to evacuate or move to a safer location. Their portability is a significant advantage in situations where mobility is necessary.

4. **Nutritional Content**: These products are often fortified with essential vitamins and minerals to ensure that you receive balanced nutrition, even during an extended crisis. They are designed to meet daily nutritional requirements, which can be particularly beneficial in situations where access to fresh food is limited.

Drawbacks:

1. **Cost**: One of the primary drawbacks of commercially prepared emergency rations is their cost. High-quality freeze-dried meals and MREs can be expensive, especially when purchasing enough to sustain a family for an extended period. This can make it challenging to build a comprehensive stockpile on a budget.

2. **Limited Variety**: While there are many different products available, relying solely on pre-packaged foods can lead to a lack of variety in your diet. Eating the same meals repeatedly can cause "meal fatigue," reducing appetite and the overall enjoyment of food, which can be detrimental to morale during a crisis.

3. **Taste and Texture**: Despite advances in food preservation technology, some pre-packaged foods may not taste as good as fresh or home-cooked meals. Freeze-dried and dehydrated foods can have a different texture, and the flavor may not be as vibrant. This can be a significant drawback for those who are accustomed to a varied and flavorful diet.

4. **Nutritional Limitations**: Although these foods are designed to be nutritionally balanced, they may not meet all dietary needs, particularly for individuals with specific health conditions or dietary restrictions. The heavy reliance on preservatives and sodium in some products could be problematic for those managing conditions like hypertension.

5. **Dependency on Commercial Products**: Over-reliance on commercially prepared foods can create a dependency on products that may become unavailable during prolonged crises or supply chain disruptions. This makes it important to also consider other methods of food storage and preservation, such as canning, dehydrating, or growing your own food.

While long-lasting prepared and packaged foods are an integral part of any comprehensive food storage plan, it's essential to be aware of their benefits and limitations. These products offer convenience, a long shelf life, and portability, making them ideal for emergency situations. They can be expensive, and their reliance on processed ingredients may not appeal to everyone's taste or nutritional needs. Therefore, it's wise to use these foods as part of a broader strategy that includes a variety of food storage methods, ensuring a balanced, sustainable, and enjoyable diet during any emergency.

Rotating and Maintaining Your Food Reserve

Establishing a Food Rotation System

A well-organized food rotation system is essential for maintaining the freshness and effectiveness of your emergency food stockpile. Without a system in place, you risk allowing food to spoil, wasting valuable resources, and potentially leaving yourself with inedible supplies when you need them most. Establishing a robust food rotation system ensures that older food is consumed first, keeping your stockpile fresh and reducing waste.

Techniques for Organizing and Using Your Stockpile Effectively

To effectively manage your food reserves, it's crucial to organize them in a way that makes it easy to monitor and rotate items regularly. One of the most common and effective techniques is the **First-In, First-Out (FIFO) method**. This system is simple: the first items that go into your stockpile are the first items that should be used. This method ensures that food is consumed before it reaches the end of its shelf life.

Begin by organizing your food storage area so that newer items are placed behind older ones. This can be done by grouping similar items together (e.g., all canned vegetables in one section, all grains in another) and labeling them clearly with their purchase or expiration date. Shelves should be arranged so that you can easily see and access the oldest items first. For example, if you store canned goods, place the ones with the earliest expiration dates at the front of the shelf and newer purchases at the back.

Another useful technique is the **category system**, where food items are grouped by type (e.g., proteins, grains, fruits, and vegetables) and then further divided by shelf life. This system allows you to quickly identify which categories need to be used up sooner and which can be stored for longer periods. For example, grains might be grouped together, with those that have a shorter shelf life, like whole wheat flour, stored in a more accessible spot, while long-lasting items like white rice are stored further back.

In addition to organizing by date and category, consider **color-coding** your storage containers or shelves to visually distinguish between different stages of freshness. For instance, red labels could indicate items that need to be used within the next month, yellow for items with three to six months left, and green for those that can be stored for a year or more. This visual system makes it easier to quickly assess your inventory and make decisions about what to use next.

For perishable items or those with shorter shelf lives, consider integrating them into your regular meal planning. This approach not only helps rotate your stockpile but also familiarizes you and your family with the foods you'll rely on in an emergency. Incorporating these items into your daily diet ensures they are regularly consumed and replaced, keeping your stockpile fresh and reducing the chance of waste.

Methods to Ensure Older Food Is Consumed First, Maintaining Freshness

To maintain freshness and prevent spoilage, it's essential to establish a routine for checking and rotating your stockpile. Regularly inspect your food storage area, ideally on a monthly basis, to identify items that are approaching their expiration date. Make a habit of using these items in your cooking before they spoil.

When adding new items to your stockpile, always place them behind or beneath older items to ensure the FIFO method is followed. If you have multiple storage locations (e.g., a pantry, basement, or garage), consider setting up a rotation schedule that allows you to move older items from one location to another for immediate use.

One effective strategy is to create a **"use now" section** in your pantry or kitchen. This section should include items from your emergency stockpile that need to be consumed soon. By incorporating these items into your weekly meal planning, you can ensure that they are used before they expire. For example, if you notice that canned beans are nearing their expiration date, plan to make a dish like chili or bean soup that week. This approach not only keeps your stockpile fresh but also reduces the need for last-minute grocery trips.

For those who prefer a more automated approach, **inventory management apps** or spreadsheets can be valuable tools. These tools allow you to track expiration dates, monitor stock levels, and receive alerts when items need to be used or replaced. By keeping a digital record, you can easily manage large stockpiles and ensure that no item is overlooked.

In summary, establishing a food rotation system is key to maintaining the freshness and quality of your emergency food supply. By organizing your stockpile effectively and consistently using older items first, you can minimize waste, save money, and ensure that your family always has access to fresh, nutritious food in an emergency.

Monitoring Food Quality and Shelf Life

Maintaining a long-term food storage system requires regular monitoring to ensure that your supplies remain in good condition and are safe to consume. Even with careful planning, factors like temperature fluctuations, humidity, and pests can impact the quality of your stored food. Regular inspections help you identify potential issues early, allowing you to take corrective action before your food becomes spoiled or unsafe.

Signs of Spoilage and How to Check the Condition of Stored Foods

Knowing how to recognize the signs of spoilage is crucial for maintaining the integrity of your stockpile. Spoiled food can lead to foodborne illnesses, which are especially dangerous during an emergency when medical resources may be limited.

Visual inspection is the first step in checking your stored foods. Look for signs of discoloration, mold, or unusual textures, which can indicate spoilage. For example, canned goods should be free from rust, dents, or bulging, as these can indicate compromised seals or contamination. If you notice any of these signs, it's best to discard the item immediately.

For dried goods like grains, pasta, and legumes, check for any signs of moisture, clumping, or the presence of pests. Moisture can cause mold growth, while clumping may indicate that the food has absorbed humidity and is no longer safe to eat. If you find evidence of pests, such as weevils or larvae, it's important to dispose of the affected items and inspect nearby foods to prevent further contamination.

Smell is another key indicator of food spoilage. When opening a container or package, take a moment to smell the contents. A sour, rancid, or off odor is a strong sign that the food has gone bad. This is particularly important for items like oils, nuts, and grains, which can turn rancid if not stored properly.

For foods stored in **Mylar bags** or vacuum-sealed containers, be mindful of any changes in the integrity of the packaging. If a vacuum-sealed bag has lost its seal or a Mylar bag has become punctured, the food inside may no longer be safe to eat. Inspect these packages regularly and reseal or replace them as needed.

Tasting should be the last step, only after visual and smell checks indicate that the food is likely still good. If the taste is off or unusual, it's better to discard the item than risk consuming something that could cause illness.

Tips for Regularly Inspecting and Replacing Items as Needed

To maintain a reliable food stockpile, establish a routine inspection schedule. Monthly inspections are ideal for catching potential issues before they escalate. During these inspections, check the condition of each item, paying special attention to those with nearing expiration dates or signs of spoilage.

Keep a **detailed inventory** of your stockpile, including purchase dates, expiration dates, and storage conditions. This inventory helps you stay organized and makes it easier to identify items that need to be used or replaced. Update your inventory regularly, especially after inspections or when adding new items to your stockpile.

When replacing items, ensure that the new items are placed behind or beneath older ones, in line with the FIFO method. This helps maintain a consistent rotation and reduces the risk of accidentally letting food expire.

Consider setting aside a specific day each month for **stockpile maintenance**. On this day, review your inventory, inspect your food storage areas, and make note of any items that need to be used soon. By dedicating time to this task, you can ensure that your stockpile remains in optimal condition and is ready to serve its purpose when needed.

Monitoring food quality and shelf life is an essential part of maintaining a long-term food storage system. By regularly inspecting your stockpile and knowing the signs of spoilage, you can prevent waste, ensure the safety of your food, and keep your emergency supplies fresh and ready for use. With diligent care and attention, your food stockpile will remain a valuable resource in any crisis.

Incorporating Stockpiled Food into Daily Meals

Incorporating stockpiled food into your daily meals is a smart strategy to prevent waste, ensure freshness, and familiarize yourself with the ingredients you'll rely on during an emergency. By regularly using your stored food in everyday cooking, you can maintain a well-rotated stockpile while also ensuring that your family is accustomed to these foods before a crisis strikes. This chapter explores effective strategies for integrating stockpiled food into your daily meals and offers tips on adapting your cooking practices to maximize the use of your food reserves.

Strategies for Using Stored Food in Everyday Cooking to Prevent Waste

One of the most effective ways to prevent food waste and keep your stockpile fresh is by regularly incorporating it into your meal planning. This not only helps rotate your stockpile but also reduces the need for frequent grocery shopping, making it a practical approach even during non-emergency times.

Start by taking inventory of the items in your stockpile that are approaching their expiration dates. Plan your weekly meals around these items, ensuring that they are used before they expire. For example, if you have canned beans, dried pasta, and tomato sauce nearing the end of their shelf life, plan to make a hearty pasta dish or a bean-based soup. By consistently using these items in your meals, you ensure that your stockpile remains fresh and avoid the need to discard expired food.

Another strategy is to designate specific days each week as "pantry meal" days, where the focus is on using ingredients from your stockpile. These meals can be simple, such as rice and beans, or more elaborate, depending on what you have stored. The key is to regularly incorporate these foods into your diet, so they are consumed in a timely manner.

When cooking with stockpiled food, think creatively about how to combine ingredients in new ways. For example, canned vegetables can be used in soups, stews, casseroles, or stir-fries, while dried grains can be used as a base for salads, side dishes, or as a filling for stuffed vegetables. The more versatile your meals, the easier it is to incorporate a variety of stockpiled items into your cooking.

Consider batch cooking or meal prepping using stockpiled foods. Preparing large quantities of meals that can be frozen and eaten later not only saves time but also ensures that your stockpile is used consistently. For instance, you can cook a large pot of chili using canned beans and tomatoes, then freeze portions for future meals. This method is particularly useful for managing items that come in bulk or that you want to use up before replenishing your stockpile.

How to Adapt Your Cooking Practices to Make the Most of Your Stockpile

Adapting your cooking practices to include stockpiled food requires some flexibility and creativity. One approach is to learn how to make basic, versatile dishes that can be easily adapted based on what you have on hand. For example, learning to make a basic soup or stew allows you to use a variety of canned vegetables, beans, and grains, depending on what needs to be rotated out of your stockpile.

Another important aspect is learning how to **reconstitute dried or dehydrated foods**. Many stockpiled foods, such as dehydrated vegetables or freeze-dried meals, require rehydration before use. Understanding how much water is needed and the best methods for rehydrating these foods can help you incorporate them seamlessly into your meals. For instance, rehydrated vegetables can be added to soups, casseroles, or even baked into breads and muffins.

If your stockpile includes a lot of canned goods, consider how to reduce the sodium content, as many canned items are high in salt. Rinsing canned beans or vegetables under cold water before using them can help reduce sodium levels, making these items healthier to consume regularly. You can balance high-sodium items with fresh or low-sodium ingredients to create a more balanced meal.

To make the most of your stockpile, **experiment with new recipes** that specifically use long-lasting ingredients. This not only helps you use your stored food but also expands your culinary repertoire, making it easier to create satisfying meals even when fresh ingredients are scarce. For example, try making a casserole using canned tuna, dried pasta, and canned vegetables, or experiment with a stir-fry made from dehydrated vegetables and canned meat.

Incorporating herbs, spices, and flavorings into your cooking is another way to enhance the taste of stockpiled foods, which can sometimes be bland. Stock up on dried herbs, spices, and seasonings that can be used to add variety and depth to your meals. For instance, a simple can of beans can be transformed into a flavorful dish with the addition of cumin, chili powder, and garlic.

Practice **portion control** and mindful cooking to avoid over-preparing and wasting food. By cooking only what you need and storing leftovers properly, you can extend the life of your stockpile and ensure that nothing goes to waste.

Incorporating stockpiled food into your daily meals is an essential practice for maintaining a fresh and effective food reserve. By using your stored foods regularly and adapting your cooking practices, you not only prevent waste but also ensure that your family is familiar with the foods they will rely on during an emergency. This approach fosters a sustainable, efficient food storage system that will keep you well-prepared and resilient in any situation.

Video BONUS

Chapter 5: Water Security and Purification

Securing a Reliable Water Supply

Assessing Water Needs for Your Household

Water is one of the most critical resources for survival, and understanding your household's water needs is the first step in securing a reliable supply. Proper planning ensures that you have enough water not only for drinking but also for cooking, hygiene, and other essential uses during an emergency.

Determining Daily Water Requirements for Drinking, Cooking, and Hygiene

The average person needs about one gallon of water per day for basic needs, including drinking, cooking, and minimal hygiene. This is a baseline estimate and actual requirements can vary depending on several factors, such as age, health, activity level, and climate. In hotter climates or during periods of increased physical activity, water needs can easily double. Therefore, it's crucial to plan for at least one to two gallons of water per person per day.

For drinking alone, each person typically requires about half a gallon of water per day to stay properly hydrated. Cooking can require an additional half gallon, depending on the types of meals you are preparing and whether you're using water-intensive methods like boiling or rehydrating dried foods. Hygiene needs, including washing hands, brushing teeth, and basic cleaning, may require at least another half gallon per person per day, although this can vary greatly based on your water conservation practices.

Beyond these daily needs, you should also consider other uses of water, such as pet care, laundry, and sanitation. If you have pets, especially large ones like dogs, their water needs should be included in your overall calculations. In emergency situations where hygiene becomes critical to preventing disease, water for washing clothes or maintaining a clean environment may also be necessary.

Accounting for Special Needs and Emergency Scenarios

When planning for water storage, it's essential to consider any special needs within your household. Infants, elderly family members, or those with medical conditions may require additional water. For example, babies who are formula-fed will need extra water for mixing formula and cleaning bottles. Similarly, someone who is ill or has compromised immune function may require more water for hygiene and care.

In addition to regular needs, consider scenarios where your water usage might increase unexpectedly. During an emergency, access to running water could be limited or completely unavailable, which might necessitate the use of stored water for tasks that you would typically rely on your municipal supply for. For instance, you may need additional water for sanitation purposes, such as flushing toilets with bucket water if the plumbing system is compromised.

Emergency scenarios also demand that you plan for potential long-term disruptions. While a three-day supply of water is a good starting point, it's advisable to aim for at least two weeks' worth of water storage for each person in your household. This extended supply will provide a critical buffer in the event of prolonged emergencies, such as natural disasters, infrastructure failures, or extended quarantine situations.

Accurately assessing your household's water needs involves calculating the daily requirements for each person and accounting for special needs and potential emergencies. By planning for one to two gallons of water per person per day and considering additional factors like climate, health, and the likelihood of extended disruptions, you can ensure that your household is well-prepared to meet its water needs in any situation.

Identifying Local Water Sources

In addition to storing water, it's essential to identify and evaluate local water sources that could be used in an emergency. Understanding the availability and safety of these sources is crucial for ensuring that your household has a reliable water supply even if your stored water runs out.

Evaluating Nearby Natural Water Sources

Natural water sources, such as rivers, lakes, and wells, can provide an alternative water supply during emergencies. The availability and quality of these sources can vary significantly, and not all are safe for direct consumption without treatment.

Rivers and streams are common natural water sources, but they are highly variable in both availability and quality. These water bodies are often subject to contamination from agricultural runoff, industrial waste, and sewage, making them unsafe for drinking without proper filtration and purification. Before relying on a river or stream, it's important to assess its water flow, potential sources of contamination, and accessibility. Ideally, choose a water source that is upstream from any potential contaminants and far from urban or industrial areas.

Lakes and ponds are more stable sources of water compared to rivers, as they are less affected by seasonal changes. They are still vulnerable to pollution, algae blooms, and other environmental factors that can degrade water quality. When considering a lake or pond as a water source, evaluate its size, depth, and surrounding environment. Larger, deeper lakes are generally less prone to contamination, but all surface water should be treated before use.

Wells are another reliable source of water, especially if they are deep and properly maintained. Groundwater from wells is typically safer than surface water, as it is filtered naturally through soil and rock. Wells can still be contaminated by nearby septic systems, agricultural chemicals, or industrial pollutants. If you have a well on your property, regular testing for contaminants is essential to ensure its safety. In an emergency, well water may require additional treatment, such as chlorination or filtration, depending on the results of these tests.

If you do not have immediate access to a natural water source, consider alternatives such as **rainwater harvesting** or **collecting dew**. These methods require proper collection and storage systems to ensure the water remains clean and usable.

Assessing the Reliability and Safety of Municipal Water Systems During Crises

Municipal water systems are generally reliable, but they are not immune to disruption, especially during large-scale emergencies like natural disasters, power outages, or contamination events. Understanding the vulnerabilities of your local water supply can help you prepare for potential outages or water quality issues.

Municipal systems can be disrupted by events such as earthquakes, hurricanes, or widespread power failures that affect water treatment plants and distribution networks. Even in the absence of a disaster, municipal water supplies can become contaminated due to aging infrastructure, chemical spills, or biological hazards. In some cases, boil water advisories may be issued, indicating that the water is unsafe to drink without treatment.

To assess the reliability of your local water system, consider the following factors:

1. **History of outages or advisories**: Research whether your area has experienced water outages, boil water advisories, or contamination events in the past. This information can give you insight into the potential risks and how quickly issues are typically resolved.

2. **Proximity to water treatment facilities**: Living close to a water treatment plant can be an advantage, as water from the source may reach your home more quickly and with fewer opportunities for contamination. Proximity to industrial areas or large-scale agriculture can also increase the risk of contamination.

3. **Redundancy and backup systems**: Investigate whether your local water utility has backup systems in place, such as emergency generators or alternative water sources, to maintain service during a crisis. Utilities that have robust contingency plans are more likely to provide uninterrupted service during emergencies.

4. **Communication and alerts**: Ensure that you are signed up for local emergency alerts and notifications from your water utility. These alerts can provide timely information about water safety, outages, and any necessary actions, such as boiling water before use.

Securing a reliable water supply requires not only storing sufficient quantities of water but also identifying and evaluating alternative sources. By assessing the availability and safety of nearby natural water sources and understanding the vulnerabilities of your municipal water system, you can develop a comprehensive plan to ensure that your household has access to clean, safe water in any emergency scenario.

Setting Up a Rainwater Harvesting System

Rainwater harvesting is a practical and sustainable method for securing an additional water supply, particularly in areas prone to drought or where municipal water systems may be unreliable during emergencies. By collecting and storing rainwater, you can ensure a steady supply of water for non-potable uses, and with proper treatment, even for drinking. This chapter will guide you through the basics of collecting and storing rainwater, as well as the legal considerations you should be aware of before setting up your system.

Basics of Collecting and Storing Rainwater

At its core, rainwater harvesting involves capturing runoff from a surface—most commonly a roof—and channeling it into a storage system for later use. Setting up a basic rainwater harvesting system is relatively straightforward and can be scaled to fit your household's needs, from small barrel systems to more extensive cistern setups.

1. Collecting Rainwater

The first step in setting up a rainwater harvesting system is selecting the appropriate collection surface. Roofs are the most common collection surfaces due to their large surface area and natural incline, which facilitates water runoff. The type of roofing material you have can affect water quality; metal roofs are typically preferred for potable water harvesting, as they are less likely to leach harmful chemicals compared to asphalt shingles.

Gutters are installed along the edges of the roof to collect rainwater as it flows off. These gutters should be made of non-toxic materials and equipped with leaf guards or screens to prevent debris from entering the system. From the gutters, water is channeled into downspouts that lead to a filtration system before entering the storage container. It's crucial to install a first flush diverter in the system, which allows the initial runoff (often containing contaminants like dust, bird droppings, and leaves) to be discarded, ensuring that cleaner water is stored.

2. Storing Rainwater

Once collected, rainwater must be stored in a way that maintains its quality and prevents contamination. Storage options range from small rain barrels to large cisterns, depending on the amount of water you plan to harvest and the space available.

Rain barrels are an easy and cost-effective solution for small-scale rainwater harvesting. Typically holding 50 to 100 gallons of water, these barrels can be placed under downspouts to collect runoff directly. They are ideal for watering gardens, washing cars, or other non-potable uses. However, due to their limited capacity, rain barrels are not sufficient for providing a significant backup water supply for larger households.

For more extensive storage needs, consider installing a **cistern**. Cisterns can hold several thousand gallons of water and are often buried underground or placed in a shaded area to prevent algae growth and reduce evaporation. These larger tanks are typically made from food-grade plastic, fiberglass, or concrete, ensuring that the water remains safe for various uses. Cisterns can be fitted with pumps to facilitate water distribution throughout your home, making them a more integrated solution for emergency water supply.

Regardless of the size of your storage system, it's important to ensure that the container is sealed to prevent contamination from insects, animals, and environmental pollutants. Regular maintenance, such as cleaning gutters and checking filters, is necessary to keep the system functioning efficiently and the stored water safe for use.

Legal Considerations and Guidelines for Rainwater Harvesting

Before installing a rainwater harvesting system, it's important to familiarize yourself with the regulations governing rainwater collection and usage in your area. Rules can differ greatly depending on state and local jurisdictions—some places actively promote rainwater harvesting, while others may impose restrictions.

In many areas, collecting rainwater is allowed and even encouraged as a way to reduce pressure on municipal water supplies and help manage stormwater runoff. Some states, such as Colorado and Texas, have specific guidelines that outline how rainwater can be harvested and used. For example, in Colorado, rainwater collection is limited to two barrels with a combined capacity of 110 gallons, and the water can only be used for outdoor purposes like irrigating plants. In contrast, Texas offers incentives, including exemptions from state sales tax for purchasing rainwater harvesting equipment.

In regions where water rights are a significant concern, such as the western United States, rainwater harvesting might be subject to more stringent rules. In these areas, collecting rainwater could be seen as diverting water that would otherwise flow into rivers and streams, potentially affecting the rights of downstream users. It's essential to consult your local water authority or state government to understand the specific rules that apply in your area.

Additionally, it's important to take local building codes and zoning requirements into account. Some municipalities may require permits for larger rainwater systems, especially if they involve plumbing modifications or structural changes to your property. Ensuring your system complies with these regulations is crucial to avoid penalties.

Maintaining the quality of your harvested rainwater is also key. This includes using non-toxic materials for your system, regularly cleaning storage tanks and filters, and treating the water if you intend to use it for drinking. If potable water use is your goal, additional filtration and disinfection methods, such as UV treatment or chlorination, will be necessary to ensure safety.

Installing a rainwater harvesting system is a practical, sustainable way to secure a supplemental water supply for your household. By understanding the basics of collection and storage, along with the regulatory framework in your area, you can design a system that fits your needs while staying compliant with local guidelines. With proper setup and maintenance, rainwater harvesting can be an invaluable resource, offering self-sufficiency and peace of mind during emergencies.

Storage Solutions for Long-Term Use

Choosing the Right Water Storage Containers

Selecting the appropriate water storage containers is a critical step in ensuring that your water supply remains safe and accessible during an emergency. The type of container you choose can affect the longevity and quality of your stored water, making it important to understand the advantages and disadvantages of various options.

Comparing Different Types of Containers

When it comes to storing water, there are several types of containers to consider, each with its own benefits and limitations. The most common materials used for water storage containers include plastic, glass, and metal, each suitable for different storage needs and environments.

Plastic Barrels: Plastic is one of the most popular materials for water storage due to its affordability, durability, and versatility. Large plastic barrels, often made from high-density polyethylene (HDPE), are widely used for long-term water storage. These barrels typically hold 55 gallons or more and are designed to be food-grade, meaning they are safe for storing potable water. HDPE is resistant to impact, chemicals, and temperature fluctuations, making it an ideal choice for both indoor and outdoor storage. It's important to ensure that the plastic is BPA-free to avoid potential chemical leaching, especially if the containers are exposed to heat or direct sunlight.

Glass Containers: Glass is another option for water storage, particularly for smaller quantities. It is impermeable and does not leach chemicals, which makes it an excellent choice for preserving the purity of your water. Glass containers are typically used for short-term storage or for storing smaller volumes of water, such as in gallon jugs or bottles. Glass is heavy, fragile, and can break if dropped, making it less practical for large-scale or long-term storage. It is also more expensive compared to plastic or metal alternatives.

Metal Tanks: Metal containers, particularly those made from stainless steel, are highly durable and can be used for both short-term and long-term water storage. Stainless steel is resistant to corrosion and does not leach chemicals into the water, making it a safe option for storing potable water. Metal tanks are often used in larger systems, such as rainwater harvesting or for storing large volumes of water in industrial settings. Metal tanks can be expensive and heavy, and they require careful maintenance to prevent rust and corrosion over time.

When choosing a container, consider the amount of water you need to store, the available storage space, and how you plan to access the water in an emergency. Large plastic barrels or metal tanks are ideal for long-term storage, while smaller glass containers can be used for short-term needs or for storing water in easily accessible locations.

Understanding the Importance of Food-Grade Materials and UV Protection

When selecting water storage containers, it is crucial to ensure that they are made from **food-grade materials**. Food-grade containers are specifically designed to store consumable products without contaminating them. This means that the materials used do not leach harmful chemicals or toxins into the water, even over extended periods. HDPE plastic, for example, is a common food-grade material used in water barrels, jugs, and tanks. Containers that are not food-grade may contain chemicals that can seep into the water, especially when exposed to heat or sunlight, posing a health risk over time.

Another critical consideration is **UV protection**. Exposure to sunlight can cause several problems for stored water, including the growth of algae and bacteria, as well as the degradation of the container material itself. Containers that are not UV-resistant can allow sunlight to penetrate, encouraging microbial growth and leading to potential contamination. To prevent this, choose containers that are either opaque or specifically labeled as UV-resistant. Storing water containers in a cool, dark place further reduces the risk of UV exposure and helps maintain the quality of your stored water.

Storing Water for Short-Term vs. Long-Term Needs

The strategies for storing water vary depending on whether you are preparing for short-term emergencies, such as a power outage or natural disaster, or for long-term situations where access to clean water may be disrupted for an extended period.

Strategies for Short-Term Water Storage (Up to 72 Hours)

For short-term emergencies, it's essential to have enough water stored to last your household for at least 72 hours. This is often referred to as a "72-hour kit," and the water stored in it should be easily accessible and portable.

Bottled Water: One of the simplest solutions for short-term water storage is commercially bottled water. Bottled water is convenient, portable, and has a relatively long shelf life, typically around one to two years. It's recommended to store at least one gallon of water per person per day for three days, which covers drinking, cooking, and basic hygiene needs. Bottled water should be stored in a cool, dark place, away from direct sunlight and chemicals, to ensure it remains safe for consumption.

Small Containers: For those who prefer not to rely solely on bottled water, small food-grade plastic or glass containers can be used to store water for short-term needs. These containers should be thoroughly cleaned and sanitized before use. Fill them with tap water, add a few drops of unscented household bleach if necessary to prevent microbial growth, and seal them tightly. Label the containers with the date and rotate them every six months to ensure freshness.

Portable Water Filters: In addition to storing water, it's a good idea to have portable water filters on hand. These can be used to purify water from nearby sources, such as rivers, streams, or lakes, if your stored water runs out. Portable filters are lightweight, easy to use, and can remove bacteria, protozoa, and, in some cases, viruses from untreated water, making them a valuable addition to your short-term water storage plan.

Techniques for Long-Term Water Storage (Months to Years)

Long-term water storage requires more planning and consideration to ensure that the water remains safe and potable over an extended period. The following techniques can help you maintain a reliable water supply for months or even years.

Large Containers and Barrels: For long-term storage, larger containers like 55-gallon plastic barrels or metal tanks are ideal. These containers should be food-grade and designed for storing water. Before filling them, clean and sanitize the containers thoroughly. It's recommended to use a water treatment solution, such as chlorine bleach or commercially available water preservatives, to prevent the growth of bacteria and algae. After filling the containers, seal them tightly and store them in a cool, dark place, such as a basement or garage, to minimize exposure to temperature fluctuations and sunlight.

Water Rotation and Treatment: Even with proper storage, water should be rotated periodically to ensure its freshness. As a general rule, water stored in plastic containers should be rotated every six to twelve months, while water in stainless steel tanks can last longer, especially if treated with preservatives. Regularly check the condition of your stored water, looking for signs of contamination, such as cloudiness or an unusual odor. If in doubt, re-treat the water with bleach or another suitable disinfectant before use.

Emergency Wells or Rainwater Harvesting: For truly long-term preparedness, consider alternative water sources like a well or a rainwater harvesting system. Wells provide a continuous source of groundwater, but they require proper maintenance and occasional testing to ensure the water remains safe. Rainwater harvesting systems can collect and store large amounts of water, which can be treated and used during prolonged emergencies. These systems require an investment in infrastructure but offer a sustainable water supply when other sources are unavailable.

Choosing the right water storage containers and understanding the differences between short-term and long-term storage strategies are crucial for ensuring that your household has a reliable supply of safe water in any emergency. By selecting appropriate containers, ensuring they are food-grade and UV-protected, and following best practices for water storage, you can protect your water supply from contamination and ensure it remains safe for your family when needed most.

Preventing Contamination in Stored Water

Ensuring that your stored water remains clean and safe over time is critical for maintaining a reliable emergency supply. Contaminated water can pose serious health risks, so it's essential to follow best practices for preventing contamination and to conduct regular maintenance and inspections of your water storage systems. This chapter will explore how to keep stored water safe and outline the steps you can take to monitor and maintain your water storage effectively.

Best Practices for Keeping Stored Water Clean and Safe

To prevent contamination in stored water, it's important to start with clean, sanitized containers and to use proper storage methods that minimize the risk of introducing harmful bacteria, algae, or other pollutants. Here are the key steps to maintaining the purity of your stored water:

1. Start with Clean Containers and Water:

The first step in preventing contamination is to ensure that the containers you use for water storage are thoroughly cleaned and sanitized before filling them. Even if a container appears clean, it may harbor bacteria or other microorganisms that can proliferate once the container is sealed.

To sanitize your containers, wash them with hot, soapy water, then rinse thoroughly. After rinsing, you can further sanitize the containers by using a solution of one teaspoon of unscented liquid household bleach (containing 5% to 9% sodium hypochlorite) per gallon of water. Let the solution sit in the container for at least 30 seconds before rinsing again with clean water.

When filling your containers, use water from a reliable, potable source. If you are filling containers from a municipal tap, ensure that the water is chlorinated or otherwise treated to kill pathogens. If the water is untreated or comes from a questionable source, consider adding a small amount of bleach to the water to further reduce the risk of contamination. For most water, adding 1/8 teaspoon of unscented bleach per gallon will be sufficient to disinfect it.

2. Use Airtight, UV-Protected Containers:

Properly sealing your containers is crucial for preventing airborne contaminants from entering your stored water. Make sure all lids and caps are screwed on tightly, and use containers that are specifically designed to be airtight. Containers should also be opaque or made from UV-resistant materials to block sunlight, which can promote the growth of algae and other microorganisms.

If you are using large barrels or tanks for long-term storage, consider adding additional layers of protection, such as sealing the tops with plastic wrap or using secure, locking lids. These measures help prevent insects, dust, and other contaminants from entering the water.

3. Store Water in a Cool, Dark Place:

Temperature and light are significant factors in maintaining the quality of stored water. Heat can accelerate chemical reactions that lead to the degradation of the container material or the growth of bacteria, while exposure to light, particularly sunlight, can encourage algae growth.

To minimize these risks, store your water containers in a cool, dark place, such as a basement, cellar, or interior closet. Avoid areas that experience temperature fluctuations, such as garages or attics, where heat can build up during the day and drop at night. Keeping the storage area clean and free of pests is also important, as rodents and insects can damage containers and introduce contaminants.

4. Regularly Rotate Your Water Supply:

Even with the best storage practices, water should not be stored indefinitely. Regularly rotating your water supply helps ensure that it remains fresh and safe to drink. A good rule of thumb is to rotate your water every six to twelve months, depending on storage conditions and the type of container used.

When rotating your water, use the old supply for tasks like watering plants, cleaning, or washing vehicles, and replace it with fresh water. This practice not only maintains the quality of your emergency supply but also familiarizes you with the process of accessing and using your stored water.

Regular Maintenance and Inspection of Water Storage Systems

Ongoing maintenance and inspection are essential to ensure that your water storage system remains in good condition and that your stored water is safe to use. Regular checks can help you catch any issues early, preventing small problems from becoming serious threats to your water supply.

1. Conduct Routine Inspections:

Set a schedule for regular inspections of your water storage containers and systems. Monthly checks are recommended, especially if your water is stored in large barrels, tanks, or in areas prone to temperature fluctuations or pest activity.

During these inspections, look for any signs of contamination or damage to the containers. Check for leaks, cracks, or bulging in the containers, which could indicate a problem. If you notice any mold, algae, or sediment in the water, this could be a sign of contamination, and the water should be treated or replaced.

Inspect the seals and lids to ensure they remain airtight. Over time, seals can degrade, leading to potential contamination. If you detect any issues with the seals or lids, replace them immediately to maintain the integrity of the containers.

2. Clean and Sanitize Containers Periodically:

In addition to rotating your water supply, it's important to clean and sanitize your containers periodically, especially for long-term storage. Empty the containers, clean them with hot, soapy water, and sanitize them using a bleach solution as described earlier. This process should be done at least once a year, or more frequently if you notice any signs of contamination.

If you are using large storage tanks, such as those used in rainwater harvesting systems, consider draining and cleaning them every one to two years. Use a brush or pressure washer to remove any buildup of sediment, algae, or debris from the interior walls of the tank. After cleaning, rinse thoroughly and allow the tank to dry completely before refilling it with fresh water.

3. Monitor Water Quality:

Even with careful storage, it's important to periodically test the quality of your stored water. Simple water testing kits are available that can detect common contaminants such as bacteria, chlorine levels, pH balance, and hardness. Testing your water every six months can give you peace of mind and help you identify any potential issues early.

If you detect any irregularities in your water quality, such as unusual taste, odor, or color, treat the water with an appropriate disinfectant or replace it entirely. In an emergency, always have a backup plan for water treatment, such as portable filters, purification tablets, or a boiling method, to ensure your water remains safe to drink.

4. Keep an Emergency Water Treatment Plan:

Despite your best efforts, there's always a chance that your stored water could become compromised. Having an emergency water treatment plan in place ensures that you can still have access to safe drinking water when needed. This plan should include methods such as boiling, using chlorine bleach, or employing commercial water filters to purify contaminated water.

Store these treatment supplies near your water storage so they are easily accessible in an emergency. Familiarize yourself and your household with the treatment process, including how to properly measure and apply disinfectants.

Preventing contamination in stored water is a critical aspect of maintaining a safe and reliable emergency water supply. By following best practices for storing water, conducting regular maintenance and inspections, and being prepared to treat water if necessary, you can ensure that your household is well-equipped to handle any situation where clean drinking water is needed. With these steps, you protect not only the quality of your stored water but also the health and well-being of your family.

Purification Techniques: Ensuring Safe Drinking Water

Understanding Common Water Contaminants

Water is a fundamental necessity, but in an emergency or survival situation, ensuring that your water supply is free from contaminants is crucial for maintaining health and safety. Contaminants can be present in both natural and municipal water sources, making it essential to understand the types of potential hazards and the health risks they pose.

Types of Contaminants to Be Aware Of (Biological, Chemical, Physical)

Contaminants in water can be broadly categorized into three groups: biological, chemical, and physical. Each type presents its own set of challenges and requires specific methods for detection and removal.

Biological Contaminants: These are microorganisms that can cause waterborne diseases. The most common biological contaminants include bacteria, viruses, protozoa, and parasites. Pathogens such as E. coli, Salmonella, and Giardia are examples of bacteria and protozoa that can cause severe gastrointestinal illnesses. Viruses like Hepatitis A and Norovirus can also be present in contaminated water and pose significant health risks. Biological contaminants are typically introduced into water through human and animal waste, decomposing organic matter, and contaminated surfaces.

Chemical Contaminants: Chemical pollutants can come from various sources, including agricultural runoff, industrial discharges, and even naturally occurring minerals. Common chemical contaminants include pesticides, herbicides, heavy metals (such as lead, mercury, and arsenic), and toxic chemicals like benzene and chloroform. These substances can cause a range of health problems, from acute poisoning to long-term effects like cancer, reproductive issues, and neurological damage. Chemical contaminants can be particularly challenging to detect, as they are often colorless, tasteless, and odorless.

Physical Contaminants: Physical contaminants are any solid materials that are present in water. These can include sediments, silt, organic debris, and microplastics. While physical contaminants are generally less harmful than biological or chemical ones, they can still pose health risks, especially if they carry pathogens or chemicals. Physical contaminants can clog filters and make water purification more difficult. They are usually introduced into water through erosion, runoff, and inadequate filtration systems.

Health Risks Associated with Contaminated Water

The health risks associated with consuming contaminated water vary depending on the type and level of contamination, as well as the overall health and immunity of the individual. Some general health risks are commonly associated with each type of contaminant.

Biological Contaminants: Drinking water contaminated with pathogens can lead to waterborne diseases, which are a major cause of illness and death in many parts of the world. Symptoms of bacterial infections, such as those caused by E. coli or Salmonella, typically include diarrhea, vomiting, stomach cramps, and fever. In severe cases, these infections can lead to dehydration, organ failure, and even death, particularly in vulnerable populations like children, the elderly, and those with weakened immune systems. Protozoa like Giardia can cause prolonged gastrointestinal issues, including severe diarrhea and malabsorption of nutrients.

Chemical Contaminants: The health effects of chemical contaminants can be acute or chronic, depending on the substance and exposure level. Acute exposure to high levels of chemicals like pesticides or heavy metals can result in immediate poisoning, with symptoms such as nausea, vomiting, headaches, and in extreme cases, organ failure or death. Chronic exposure to lower levels of chemicals, such as lead or arsenic, can lead to long-term health issues, including developmental problems in children, kidney damage, cancer, and neurological disorders.

Physical Contaminants: While physical contaminants may not directly cause illness, they can exacerbate the effects of other contaminants. For example, sediments and debris can shield pathogens from disinfection processes, making it harder to remove biological contaminants from the water. Ingesting microplastics, which are becoming increasingly prevalent in water sources, is a growing concern, though the long-term health effects are still being studied. Physical contaminants can also make water unpalatable and unfit for consumption, even if it is otherwise safe.

Understanding these common water contaminants and their associated health risks is the first step in protecting yourself and your family during an emergency. By recognizing the potential dangers, you can take proactive measures to purify and protect your water supply.

Boiling and Basic Filtration Methods

Once you understand the types of contaminants that may be present in your water, the next step is to employ effective purification methods to ensure it is safe for consumption. Two of the most accessible and reliable methods for purifying water are boiling and basic filtration. These techniques can be used alone or in combination to remove or kill a wide range of contaminants.

How to Effectively Boil Water to Kill Pathogens

Boiling is one of the simplest and most effective methods for purifying water, particularly when the primary concern is biological contamination. The process of boiling water kills most bacteria, viruses, and protozoa, making it safe to drink.

To effectively purify water through boiling:

1. **Bring Water to a Rolling Boil**: Heat the water until it reaches a full, rolling boil. A rolling boil is when the water is bubbling vigorously and cannot be easily disturbed by stirring or shaking. This level of heat is necessary to ensure that the water reaches the temperature required to kill most pathogens.

2. **Maintain the Boil for At Least One Minute**: Once the water reaches a rolling boil, continue boiling for at least one minute. At high altitudes (above 5,000 feet), where water boils at a lower temperature, extend the boiling time to three minutes to ensure that all pathogens are effectively killed.

3. **Cool and Store Safely**: After boiling, allow the water to cool naturally before storing it in a clean, covered container. Be sure to use sanitized containers to prevent recontamination. If the water tastes flat after boiling, you can aerate it by pouring it back and forth between two clean containers to restore some oxygen and improve the flavor.

Boiling is a highly effective method for killing pathogens, but it does not remove chemical contaminants or physical debris. Therefore, if the water source is suspected of containing chemicals or is visibly dirty, additional filtration may be necessary before boiling.

Simple Filtration Techniques Using Cloth, Sand, or Charcoal

Filtration is a physical process that removes particles and, to some extent, certain contaminants from water. While basic filtration methods may not eliminate all pathogens, they are effective at reducing turbidity (cloudiness) and removing larger contaminants such as sediments, debris, and some microorganisms.

Cloth Filtration: One of the simplest filtration methods involves using a clean cloth, such as cotton or a fine-mesh fabric, to filter water. Pour the water through the cloth into a clean container. The cloth acts as a basic filter, removing larger particles like dirt, sand, and organic debris. While this method does not remove pathogens or chemicals, it can be a useful first step in a multi-stage purification process.

Sand Filtration: Sand filtration is a more advanced method that uses layers of sand and gravel to filter water. This technique mimics natural filtration processes found in the environment. To create a basic sand filter:

1. **Layer a Container with Gravel and Sand**: Use a clean container or bucket and layer it with coarse gravel at the bottom, followed by fine sand on top. The gravel helps prevent the sand from washing out and provides additional filtration.

2. **Pour Water Through the Filter**: Slowly pour the water into the top of the sand filter. The water will percolate down through the sand and gravel, which traps particles and some microorganisms. The filtered water can then be collected from the bottom of the container.

3. **Multiple Filtrations**: For better results, you can filter the water multiple times through the sand filter. Each pass through the filter will further reduce turbidity and improve water clarity.

Charcoal Filtration: Charcoal, particularly activated charcoal, is highly effective at removing impurities, including some chemicals, from water. It works by adsorbing (binding) contaminants to its surface, trapping them as water passes through.

1. **Prepare the Charcoal**: Use activated charcoal, which has been treated to increase its surface area and adsorption capacity. If you don't have activated charcoal, you can use charcoal from a fire (as long as it is free of additives), but it will be less effective.

2. **Layer the Charcoal in a Filter**: Similar to sand filtration, layer the charcoal in a clean container or filter system. You can combine it with sand and gravel layers for additional filtration.

3. **Filter the Water**: Pour the water through the charcoal filter. The charcoal will adsorb many organic compounds, chlorine, and other chemicals, as well as improving the taste and odor of the water. Collect the filtered water and, if necessary, boil it afterward to kill any remaining pathogens.

These basic filtration techniques can significantly improve the quality of your water by removing physical contaminants and, in the case of charcoal, reducing certain chemical impurities. Combining filtration with boiling or another disinfection method is recommended to ensure that the water is safe to drink.

Understanding the types of water contaminants and utilizing effective purification methods such as boiling and filtration are essential for maintaining a safe and reliable water supply. By implementing these techniques, you can protect yourself and your family from the health risks associated with contaminated water, ensuring that you are prepared for any emergency.

Advanced Water Purification Systems

In situations where water quality is a concern, advanced purification systems can provide an added layer of security, ensuring that your water supply is safe for drinking and other essential uses. These systems are designed to remove a wide range of contaminants, from pathogens to chemical pollutants, and are particularly useful in both long-term preparedness scenarios and emergency situations.

Overview of Commercial Water Filters (e.g., Reverse Osmosis, UV Purifiers)

Commercial water purification systems offer a variety of technologies designed to address specific types of contaminants. Understanding the capabilities and limitations of these systems can help you choose the right one for your needs.

Reverse Osmosis (RO) Systems: Reverse osmosis is a highly effective water purification method that removes a wide range of contaminants, including bacteria, viruses, heavy metals, and dissolved solids. An RO system works by forcing water through a semi-permeable membrane, which blocks larger molecules and contaminants while allowing clean water to pass through. These systems are particularly effective at removing chemical contaminants like arsenic, fluoride, and lead, making them ideal for households concerned about chemical pollutants in their water supply.

Reverse osmosis systems also have some drawbacks. They require a consistent source of water pressure to operate efficiently, and the process can be relatively slow, producing a limited amount of purified water each day. RO systems typically waste a significant amount of water—up to three gallons for every gallon of purified water— making them less efficient in areas where water conservation is a priority.

UV Purifiers: Ultraviolet (UV) water purifiers use UV light to kill or inactivate microorganisms, including bacteria, viruses, and protozoa. This method is highly effective at eliminating biological contaminants without the use of chemicals, making it a safe and environmentally friendly option. UV purifiers are often used in conjunction with other filtration systems, such as carbon filters, to address chemical and physical contaminants.

One of the main advantages of UV purification is its speed—water can be treated almost instantly as it flows through the UV chamber. UV systems do not remove chemical or physical contaminants, so they should be used in combination with other filtration methods if these contaminants are a concern. UV purifiers require electricity to operate, which may limit their usefulness in off-grid or emergency situations unless a backup power source is available.

Activated Carbon Filters: Activated carbon filters are commonly used in water purification systems to remove chlorine, volatile organic compounds (VOCs), and other chemicals that can affect the taste and odor of water. These filters work by adsorbing contaminants onto the surface of the carbon granules as water passes through the filter. While carbon filters are effective at improving water quality and taste, they are less effective at removing pathogens and heavy metals, so they are often used in combination with other purification technologies.

Pros and Cons of Portable Water Purifiers and Treatment Tablets

For those who need a portable and versatile solution, portable water purifiers and treatment tablets offer a convenient way to ensure access to clean water in the field or during emergencies. These options are particularly useful for hikers, campers, and preppers who may need to purify water from natural sources like rivers, lakes, or streams.

Portable Water Purifiers: Portable water purifiers come in various forms, including pump filters, gravity filters, and straw-style filters. These devices are designed to remove pathogens and physical contaminants from water on the go. For example, pump filters use a hand pump to force water through a filter cartridge, removing bacteria, protozoa, and sediments. Gravity filters rely on gravity to pass water through a filter, making them easy to use and requiring minimal effort. Straw-style filters, such as the popular LifeStraw, allow users to drink directly from a water source, filtering contaminants as the water is drawn through the straw.

The main advantages of portable water purifiers are their ease of use, portability, and effectiveness at removing biological contaminants. They may have limitations in terms of filter lifespan and their ability to remove chemical pollutants. Some portable purifiers require regular maintenance, such as cleaning or replacing filter cartridges, to ensure continued effectiveness.

Water Treatment Tablets: Water treatment tablets are another portable solution for purifying water in the field. These tablets typically contain chlorine, iodine, or chlorine dioxide, which disinfect water by killing bacteria, viruses, and protozoa. To use, simply add the tablet to a container of water, stir, and wait for the recommended time (usually 30 minutes to 4 hours, depending on the tablet and water temperature) before drinking.

The primary benefit of water treatment tablets is their convenience—they are lightweight, easy to carry, and require no special equipment. They are also effective against a broad spectrum of pathogens. They do not remove chemical contaminants or physical debris from the water, so pre-filtering through a cloth or other method may be necessary before treatment. Some people may be sensitive to the taste of treated water, particularly with iodine-based tablets, which can leave an aftertaste.

Advanced water purification systems, including reverse osmosis, UV purifiers, and portable options like filters and treatment tablets, offer a range of solutions for ensuring safe drinking water. Each method has its own strengths and limitations, making it important to choose the right system based on your specific needs, whether at home or in the field.

Building a DIY Water Purification System

For those looking to create a more self-sufficient approach to water purification, building a DIY system can be an effective and rewarding solution. Whether you need a home setup for long-term use or an emergency method for purifying water in the field, constructing your own purification system allows you to tailor the process to your specific needs.

Step-by-Step Guide to Constructing a Basic Home Water Purification Setup

Creating a basic home water purification system involves combining several methods to ensure comprehensive filtration and disinfection. Here's a simple guide to constructing a system that can handle a variety of contaminants:

1. **Collect and Pre-Filter Water**: Begin by collecting water from your source and running it through a pre-filter to remove large particles and debris. This can be done using a simple cloth or mesh filter. If the water is particularly dirty, consider running it through a sand or gravel filter for additional sediment removal.

2. **Set Up a Gravity-Fed Filtration System**: Gravity-fed systems are ideal for home use because they require no electricity and are easy to maintain. To build one, you'll need two containers: an upper container for untreated water and a lower container to collect the filtered water. Drill a hole in the bottom of the upper container and fit it with a ceramic or activated carbon filter. As water passes through the filter, it will be purified and collected in the lower container.

3. **Add a Chemical Disinfection Stage**: After filtration, the water should be disinfected to kill any remaining pathogens. This can be done by adding a few drops of unscented chlorine bleach (typically 8 drops per gallon) or using a UV light purifier if available. Stir the water and allow it to sit for at least 30 minutes before use. If using bleach, be sure to let the water sit until there is no longer a chlorine odor.

4. **Store Water Safely**: Once purified, store the water in clean, airtight containers. Glass or food-grade plastic containers are ideal for preventing contamination. Keep the containers in a cool, dark place to maintain water quality.

Emergency Methods for Purifying Water in the Field

In emergency situations where access to sophisticated purification systems is limited, knowing how to purify water using basic materials and methods can be life-saving. Here are a few field-ready techniques:

1. **Boiling**: As discussed in previous sections, boiling is one of the most reliable methods for killing pathogens. In the field, you can boil water over a campfire or portable stove. Allow the water to reach a rolling boil for at least one minute (or three minutes at higher altitudes) before cooling and using.

2. **Improvised Charcoal Filter**: If you don't have a commercial filter on hand, you can create a simple charcoal filter using materials found in nature. Burn hardwood to create charcoal, then crush it into small pieces. Layer the crushed charcoal with sand and gravel inside a container, such as a plastic bottle with the bottom cut off. Pour water through the layers to filter out contaminants. Boil the filtered water afterward to ensure it's safe to drink.

3. **Solar Disinfection (SODIS)**: Solar disinfection is a method that uses UV rays from the sun to kill pathogens in water. Fill a clear plastic bottle with water and place it in direct sunlight for at least six hours. The UV rays and heat will help to disinfect the water. This method works best with clear water, as turbidity can reduce the effectiveness of the UV rays.

4. **Improvised Distillation**: If chemical contaminants are a concern, distillation can be an effective purification method. In the field, you can create an improvised distillation setup by boiling water and capturing the steam in a clean cloth or plastic sheet, then allowing the condensed steam to drip into a clean container. This method removes most contaminants, including salts and heavy metals, though it may be more labor-intensive.

Building a DIY water purification system and understanding emergency purification methods are essential skills for anyone interested in preparedness and self-sufficiency. By combining different techniques, you can ensure access to safe drinking water, whether at home or in challenging conditions in the field.

Video BONUS

Chapter 6: Off-Grid Energy Solutions

Powering Your Home Without the Grid

Assessing Your Energy Needs

When planning to power your home without relying on the grid, the first critical step is understanding your household's energy consumption. Knowing how much energy you use on a daily basis allows you to design an off-grid system that meets your needs, while also helping you prioritize which appliances and systems are most essential during an outage.

How to Calculate Your Household's Energy Consumption

To begin assessing your energy needs, you'll want to calculate the total amount of electricity your household consumes. This process involves understanding both your average daily usage and peak energy demands.

1. **Gathering Data from Utility Bills**: Start by reviewing your past utility bills, which typically list your monthly energy consumption in kilowatt-hours (kWh). To get a more precise estimate of your daily usage, divide the monthly kWh by the number of days in the billing cycle. This gives you a baseline for your average daily consumption.

2. **Identifying Key Appliances and Systems**: Make a list of all the electrical appliances and systems in your home, including major items like refrigerators, heating and cooling systems, water heaters, and lighting, as well as smaller devices like computers, televisions, and kitchen appliances. For each item, note the power rating in watts (usually found on the appliance's label or manual) and estimate how many hours per day each appliance is used.

3. **Calculating Energy Use**: Multiply the wattage of each appliance by the number of hours it's used daily to find its energy consumption in watt-hours (Wh). To convert this to kilowatt-hours (kWh), divide by 1,000. For example, if a 100-watt light bulb is used for 5 hours a day, it consumes 500 Wh, or 0.5 kWh daily. Repeat this calculation for each appliance and add up the totals to determine your household's daily energy consumption.

4. **Accounting for Peak Usage**: In addition to average consumption, consider your household's peak energy usage—times when multiple high-power devices are operating simultaneously. Understanding these peak periods is crucial for designing an off-grid system that can handle maximum demand without overloading.

Prioritizing Essential Appliances and Systems During a Power Outage

Once you have a clear understanding of your energy consumption, the next step is to prioritize which appliances and systems are most important during a power outage. This prioritization ensures that you allocate your off-grid energy resources effectively, focusing on the items that are crucial for your household's safety and comfort.

1. **Identify Essential Systems**: Essential systems typically include those that maintain your home's livability, such as refrigeration, heating or cooling, and water pumping. Medical equipment, if needed, also falls into this category. These systems should be given top priority when planning your off-grid setup.

2. **Categorize Appliances by Necessity**: Divide your appliances into categories based on necessity. High-priority items, such as refrigerators, freezers, and communication devices, should be powered first. Medium-priority items might include lighting and cooking appliances, which are important but can be used more sparingly. Low-priority items, like entertainment systems, should be considered last and only powered if sufficient energy is available.

3. **Consider Backup Solutions**: For less critical items, consider manual or alternative backup solutions. For example, you could use battery-powered lanterns instead of electric lights or a gas stove instead of an electric one during a power outage. This reduces the overall load on your off-grid system and ensures that the most important devices remain operational.

4. **Prepare for Extended Outages**: If you anticipate long-term power outages, plan for rotating power usage. This might involve running certain appliances only during specific times of the day or alternating which systems are powered to conserve energy.

Designing an Off-Grid Energy System

Designing an off-grid energy system involves more than just installing solar panels or a generator. It requires a comprehensive approach that considers all components necessary for generating, storing, and distributing power effectively. Integrating multiple energy sources can enhance reliability and ensure that your household remains powered in various conditions.

Key Components of an Off-Grid Energy Setup

An off-grid energy system typically consists of several key components, each playing a vital role in ensuring a steady supply of electricity:

1. **Energy Generation**: The most common methods of generating electricity off-grid include solar panels, wind turbines, and generators. Solar panels convert sunlight into electricity, while wind turbines harness the power of the wind. Generators, which can be powered by gasoline, diesel, or propane, provide backup power when renewable sources are insufficient. The choice of generation method depends on your location, climate, and energy needs.

2. **Energy Storage**: Since renewable energy sources like solar and wind are intermittent, storing the generated electricity is crucial. Batteries are the primary method of energy storage in off-grid systems. Lead-acid batteries have traditionally been used, but newer technologies like lithium-ion batteries offer higher efficiency, longer lifespan, and greater energy density. The size and capacity of your battery bank should be sufficient to store enough energy to meet your household's needs during periods of low generation.

3. **Inverter**: The inverter converts the direct current (DC) electricity stored in your batteries into alternating current (AC), which is the standard form of electricity used by most household appliances. Inverters come in various sizes and capacities, so choosing the right one depends on the total power demand of your home. Some inverters also have built-in chargers, allowing them to convert AC from a generator or the grid back into DC to recharge your batteries.

4. **Charge Controller**: The charge controller regulates the flow of electricity from your solar panels or wind turbines to the batteries, preventing overcharging and extending battery life. Maximum Power Point Tracking (MPPT) controllers are commonly used in modern systems because they optimize the energy harvest from your solar panels.

5. **Distribution System**: This includes all the wiring, breakers, and switches necessary to distribute electricity throughout your home. A well-designed distribution system ensures that power is delivered efficiently and safely to each appliance and system in your home.

Integrating Multiple Energy Sources for Reliability

Relying on a single source of energy can be risky, especially in off-grid situations where weather conditions or fuel availability can fluctuate. By integrating multiple energy sources into your system, you can increase reliability and ensure a continuous power supply.

1. **Combining Solar and Wind**: Solar panels and wind turbines are complementary in many locations—solar power is often strongest during the day and in summer, while wind power may be more consistent

at night and during winter. By combining these two sources, you can create a more balanced energy generation profile, reducing your dependence on any single source.

2. **Incorporating a Generator**: A generator serves as a reliable backup for times when solar and wind energy are insufficient. It can be used to recharge batteries during extended periods of cloudy weather or calm winds. Generators are also useful for meeting peak demand when your renewable sources and batteries are not enough to power all essential systems. Some modern systems use automatic generator start features, where the generator kicks in automatically when battery levels drop below a certain threshold.

3. **Using Hybrid Systems**: Hybrid systems that combine solar, wind, and generator power, along with battery storage, offer the best of all worlds. These systems are highly adaptable and can be tailored to fit your specific energy needs and environmental conditions. Hybrid inverters are available that can manage inputs from multiple sources, seamlessly switching between them as needed.

4. **Energy Management and Monitoring**: To maximize the efficiency of your off-grid system, it's important to implement an energy management and monitoring system. These systems track your energy production, storage, and consumption in real-time, allowing you to make informed decisions about when to use or conserve power. Advanced systems can automate the process, prioritizing energy use based on preset criteria, such as maintaining battery charge or minimizing generator use.

By carefully assessing your energy needs and designing an off-grid system that integrates multiple sources of energy, you can create a reliable and sustainable power supply for your home. This approach not only ensures that you have the electricity needed to maintain comfort and safety during an outage but also provides the flexibility to adapt to changing conditions and future energy demands.

Backup Power Sources

In an off-grid energy system, having reliable backup power sources is crucial for maintaining a continuous power supply, especially during extended outages or periods of low energy generation. Batteries and other energy storage solutions play a vital role in ensuring that your household remains powered when primary energy sources, such as solar panels or wind turbines, are insufficient. This chapter explores the importance of energy storage solutions and offers strategies to ensure a steady power supply during prolonged disruptions.

The Role of Batteries and Energy Storage Solutions

Batteries are the cornerstone of any off-grid energy system. They store the electricity generated by your solar panels, wind turbines, or other energy sources, allowing you to use it when production is low or demand is high. The effectiveness of your energy storage system depends on several factors, including the type of batteries you choose, their capacity, and how well they are maintained.

1. Types of Batteries

The most common types of batteries used in off-grid systems include lead-acid, lithium-ion, and nickel-iron (NiFe) batteries. Each type has its advantages and disadvantages, which can affect your choice depending on your specific needs and budget.

- **Lead-Acid Batteries**: These are the most traditional and widely used batteries for off-grid energy storage. They come in two main varieties: flooded lead-acid and sealed lead-acid (such as AGM or gel batteries). Flooded lead-acid batteries are known for their reliability and affordability, but they require regular maintenance, including checking electrolyte levels and ensuring proper ventilation. Sealed lead-acid batteries are maintenance-free and safer for indoor use, but they generally have a shorter lifespan compared to flooded varieties.

- **Lithium-Ion Batteries**: Lithium-ion batteries have become increasingly popular in recent years due to their high energy density, long lifespan, and low maintenance requirements. They are more efficient than lead-acid batteries, meaning they can store more energy in a smaller space and provide longer-lasting power. However, lithium-ion batteries are more expensive upfront, making them a significant investment. Despite the cost, their long-term benefits often outweigh the initial expense, especially in systems where space and weight are considerations.

- **Nickel-Iron (NiFe) Batteries**: NiFe batteries are known for their durability and extremely long lifespan, often exceeding 20 years. They are resistant to overcharging, deep discharging, and extreme temperatures, making them ideal for harsh environments. They are less efficient than lithium-ion batteries and have a higher self-discharge rate, meaning they lose stored energy more quickly when not in use. NiFe batteries also require more maintenance and have a higher initial cost.

2. Battery Capacity and Sizing

The capacity of your battery bank is a critical factor in ensuring that you have enough stored energy to meet your needs during extended outages. Battery capacity is typically measured in kilowatt-hours (kWh), which indicates how much energy the battery can store and deliver over time.

To determine the appropriate battery capacity for your system, you'll need to consider your household's daily energy consumption and the number of days you want to be able to go without recharging the batteries. For example, if your household consumes 10 kWh per day and you want a three-day backup supply, you would need a battery bank with at least 30 kWh of usable capacity.

It's also important to account for the depth of discharge (DoD) when sizing your battery bank. The DoD refers to the percentage of a battery's capacity that can be used before it needs to be recharged. For instance, a battery with a 50% DoD can only use half of its total capacity without reducing its lifespan. Lithium-ion batteries typically have a higher DoD (around 80-90%) compared to lead-acid batteries, which usually have a DoD of 50%.

3. Battery Maintenance and Longevity

Proper maintenance is essential for prolonging the lifespan of your batteries and ensuring they perform efficiently. Regularly inspect your batteries for signs of wear, such as corrosion on terminals or bulging cases, and clean any build-up on the terminals. For flooded lead-acid batteries, check and top off the electrolyte levels with distilled water as needed.

Temperature management is also crucial, as extreme heat or cold can reduce battery efficiency and lifespan. Ideally, batteries should be stored in a controlled environment where temperatures are kept stable. If you live in an area with extreme temperatures, consider investing in a temperature-regulated battery enclosure.

How to Ensure Continuous Power Supply During Extended Outages

Ensuring a continuous power supply during extended outages requires more than just a robust battery system. It involves a combination of energy storage, backup generation, and strategic energy management.

1. Integrating Backup Generators

A backup generator is an essential component of any off-grid system, providing power when your renewable energy sources and batteries are unable to meet demand. Generators can run on various fuels, including gasoline, diesel, propane, or natural gas. Choosing the right generator depends on your energy needs, fuel availability, and budget.

When integrating a generator into your off-grid system, consider installing an automatic transfer switch (ATS). An ATS detects when your primary energy sources fail and automatically starts the generator to provide power without manual intervention. This feature is particularly useful during extended outages when you may not be immediately available to start the generator manually.

2. Managing Energy Usage

During an extended outage, it's crucial to manage your energy consumption carefully to stretch your stored power as far as possible. This may involve prioritizing essential systems and appliances, as discussed in the previous section, and minimizing the use of non-essential items.

Consider implementing a load-shedding plan, where you temporarily disconnect certain appliances or systems to reduce overall demand on your batteries and generator. For example, you might only run your refrigerator and critical medical equipment during the day and switch to using lights and communication devices at night.

3. Using Smart Energy Management Systems

Smart energy management systems can optimize your off-grid setup by monitoring and controlling energy production, storage, and consumption in real-time. These systems can automatically adjust power usage based on available energy, prioritize charging your batteries during peak solar or wind generation, and alert you when it's time to activate your backup generator.

Some advanced systems even allow for remote monitoring and control, enabling you to manage your energy usage from a smartphone or computer. This level of automation ensures that your off-grid system operates as efficiently as possible, maximizing the lifespan of your batteries and minimizing fuel consumption by your generator.

4. Planning for Extended Outages

Finally, planning for extended outages involves ensuring that you have sufficient fuel supplies for your generator, spare parts for your energy system, and a clear understanding of how to troubleshoot and repair common issues. Keep an emergency kit with essential tools, spare fuses, and extra fuel or oil for your generator.

Regularly test your backup power system under load conditions to ensure that it functions properly when needed. Familiarize yourself with the system's operation and maintenance procedures, and educate other household members on how to manage the system during an outage.

Backup power sources are an indispensable part of any off-grid energy system. By selecting the right batteries, integrating reliable backup generators, and employing smart energy management strategies, you can ensure a continuous power supply even during extended outages. This comprehensive approach not only enhances the resilience of your off-grid system but also provides peace of mind, knowing that your household will remain powered and secure in any situation.

Exploring Solar, Wind, and Generator Options

Solar Power Systems

Solar power is one of the most popular and accessible forms of renewable energy for off-grid living. Harnessing the power of the sun allows homeowners to generate electricity independently, reducing reliance on traditional power grids. Understanding the types of solar panels available and how to properly size and install a solar power system for your home is essential for maximizing efficiency and meeting your energy needs.

Types of Solar Panels and How They Work

Solar panels are made up of photovoltaic (PV) cells, which convert sunlight into electricity. When sunlight hits the PV cells, it excites electrons, creating a flow of electric current. This direct current (DC) electricity can then be used to power your home, stored in batteries, or converted to alternating current (AC) by an inverter for use with standard household appliances.

There are three main types of solar panels commonly used in residential settings: monocrystalline, polycrystalline, and thin-film.

1. **Monocrystalline Solar Panels**: These panels are made from a single, continuous crystal structure, which gives them a high efficiency rate—typically around 17% to 22%. Monocrystalline panels are known for their longevity and space efficiency, making them ideal for homes with limited roof space. They tend to be more expensive than other types due to their manufacturing process.

2. **Polycrystalline Solar Panels**: Polycrystalline panels are made from multiple silicon crystals melted together, resulting in a lower efficiency rate—around 15% to 17%. These panels are generally less expensive than monocrystalline panels and are a good option for homeowners with ample roof space. While slightly less efficient, they still provide a reliable source of solar power.

3. **Thin-Film Solar Panels**: Thin-film panels are made by depositing a thin layer of photovoltaic material onto a substrate, such as glass, plastic, or metal. They are lightweight, flexible, and can be used in a variety of applications, including rooftops, facades, and even portable solar solutions. Thin-film panels have a lower efficiency rate—around 10% to 12%—and typically require more space to generate the same amount of electricity as crystalline panels. They are also less durable and have a shorter lifespan.

Sizing and Installing a Solar Power System for Your Home

Properly sizing your solar power system is crucial to ensure that it meets your energy needs without overspending on unnecessary capacity. Sizing involves determining how many solar panels you need based on your energy consumption, the available sunlight in your area, and the efficiency of the panels you choose.

1. **Calculating Energy Needs**: Begin by calculating your household's average daily energy consumption in kilowatt-hours (kWh). This information can be found on your utility bills. Next, consider your energy goals: do you want to offset all of your energy consumption with solar, or just a portion? This will help determine the size of your system.

2. **Assessing Sunlight Availability**: The amount of sunlight your location receives directly affects the output of your solar panels. Use tools like solar calculators or consult with a solar installer to determine the average sunlight hours per day in your area. Areas with more sunlight hours will require fewer panels to generate the same amount of electricity as areas with less sunlight.

3. **Determining System Size**: To estimate the size of your solar power system, divide your daily energy consumption by the average sunlight hours per day, then divide that number by the efficiency of your solar panels. For example, if your household uses 30 kWh per day, receives 5 hours of sunlight per day, and you're using panels with an efficiency of 18%, you would need approximately 33.3 kW of installed capacity (30 kWh / 5 hours / 0.18 efficiency = 33.3 kW).

4. **Installation Considerations**: Solar panels are typically installed on rooftops, but they can also be mounted on the ground if roof space is limited. The orientation and tilt of the panels are important factors in maximizing energy production. In the Northern Hemisphere, panels should generally face south and be tilted at an angle equal to your latitude to capture the most sunlight throughout the year.

When installing a solar power system, it's also important to consider shading from trees, buildings, or other obstructions that could reduce the panels' exposure to sunlight. An experienced solar installer can conduct a site assessment to optimize panel placement.

Ensure your system is properly connected to an inverter, which will convert the DC electricity produced by the panels into usable AC power for your home. If you're planning to go completely off-grid, you'll also need a battery storage system to store excess electricity for use when the sun isn't shining.

Wind Power Solutions

Wind power is another viable option for generating electricity off-grid, particularly in areas with consistent wind patterns. Wind turbines convert the kinetic energy of the wind into mechanical power, which can then be used to generate electricity. Understanding how wind turbines work and assessing the suitability of wind power for your location are key steps in determining if this renewable energy source is right for your home.

Understanding Wind Turbines and Their Effectiveness

Wind turbines consist of a tower, blades, a rotor, and a generator. As the wind blows, it turns the blades, which spin the rotor connected to the generator. The generator then converts the mechanical energy into electricity.

The effectiveness of a wind turbine depends on several factors, including wind speed, turbine height, and rotor size.

1. **Wind Speed**: Wind speed is the most critical factor in determining the effectiveness of a wind turbine. Generally, a minimum wind speed of 10 to 12 mph (16 to 19 km/h) is needed to generate a meaningful amount of electricity. The power output of a wind turbine increases exponentially with wind speed, meaning that small increases in wind speed can result in significantly higher electricity generation.

2. **Turbine Height**: Wind speeds tend to increase with height above the ground, so taller towers typically result in better turbine performance. Small residential wind turbines are usually mounted on towers ranging from 30 to 100 feet tall. The higher the turbine, the more consistent and stronger the wind it can capture, leading to higher energy output.

3. **Rotor Size**: The size of the rotor, or the diameter of the area swept by the turbine blades, also affects the amount of energy a wind turbine can generate. Larger rotors capture more wind, which increases the turbine's energy production. Larger rotors also require stronger, more expensive towers and may be subject to local zoning regulations.

4. **Efficiency and Maintenance**: Wind turbines are highly efficient in converting wind energy to electricity, but they do require regular maintenance, especially in harsh environments. Turbine components, such as blades and bearings, can wear out over time and may need to be replaced. It's important to consider the maintenance requirements and associated costs when evaluating wind power for your home.

Assessing the Suitability of Wind Power Based on Your Location

Wind power is not suitable for every location, so it's crucial to assess whether your home is in an area with adequate wind resources before investing in a wind turbine.

1. **Wind Resource Assessment**: Begin by assessing the wind resources in your area. You can use wind maps, which provide estimates of average wind speeds at various heights, or install an anemometer on your property to measure wind speed directly over a period of time. Ideally, your location should have average wind speeds of at least 10 mph to make wind power viable.

2. **Local Zoning and Regulations**: Check local zoning laws and regulations, as they may restrict the height or placement of wind turbines. Some areas may require permits or have specific setbacks from property lines, roads, or buildings. Noise restrictions or aesthetic considerations may influence where and how a wind turbine can be installed.

3. **Obstructions and Terrain**: The terrain and surrounding structures can significantly impact wind flow. Open, flat areas with minimal obstructions, such as trees or buildings, are ideal for wind turbines. In contrast, areas with significant obstructions or in valleys where wind can be turbulent may be less suitable for wind power.

4. **Hybrid Systems**: In many cases, a hybrid system that combines wind and solar power can provide a more reliable and consistent energy supply. Wind turbines can generate electricity during cloudy or rainy days when solar panels are less effective, and vice versa. This approach can help balance energy production and increase the overall resilience of your off-grid system.

Both solar and wind power offer viable solutions for generating electricity off-grid. By understanding the types of solar panels and wind turbines available, how they work, and how to properly size and install these systems, you can harness renewable energy to meet your household's needs. Whether you choose to rely solely on one energy source or integrate multiple sources for greater reliability, these technologies provide the foundation for a sustainable and self-sufficient energy future.

Using Generators for Backup Power

Generators are a crucial component of any off-grid energy system, providing a reliable source of power when renewable energy sources like solar or wind are insufficient. Understanding the different types of generators available and the best practices for their safe and efficient use is essential for ensuring that your home remains powered during outages or periods of low energy generation.

Different Types of Generators (Portable, Standby, Dual-Fuel)

Generators come in various types, each suited to different needs and circumstances. The main categories include portable generators, standby generators, and dual-fuel generators, each offering unique advantages and considerations.

1. **Portable Generators**: Portable generators are versatile, movable units that are typically powered by gasoline or diesel. They are ideal for temporary power needs, such as during short-term outages or when you need to power specific appliances. Portable generators range in size and capacity, from small units capable of powering a few essential devices to larger models that can handle multiple appliances or even a small home.

Portable generators are relatively affordable and easy to store when not in use. They require manual setup and fueling, and they typically need to be started manually as well. Due to their mobility, portable generators are also useful for outdoor activities, such as camping or working at remote sites.

2. **Standby Generators**: Standby generators are permanently installed units that automatically kick in when the power goes out. These generators are typically connected to your home's electrical system and can power your entire house or specific circuits depending on their size. Standby generators run on natural gas, propane, or diesel and are designed to provide seamless backup power without requiring manual intervention.

The primary advantage of standby generators is their convenience and reliability. They are always ready to operate and can run for extended periods, making them ideal for homes in areas prone to frequent or prolonged outages. They are more expensive to purchase and install compared to portable generators and require regular maintenance to ensure they function properly when needed.

3. **Dual-Fuel Generators**: Dual-fuel generators offer the flexibility to run on two different types of fuel, typically gasoline and propane. This flexibility provides several advantages, such as extended run time and the ability to switch fuels depending on availability or cost. Dual-fuel generators can be particularly useful in emergencies when one type of fuel may be scarce or unavailable.

These generators combine the portability of a gasoline-powered unit with the longer storage life and cleaner-burning characteristics of propane. Dual-fuel generators are versatile and convenient for both home backup and outdoor use. They tend to be more expensive than single-fuel portable generators and may require more complex maintenance.

Safety Considerations and Maintenance Tips for Generators

While generators are invaluable for providing backup power, they also come with safety risks and maintenance requirements that must be carefully managed.

1. **Safety Considerations**:

    o **Carbon Monoxide (CO) Risk**: One of the most significant safety hazards associated with generators is carbon monoxide poisoning. Generators produce CO, a colorless, odorless gas that can be deadly if inhaled. It is crucial never to operate a generator indoors, in an enclosed space, or near windows and doors where exhaust could enter the home. Always place the generator outside, at least 20 feet away from your home, and direct the exhaust away from occupied areas.

    o **Electrical Safety**: To avoid electrical hazards, never plug a generator directly into a wall outlet—a practice known as "backfeeding." This can create dangerous conditions for utility workers and damage your home's electrical system. Instead, use a transfer switch to connect the generator to your home's electrical panel or plug appliances directly into the generator using heavy-duty extension cords rated for outdoor use.

- o **Fuel Storage and Handling**: Store fuel for your generator in approved containers and keep it in a well-ventilated area away from living spaces. Fuel should be kept away from open flames, sparks, and heat sources. Check local regulations regarding fuel storage limits and follow guidelines for proper storage and disposal of old or contaminated fuel.

2. **Maintenance Tips**:

- o **Regular Testing**: Periodically run your generator to ensure it is in good working condition. For standby generators, many systems offer a self-test feature that runs the generator automatically on a set schedule. For portable generators, manually start the unit every month or two and let it run for a short period to keep the engine lubricated and the battery charged.

- o **Oil and Filter Changes**: Just like a car, generators require regular oil and filter changes to maintain optimal performance. Check the manufacturer's recommendations for the appropriate oil type and change intervals. Regularly inspect and replace the air filter to prevent dust and debris from entering the engine.

- o **Battery Maintenance**: If your generator relies on a battery for starting, ensure the battery is charged and in good condition. Standby generators usually include a trickle charger to keep the battery charged, but it's still important to check the battery regularly and replace it as needed.

- o **Fuel System Maintenance**: Fuel left in the generator's tank or fuel lines can degrade over time, leading to clogs or damage to the engine. Use a fuel stabilizer if storing the generator with fuel in the tank, and periodically run the generator to circulate the stabilizer. For dual-fuel generators, regularly switch between fuel types to ensure both systems remain operational.

Hybrid Systems: Combining Solar, Wind, and Generators

Hybrid energy systems combine multiple energy sources—such as solar, wind, and generators—to create a more resilient and reliable off-grid power supply. By integrating different energy sources, you can take advantage of the strengths of each while mitigating their individual limitations. This section explores the advantages of using a hybrid system and presents case studies of effective hybrid setups.

Advantages of Using a Hybrid System for Off-Grid Energy

1. **Increased Reliability**: One of the primary benefits of a hybrid system is its ability to provide continuous power regardless of environmental conditions. Solar panels generate electricity during the day when the sun is shining, while wind turbines can produce power at night or during cloudy weather. When both solar and wind resources are low, a generator can kick in to provide the necessary power, ensuring that your home remains powered at all times.

2. **Optimized Energy Production**: Hybrid systems allow you to optimize energy production by utilizing the most efficient and available source at any given time. For example, during sunny days, your system can prioritize solar power, reducing wear and tear on your generator and conserving fuel. On windy nights, the system can switch to wind power, further reducing the need for fuel-based generation.

3. **Cost Savings**: Although the initial setup cost of a hybrid system can be higher than a single-source system, the long-term cost savings can be significant. By relying on renewable energy sources like solar and wind, you can reduce or eliminate fuel costs associated with generator use. Hybrid systems can extend the lifespan of your generator by reducing the number of hours it needs to operate.

4. **Environmental Impact**: Hybrid systems help reduce your carbon footprint by minimizing reliance on fossil fuels. By maximizing the use of renewable energy sources, you can significantly lower greenhouse gas emissions and contribute to a more sustainable future.

Case Studies of Effective Hybrid Setups

1. **Rural Off-Grid Home in the Midwest**: A rural homeowner in the Midwest, where both sunlight and wind are abundant, installed a hybrid system combining a 5 kW solar array, a 3 kW wind turbine, and a propane-powered generator. The solar panels provide the majority of the home's electricity during the day, while the wind turbine generates power during the night and in winter months when wind speeds are higher. The generator serves as a backup during extended periods of low solar and wind output. The system is connected to a battery bank that stores excess energy, ensuring a reliable power supply even during peak demand periods. This setup has allowed the homeowner to live entirely off-grid, with minimal fuel costs and a high degree of energy independence.

2. **Coastal Off-Grid Cabin**: A coastal cabin owner installed a hybrid energy system to take advantage of the area's frequent winds and sunny weather. The system includes a 3 kW solar array, a 1.5 kW vertical-axis wind turbine, and a diesel generator. The vertical-axis wind turbine was chosen for its ability to capture wind from any direction, which is important in coastal areas where wind patterns can be unpredictable. The solar panels generate electricity during the day, while the wind turbine provides power at night and during stormy weather. The diesel generator is rarely used, only running when both solar and wind output are low. This hybrid system has allowed the cabin to remain off-grid, with the added benefit of being resilient to the area's variable weather conditions.

3. **Remote Mountain Retreat**: In a remote mountain area with limited sunlight during winter months, a hybrid system was designed to ensure a continuous power supply throughout the year. The system includes a 4 kW solar array, a 2 kW wind turbine, and a propane generator. During the summer, the solar panels provide ample electricity, while the wind turbine supplements power during the windy fall and winter seasons. The propane generator is used sparingly, primarily during the darkest winter months when solar output is minimal. This setup has enabled the retreat to remain off-grid and fully powered, with the added security of a generator for backup.

Integrating generators with solar and wind energy sources in a hybrid system offers a versatile and reliable solution for off-grid living. By combining the strengths of each energy source, you can optimize energy production, reduce costs, and ensure a continuous power supply in any weather conditions. Whether you are powering a rural home, a coastal cabin, or a remote mountain retreat, a well-designed hybrid system provides the resilience and flexibility needed for a sustainable off-grid lifestyle.

Energy Conservation Strategies

Reducing Energy Consumption at Home

Reducing energy consumption is a fundamental aspect of off-grid living, where every watt saved translates into longer battery life, reduced generator use, and overall greater system efficiency. By adopting energy-efficient practices and technologies, you can significantly lower your energy demands, making your off-grid system more sustainable and cost-effective.

Simple Steps to Minimize Energy Usage in Daily Life

Reducing energy consumption begins with simple changes in daily habits and the conscious use of appliances and systems. Here are several strategies to help you minimize energy usage:

1. **Turn Off and Unplug**: One of the easiest ways to reduce energy consumption is by turning off lights, appliances, and electronics when they are not in use. Unplugging devices that aren't being used can also prevent "phantom" or "vampire" energy drain, where devices continue to consume small amounts of power even when turned off.

2. **Use Natural Light**: Maximize the use of natural light during the day by opening curtains and blinds. This reduces the need for artificial lighting and can also help warm your home in cooler months. Consider arranging your living and working spaces to take advantage of the areas with the most natural light.

3. **Optimize Heating and Cooling**: Heating and cooling are among the largest energy consumers in most homes. To reduce this demand, set your thermostat to energy-efficient temperatures—around 68°F (20°C) in the winter and 78°F (26°C) in the summer. Use ceiling fans to circulate air and reduce the need for air conditioning. In the winter, wear warmer clothing indoors and use extra blankets at night to stay comfortable without cranking up the heat.

4. **Practice Smart Cooking**: Kitchen appliances can use significant energy, so it's important to use them wisely. When cooking, match the size of the pot or pan to the burner to avoid wasting energy. Using a microwave, slow cooker, or pressure cooker instead of a conventional oven can save a considerable amount of energy. Prepare meals in batches to reduce the frequency of cooking and reheating.

5. **Insulate Hot Water Systems**: Insulating your hot water heater and pipes can reduce heat loss, allowing you to lower the temperature setting without sacrificing comfort. Installing low-flow showerheads and faucets can also reduce the amount of hot water used, saving both water and energy.

Energy-Efficient Appliances and Technologies to Consider

Investing in energy-efficient appliances and technologies is another crucial step in reducing your overall energy consumption. These appliances are designed to perform the same tasks as their standard counterparts but use significantly less energy.

1. **Energy Star Appliances**: Look for the Energy Star label when purchasing new appliances. These appliances meet strict energy efficiency guidelines set by the U.S. Environmental Protection Agency (EPA) and can use up to 50% less energy than standard models. Common Energy Star-certified appliances include refrigerators, dishwashers, washing machines, and air conditioners.

2. **LED Lighting**: LED (light-emitting diode) bulbs use up to 80% less energy than traditional incandescent bulbs and last significantly longer. Replacing all the light bulbs in your home with LEDs can result in substantial energy savings, especially if you're off-grid and relying on battery power.

3. **High-Efficiency HVAC Systems**: If your off-grid setup includes a heating, ventilation, and air conditioning (HVAC) system, consider upgrading to a high-efficiency model. Modern HVAC systems are designed to provide the same level of comfort while using less energy. Programmable thermostats can help you manage energy use by adjusting temperatures based on your schedule.

4. **Solar Water Heaters**: Solar water heaters use the sun's energy to heat water, reducing or eliminating the need for electric or gas water heating. They are an excellent addition to any off-grid system and can significantly cut down on energy consumption, particularly in sunny climates.

5. **Energy Management Systems**: Smart energy management systems can monitor and control your home's energy use in real-time, helping you optimize consumption. These systems can automatically adjust settings based on your energy production, storage levels, and consumption patterns, ensuring that you use energy efficiently.

Seasonal Energy Conservation Tips

Energy conservation strategies should adapt to the changing demands of different seasons. By tailoring your approach to each season, you can maintain a comfortable living environment while minimizing energy use.

How to Adapt Your Energy Usage According to Seasonal Changes

1. **Winter**:
   - **Maximize Passive Solar Heating**: During the winter, take advantage of the sun's warmth by allowing sunlight to enter your home through south-facing windows. Open curtains during the day to let in sunlight, and close them at night to retain heat.

- o **Seal Drafts and Insulate**: Cold drafts can significantly increase heating costs. Seal gaps around doors and windows with weatherstripping or caulk to prevent heat loss. Insulating your home's walls, attic, and floors can keep warmth inside, reducing the need for constant heating.

- o **Use Space Heaters Wisely**: Space heaters can be an effective way to heat small areas, but they should be used with caution due to their high energy consumption. Use them to supplement your primary heating system rather than as a primary heat source. Choose energy-efficient models and avoid leaving them on unattended.

2. **Summer**:

- o **Shade Your Home**: Keep your home cool by using blinds, curtains, or shades to block out direct sunlight during the hottest parts of the day. Planting trees or installing awnings can also provide shade and reduce the amount of heat entering your home.

- o **Ventilation and Airflow**: Promote natural ventilation by opening windows during the cooler parts of the day, such as early morning or evening. Use fans to circulate air and create a cooling breeze, reducing the need for air conditioning.

- o **Cook Outdoors**: Cooking indoors can generate significant heat, making your home warmer and increasing the load on your cooling system. During the summer, consider cooking outdoors on a grill or using smaller, energy-efficient appliances like a microwave or toaster oven to minimize heat production indoors.

Insulation, Heating, and Cooling Strategies for Off-Grid Living

1. **Insulation**:

- o **Insulate Key Areas**: Proper insulation is one of the most effective ways to maintain a stable indoor temperature year-round. Focus on insulating attics, walls, and floors, as well as any spaces where air can escape or enter your home. High-quality insulation can reduce energy consumption by keeping heat in during the winter and out during the summer.

- o **Insulate Pipes and Water Heaters**: Insulating your hot water pipes and water heater can reduce energy loss and make your heating system more efficient. This is particularly important in off-grid setups where conserving every bit of energy is crucial.

2. **Heating**:

- o **Wood Stoves and Pellet Stoves**: For off-grid heating, wood stoves and pellet stoves are popular choices. They provide reliable heat without the need for electricity and can be fueled by renewable resources. Make sure your stove is properly installed and vented, and keep a supply of fuel on hand for the winter months.

- o **Radiant Floor Heating**: Radiant floor heating systems are highly efficient and can be powered by solar energy or other off-grid power sources. They provide consistent warmth throughout your home by heating the floors, which then radiate heat upward. This method is particularly effective in well-insulated homes.

3. **Cooling**:

- o **Evaporative Coolers**: In dry climates, evaporative coolers (also known as swamp coolers) are an energy-efficient alternative to traditional air conditioning. They cool the air by passing it over water-saturated pads, adding moisture to the air and lowering the temperature.

- o **Natural Cooling Techniques**: Incorporate natural cooling techniques, such as cross-ventilation, to cool your home without relying on mechanical systems. Design your home to take advantage of prevailing breezes, and use features like skylights and clerestory windows to enhance airflow.

Reducing energy consumption and implementing seasonal energy conservation strategies are essential for optimizing your off-grid system. By adopting energy-efficient habits, investing in advanced technologies, and adapting your approach based on seasonal changes, you can significantly lower your energy demands while maintaining a comfortable living environment. These practices not only contribute to the sustainability of your off-grid lifestyle but also enhance the resilience and efficiency of your energy system.

Smart Energy Management Systems

As off-grid living becomes increasingly popular and sophisticated, smart energy management systems have emerged as essential tools for monitoring and controlling energy consumption. These systems use advanced technology to optimize the efficiency of your energy use, ensuring that your resources are used wisely and sustainably. By automating energy use and providing real-time data, smart energy management systems help you maintain a balanced and efficient off-grid lifestyle.

Leveraging Technology to Monitor and Control Energy Consumption

In an off-grid environment, every watt counts. Smart energy management systems are designed to give you detailed insights into your energy production, storage, and consumption, allowing you to make informed decisions that maximize efficiency and sustainability.

1. **Real-Time Monitoring**: One of the primary benefits of smart energy management systems is the ability to monitor your energy use in real-time. These systems collect data from various components of your off-grid setup, including solar panels, wind turbines, batteries, and generators. This data is then displayed through an intuitive interface, often accessible via a smartphone app or computer dashboard. By providing a clear view of how much energy you are generating, storing, and consuming at any given moment, real-time monitoring enables you to adjust your usage patterns on the fly, ensuring that you don't exceed your system's capacity.

2. **Energy Production and Consumption Analysis**: Beyond real-time monitoring, smart energy management systems also offer in-depth analysis of your energy production and consumption over time. By analyzing trends and patterns in your energy use, these systems can help you identify inefficiencies and areas where you might be able to cut back. For example, if you notice that certain appliances or systems are consuming more energy than expected, you can take steps to reduce their usage or replace them with more efficient alternatives.

3. **Load Management**: Smart energy management systems allow you to manage your energy load more effectively by prioritizing certain appliances or systems over others. This is particularly useful during times of peak demand or when your energy resources are limited. For instance, you can program the system to automatically reduce power to non-essential devices when battery levels are low, ensuring that critical systems like refrigeration and heating continue to operate. Load management helps to prevent overloading your system and extends the life of your batteries.

4. **Remote Access and Control**: Many smart energy management systems offer remote access, allowing you to monitor and control your energy usage from anywhere in the world. This feature is particularly useful for those who travel frequently or manage multiple properties. With remote access, you can check the status of your energy system, make adjustments to your energy consumption, and even receive alerts if there are any issues, such as a drop in solar output or a low battery warning.

Automating Energy Use for Efficiency and Sustainability

Automation is a key feature of smart energy management systems, enabling you to streamline your energy use without constant manual intervention. By automating certain aspects of your energy system, you can ensure that your off-grid home operates as efficiently and sustainably as possible.

1. **Automated Energy Switching**: One of the most significant advantages of smart energy management systems is their ability to automatically switch between energy sources based on availability and demand. For example, if your solar panels are producing excess energy during the day, the system can prioritize using solar power and store any surplus in your batteries. When the sun sets and solar

production drops, the system can seamlessly switch to wind power or activate a generator if needed. This automated switching ensures that you always have access to the most efficient and sustainable energy source available, reducing reliance on fuel-based generators and lowering your overall energy costs.

2. **Smart Thermostats and Climate Control**: Integrating smart thermostats and climate control systems into your energy management setup can significantly improve your home's energy efficiency. These devices learn your heating and cooling preferences over time and automatically adjust the temperature based on your daily routine, occupancy, and even weather conditions. By optimizing your home's temperature settings, smart thermostats can reduce unnecessary energy consumption, leading to lower heating and cooling costs while maintaining comfort.

3. **Scheduled Energy Use**: Smart energy management systems allow you to schedule the operation of energy-intensive appliances during periods of peak energy production. For instance, you can program your system to run your washing machine or dishwasher during the day when solar output is highest. Similarly, you can schedule the charging of electric vehicles or other battery-powered devices during times when energy demand is low. This scheduling helps to distribute energy use more evenly throughout the day, reducing the strain on your system and ensuring that your energy resources are used efficiently.

4. **Energy Conservation Modes**: Many smart energy management systems include energy conservation modes that automatically adjust your home's energy use based on specific criteria, such as low battery levels or poor weather conditions. In conservation mode, the system might reduce power to non-essential devices, dim lights, or adjust thermostat settings to conserve energy. This proactive approach helps to extend the life of your energy resources, ensuring that you have enough power to meet your essential needs even during extended periods of low energy production.

5. **Integration with Home Automation Systems**: Smart energy management systems can be integrated with broader home automation systems, creating a fully interconnected off-grid living experience. For example, your energy management system can be linked to smart lighting, security cameras, and other smart devices, allowing them to operate in sync. This integration not only enhances convenience and security but also contributes to greater energy efficiency. For instance, lights can be programmed to turn off automatically when you leave a room, or security cameras can be set to operate only during specific hours or when motion is detected, reducing unnecessary energy use.

Smart energy management systems are indispensable tools for anyone living off-grid. By leveraging advanced technology to monitor, control, and automate energy use, these systems ensure that your home operates as efficiently and sustainably as possible. Whether you're managing energy consumption in real-time, automating energy source switching, or integrating with home automation systems, smart energy management provides the flexibility and control needed to maintain a balanced and resilient off-grid lifestyle. As technology continues to advance, the capabilities of these systems will only expand, offering even greater opportunities for energy efficiency and sustainability in the future.

Video BONUS

Chapter 7: Medical Preparedness and Home Pharmacy

Building a Comprehensive Home First Aid Kit

Basic Components of a First Aid Kit

Having a well-stocked first aid kit is crucial for addressing a wide range of injuries and medical situations, particularly in an off-grid or emergency scenario where immediate professional medical help may not be available. A comprehensive first aid kit should include essential items for wound care, infection prevention, and general health monitoring, ensuring that you can effectively manage minor to moderate injuries.

Gauze, Bandages, Antiseptics, and Wound Care Essentials

Wound care is one of the most common uses for a first aid kit, and having the right supplies on hand is vital for preventing infections and promoting healing. Here are the basic components every first aid kit should include:

1. **Gauze Pads and Rolls**: Gauze is essential for cleaning, covering, and protecting wounds. Sterile gauze pads are used to absorb blood and exudate, while gauze rolls can be wrapped around limbs or other areas to secure dressings in place. Gauze is also helpful for applying pressure to control bleeding.

2. **Adhesive Bandages**: Commonly known as Band-Aids, adhesive bandages come in various sizes and are used to cover small cuts, blisters, and abrasions. They protect the wound from dirt and bacteria while promoting faster healing. It's useful to have a variety of sizes and shapes, including fingertip and knuckle bandages.

3. **Antiseptic Wipes and Solutions**: Before applying dressings or bandages, it's crucial to clean the wound to prevent infection. Antiseptic wipes or solutions like hydrogen peroxide, iodine, or alcohol are used to disinfect the wound area. Having single-use wipes in your kit ensures that you can clean wounds without introducing additional bacteria.

4. **Medical Tape**: Medical tape is used to secure gauze, bandages, or splints. It's designed to be gentle on the skin while providing a firm hold. Waterproof varieties are particularly useful in environments where water exposure is likely.

5. **Sterile Gloves**: Wearing sterile gloves when treating wounds helps prevent the transmission of germs and reduces the risk of infection. Disposable latex or nitrile gloves are standard, but be sure to have non-latex options available for those with latex allergies.

6. **Antibiotic Ointment**: Applying an antibiotic ointment, such as Neosporin, to a wound can help prevent infection and speed up the healing process. It's a good idea to include small, single-use packets of ointment in your kit to maintain sterility.

Tools Like Scissors, Tweezers, and Thermometers

In addition to wound care supplies, your first aid kit should include a selection of basic medical tools that allow you to manage various injuries and health conditions:

1. **Scissors**: Medical scissors are designed for cutting bandages, gauze, and medical tape. Trauma scissors, which have a blunt tip to prevent accidental injury, are particularly useful for cutting through clothing to access wounds.

2. **Tweezers**: Tweezers are essential for removing foreign objects like splinters, glass, or debris from wounds. Precision tweezers with a fine tip are ideal for delicate tasks, while broader-tipped tweezers can be used for handling larger objects.

3. **Thermometer**: Monitoring body temperature is important for diagnosing fevers or infections. Digital thermometers are quick and easy to use, providing an accurate reading in a matter of seconds. For a more versatile option, consider an infrared forehead thermometer, which can take readings without direct contact.

4. **Elastic Bandages**: Elastic bandages, such as ACE wraps, are versatile tools for providing support to sprained or strained joints, securing splints, or compressing injuries to reduce swelling. They are reusable and can be adjusted to fit various body parts.

5. **Safety Pins**: Safety pins are small but incredibly useful for securing bandages, slings, or splints. They can also be used to temporarily close clothing or fabric in the absence of other fasteners.

Advanced Medical Supplies

For those preparing for more serious medical situations, or in environments where professional medical help might be delayed, adding advanced medical supplies to your first aid kit is essential. These items allow you to manage more complex injuries and emergencies, potentially saving lives when time is critical.

Suture Kits, Splints, and Emergency Tourniquets

In situations where wounds are severe or when bone injuries occur, advanced medical supplies can make a significant difference in outcomes:

1. **Suture Kits**: A suture kit contains the necessary tools to close deep cuts or lacerations. While suturing is a skill that requires training, having a kit on hand can be vital in situations where professional help is not immediately available. The kit typically includes sterile needles, sutures, forceps, and scissors. If suturing is beyond your expertise, consider adding adhesive wound-closure strips or staples, which can also close wounds effectively.

2. **Splints**: Splints are used to immobilize broken bones or sprained joints, preventing further injury and reducing pain until professional care is available. A basic first aid kit might include an adjustable aluminum splint or a SAM splint, which is lightweight, moldable, and versatile. It's important to include materials like padding or gauze to cushion the splint and avoid pressure sores.

3. **Emergency Tourniquets**: In the event of severe bleeding, a tourniquet can be a life-saving tool. Tourniquets are used to apply pressure to a limb, cutting off blood flow to the affected area and controlling hemorrhage. Modern tourniquets, such as the CAT (Combat Application Tourniquet), are designed for quick and effective use, even by those with minimal medical training. It's crucial to understand how and when to use a tourniquet, as improper application can cause serious complications.

Burn Treatments, Eye Wash Solutions, and Specialized Dressings

Burns, eye injuries, and other specialized medical situations require specific treatments that go beyond the basics of wound care:

1. **Burn Treatments**: Burns can range from minor to severe, and having the right supplies on hand is critical for managing them effectively. Your first aid kit should include burn dressings, which are sterile pads soaked in a cooling gel that helps soothe pain and protect the burn area from infection. You should also have burn ointments or creams, such as those containing aloe vera or silver sulfadiazine, which can promote healing and prevent infection in more serious burns.

2. **Eye Wash Solutions**: Eye injuries are particularly delicate and require prompt attention. An eye wash solution, typically saline-based, is used to flush out foreign particles, chemicals, or other irritants from the eye. A small, portable eye wash bottle should be included in your first aid kit, especially if you are in an environment where eye injuries are a risk. For more severe cases, consider adding an eye cup or an eye irrigation kit, which allows for more thorough flushing.

3. **Specialized Dressings**: For wounds that are more complex, such as those with heavy bleeding, or for areas prone to infection, specialized dressings may be necessary. Hydrocolloid dressings, for example, provide a moist environment that promotes faster healing for wounds like ulcers or burns. Hemostatic dressings, which contain agents that promote blood clotting, are essential for managing severe bleeding. These dressings are often used in conjunction with pressure bandages or tourniquets in emergency situations.

A well-rounded first aid kit, equipped with both basic and advanced medical supplies, is indispensable for handling a wide range of medical situations in an off-grid or emergency environment. By preparing for both minor and severe injuries, you can ensure that you are ready to provide effective care when it matters most. As always, it's important to familiarize yourself with how to use each item in your kit properly, as having the right tools is only half the battle—knowing how to use them effectively is what truly saves lives.

Customizing Your First Aid Kit for Specific Needs

A standard first aid kit provides the basics for handling common injuries and emergencies, but every family has unique health considerations that may require additional supplies. Customizing your first aid kit to address specific needs, such as allergies, chronic conditions, and the requirements of children, elderly family members, or pets, ensures that you are fully prepared for any situation.

Considerations for Allergies, Chronic Conditions, and Family-Specific Needs

1. **Allergies**:

   o **Epinephrine Auto-Injectors (EpiPens)**: If anyone in your family has severe allergies, especially to foods, insect stings, or medications, it's essential to include epinephrine auto-injectors in your first aid kit. Epinephrine can quickly counteract the symptoms of anaphylaxis, a life-threatening allergic reaction. Make sure to check the expiration dates regularly and replace them as needed.

   o **Antihistamines**: Over-the-counter antihistamines, such as diphenhydramine (Benadryl), should also be included to manage less severe allergic reactions, such as hives, itching, or minor swelling. These can be in the form of tablets, liquids, or even topical creams.

   o **Allergy-Specific Medications**: If there are specific allergies in your household, consider adding other necessary medications, such as inhalers for asthma or specialized eye drops for allergic conjunctivitis.

2. **Chronic Conditions**:

   o **Medication Management**: For family members with chronic conditions such as diabetes, heart disease, or asthma, ensure that your first aid kit includes an adequate supply of their necessary medications. This includes insulin and glucose testing supplies for diabetics, nitroglycerin for heart conditions, and rescue inhalers for asthma.

   o **Spare Medical Devices**: Consider including spare parts or backup devices for essential medical equipment, such as extra batteries for hearing aids, a backup blood pressure monitor, or an additional nebulizer for those with respiratory conditions.

   o **Health Records**: It's also wise to keep a laminated copy of essential medical information, including a list of chronic conditions, medications, allergies, and emergency contacts, within your first aid kit. This can be invaluable in an emergency when quick reference is needed.

3. **Family-Specific Needs**:

   o **Mobility Aids**: If someone in your household requires mobility aids, such as a cane, walker, or wheelchair, include items that may help with repair or adjustment, such as wrenches, screws, or spare parts. Also, consider extra padding or supports to prevent pressure sores.

○ **Vision and Hearing**: Include backup eyeglasses or contact lenses and a small eyeglass repair kit. If any family members use hearing aids, consider adding extra batteries or a portable hearing aid cleaning kit.

Adding Items for Children, Elderly Family Members, and Pets

1. **Children**:

   ○ **Child-Specific Medications**: Children often require different dosages or forms of medication than adults. Include child-specific versions of common over-the-counter medications, such as acetaminophen (Tylenol), ibuprofen (Motrin), and antihistamines in liquid or chewable form. For infants, consider adding items like infant gas drops or diaper rash cream.

   ○ **Pediatric Tools**: Include a pediatric thermometer, which is more accurate and easier to use with young children. Consider adding items like a nasal aspirator for infants and baby wipes for quick clean-ups.

   ○ **Comfort Items**: In emergencies, children may become frightened or distressed. Including a small toy, a comforting blanket, or a pacifier in your kit can help soothe a child during a stressful situation. Adhesive bandages with fun designs can make treating minor injuries less intimidating for young children.

2. **Elderly Family Members**:

   ○ **Medication Organizers**: For elderly family members who take multiple medications, include a medication organizer in your first aid kit. This can help ensure that medications are taken correctly, especially in an emergency when routines may be disrupted.

   ○ **Mobility and Comfort Aids**: Items like extra cushions, anti-slip mats, or hand grips can provide additional safety and comfort for elderly individuals who may have mobility issues. Consider adding a magnifying glass or large-print labels to make it easier for them to read medication instructions or health information.

   ○ **Hearing and Vision Considerations**: As with chronic conditions, ensure that you have extra batteries for hearing aids and a backup pair of eyeglasses. These items can be crucial for elderly family members who rely on them for daily activities and communication.

3. **Pets**:

   ○ **Pet-Specific Medications**: If you have pets, your first aid kit should include their medications, such as flea and tick prevention, heartworm medication, or any prescription drugs they may be taking. It's also important to have a copy of their vaccination records and vet contact information in case of emergencies.

   ○ **Pet Wound Care**: Include pet-specific wound care items, such as antiseptic wipes and bandages designed for animals. You may also want to add a muzzle or cone to prevent your pet from licking or biting at a wound.

   ○ **Pet Tools**: Items like tweezers for removing ticks, a small pair of scissors for trimming fur around wounds, and a soft blanket for comfort or as a makeshift stretcher can be invaluable in an emergency involving your pet. Also, consider including a collapsible water bowl and a supply of their regular food, especially if you anticipate being away from home for an extended period.

Customizing your first aid kit to address the specific needs of your household is a critical step in ensuring that you are fully prepared for any medical situation. By considering the unique health requirements of family members with allergies, chronic conditions, or other specific needs—and by including appropriate supplies for children, elderly individuals, and pets—you can create a comprehensive and versatile first aid kit. This tailored approach not only enhances your ability to respond effectively in emergencies but also provides peace of mind, knowing that you have the right tools on hand to care for your loved ones in any situation.

Essential Medications and Their Uses

Over-the-Counter Medications

Over-the-counter (OTC) medications are a crucial part of any home pharmacy, offering first-line treatment for a wide range of common ailments. These medications are readily available without a prescription and can provide relief from symptoms such as pain, inflammation, fever, allergies, colds, and digestive issues. Understanding the uses and benefits of these medications ensures that you can effectively manage minor health problems at home, especially in situations where professional medical help may not be immediately accessible.

Pain Relievers, Anti-Inflammatory Drugs, and Fever Reducers

Pain and inflammation are among the most common reasons people seek medical treatment, and having the right OTC medications on hand can help manage these symptoms effectively.

1. **Acetaminophen (Tylenol)**: Acetaminophen is widely used for pain relief and fever reduction. It's effective for treating headaches, muscle aches, arthritis, backaches, toothaches, and fevers. Unlike some other pain relievers, acetaminophen does not have anti-inflammatory properties, making it a good option for those who need pain relief without reducing inflammation. It's also gentler on the stomach, making it suitable for people who are prone to stomach issues.

2. **Ibuprofen (Advil, Motrin)**: Ibuprofen is both a pain reliever and an anti-inflammatory drug, making it ideal for conditions where inflammation is a primary concern, such as arthritis, sprains, and other musculoskeletal injuries. It's also effective for reducing fever. Ibuprofen can cause stomach irritation or ulcers with long-term use, so it should be taken with food and only as directed.

3. **Aspirin**: Aspirin is another commonly used pain reliever and anti-inflammatory drug. It's particularly noted for its blood-thinning properties, which can reduce the risk of heart attacks and strokes in certain individuals. Aspirin should be used with caution, as it can cause stomach irritation and is not recommended for children or teenagers with viral infections due to the risk of Reye's syndrome.

4. **Naproxen (Aleve)**: Naproxen is another nonsteroidal anti-inflammatory drug (NSAID) that is effective for long-lasting pain relief and inflammation reduction. It's often used for chronic conditions like arthritis, as well as acute injuries. Like other NSAIDs, it can cause gastrointestinal issues and should be taken with care.

Antihistamines, Cold Remedies, and Digestive Aids

Seasonal allergies, colds, and digestive problems are common ailments that can often be managed with OTC medications.

1. **Antihistamines**: Antihistamines are used to treat symptoms of allergies, such as sneezing, itching, watery eyes, and runny nose. They work by blocking histamine, a substance in the body that causes allergic symptoms. Common antihistamines include diphenhydramine (Benadryl), which is sedating, and loratadine (Claritin) or cetirizine (Zyrtec), which are non-drowsy options. Antihistamines are also useful for treating hives and other allergic skin reactions.

2. **Decongestants**: Decongestants like pseudoephedrine (Sudafed) are effective for relieving nasal congestion caused by colds, allergies, or sinus infections. They work by shrinking the blood vessels in the nasal passages, reducing swelling and allowing for easier breathing. Decongestants should be used with caution in people with high blood pressure or heart conditions.

3. **Cough Suppressants and Expectorants**: Cough suppressants, such as dextromethorphan (Robitussin DM), help reduce the urge to cough, making them useful for dry, irritating coughs. Expectorants, like guaifenesin (Mucinex), help thin mucus, making it easier to cough up. These medications are often combined in OTC cold remedies to address multiple symptoms simultaneously.

4. **Digestive Aids**: Digestive issues like heartburn, indigestion, diarrhea, and constipation are common and can usually be managed with OTC medications. Antacids, such as calcium carbonate (Tums) or magnesium hydroxide (Milk of Magnesia), neutralize stomach acid and provide quick relief from heartburn and indigestion. Loperamide (Imodium) is effective for controlling diarrhea, while fiber supplements or stool softeners can help alleviate constipation.

5. **Electrolyte Solutions**: In cases of severe diarrhea or vomiting, electrolyte solutions like Pedialyte can help prevent dehydration by replenishing lost fluids and electrolytes. These are particularly important for children and the elderly, who are more susceptible to dehydration.

Prescription Medications

While OTC medications are essential for managing minor health issues, prescription medications are often necessary for treating chronic conditions or more serious illnesses. Proper storage and management of these medications are crucial for ensuring their effectiveness and safety.

Storing and Managing Necessary Prescriptions for Chronic Conditions

1. **Organization and Accessibility**: It's important to keep prescription medications organized and easily accessible, especially in an emergency. Use a dedicated area in your home pharmacy, such as a labeled drawer or shelf, to store medications. Consider using a pill organizer for daily medications, which can help prevent missed doses and reduce the risk of accidental double-dosing.

2. **Maintaining an Adequate Supply**: For chronic conditions, it's essential to maintain an adequate supply of prescription medications, especially if you live in a remote area or during times when access to pharmacies may be limited. Work with your healthcare provider to ensure you have enough medication on hand to last at least a few weeks beyond your next scheduled refill. This is particularly important for medications that cannot be easily substituted or obtained over-the-counter.

3. **Medication Expiry and Storage Conditions**: Store medications in a cool, dry place away from direct sunlight, heat, and moisture, which can degrade their effectiveness. Bathrooms and kitchens, which are prone to humidity and temperature fluctuations, are not ideal storage locations. Always check the expiration dates on prescription medications, as expired drugs may lose potency or become unsafe. If a medication has expired, consult your healthcare provider before using it or replacing it.

4. **Backup Prescriptions**: If you require life-sustaining medications, consider asking your doctor for a backup prescription that you can keep in a secure location or with a trusted family member. This can be particularly useful if you travel frequently or live in an area prone to natural disasters, where access to your regular pharmacy might be disrupted.

Understanding Expiration Dates and Safe Disposal Practices

1. **Expiration Dates**: The expiration date on a medication indicates the last date the manufacturer guarantees full potency and safety. While many medications may retain some effectiveness after this date, it's not advisable to use them without consulting a healthcare professional, as the chemical composition may change over time. Medications such as insulin, nitroglycerin, and antibiotics are particularly sensitive to expiration and should be used strictly within their labeled timeframes.

2. **Safe Disposal of Medications**: Proper disposal of expired or unused medications is crucial to prevent accidental ingestion, misuse, or environmental contamination. Flushing medications down the toilet or throwing them in the trash can be harmful to the environment. Instead, many communities offer take-back programs or drop-off locations where medications can be safely disposed of. If these options are not available, the FDA recommends mixing medications (without crushing tablets or capsules) with an unpalatable substance like dirt, cat litter, or used coffee grounds, placing the mixture in a sealed plastic bag, and throwing it in the household trash. Be sure to remove or obscure any personal information on the prescription label before disposal.

3. **Handling Controlled Substances**: Controlled substances, such as opioid painkillers or certain anxiety medications, require special care in storage and disposal due to their potential for abuse. These medications should be stored securely, out of reach of children and anyone who might misuse them. When it's time to dispose of them, it's best to use a drug take-back program, as recommended by the DEA, to ensure they are handled safely.

Both over-the-counter and prescription medications are essential components of a well-prepared home pharmacy. By understanding the uses, storage requirements, and proper management of these medications, you can ensure that you are fully equipped to handle a wide range of health issues, from minor ailments to chronic conditions. This level of preparedness not only enhances your ability to provide care at home but also contributes to a safer, more organized, and effective medical response in any situation.

Natural Remedies and Supplements

Incorporating natural remedies and supplements into your home pharmacy can provide a holistic approach to health and wellness, complementing conventional medications. These alternatives can offer relief from minor ailments, boost immunity, and promote overall well-being. It's essential to understand their uses, benefits, and limitations to ensure safe and effective treatment.

Herbal Supplements for Boosting Immunity and Treating Minor Ailments

Herbal supplements have been used for centuries to support health and treat various conditions. They can be an effective addition to your home pharmacy, particularly for boosting immunity and managing minor ailments.

1. **Echinacea**: Often used to prevent or reduce the duration of colds and flu, echinacea is believed to boost the immune system. It's available in various forms, including teas, capsules, and tinctures. While echinacea is generally safe for short-term use, it's important to follow dosage recommendations to avoid potential side effects like nausea or dizziness.

2. **Ginger**: Known for its anti-inflammatory and antioxidant properties, ginger is commonly used to relieve nausea, especially from motion sickness, pregnancy, or chemotherapy. It can also help with digestion and reduce muscle pain and soreness. Fresh ginger can be used in cooking or made into tea, and ginger supplements are available in capsule or powder form.

3. **Turmeric**: Turmeric contains curcumin, a compound with potent anti-inflammatory and antioxidant effects. It's used to relieve pain and inflammation associated with conditions like arthritis and may also support digestion and liver health. Turmeric is available as a spice, in capsules, or as a liquid extract. To enhance absorption, turmeric supplements often include black pepper extract.

4. **Garlic**: Garlic has been used for its medicinal properties for thousands of years. It's believed to have antibacterial, antiviral, and antifungal properties, making it useful for boosting the immune system. Garlic supplements are available in various forms, including capsules, tablets, and oils. When using garlic as a natural remedy, it's important to consider potential interactions with medications, particularly blood thinners.

5. **Peppermint**: Peppermint is commonly used to relieve digestive issues, such as irritable bowel syndrome (IBS), indigestion, and gas. Peppermint oil, when taken in enteric-coated capsules, can help relax the muscles of the gastrointestinal tract and reduce symptoms of IBS. Peppermint tea is also popular for soothing digestive discomfort.

Essential Oils, Vitamins, and Other Alternative Treatments

In addition to herbal supplements, essential oils, vitamins, and other alternative treatments can be valuable components of a natural home pharmacy.

1. **Essential Oils**: Essential oils are concentrated extracts from plants, known for their aromatic and therapeutic properties. They can be used in various ways, including aromatherapy, topical application, and even ingestion (with caution and under professional guidance).

- **Lavender Oil**: Lavender oil is known for its calming effects and is often used to reduce anxiety, stress, and promote sleep. It can be diffused into the air, applied topically after being diluted with a carrier oil, or added to a bath for a relaxing experience.

- **Tea Tree Oil**: With its antimicrobial properties, tea tree oil is commonly used to treat minor cuts, burns, and insect bites. It can also be effective for acne and other skin conditions. When using tea tree oil, it's important to dilute it with a carrier oil to avoid skin irritation.

- **Eucalyptus Oil**: Eucalyptus oil is used for its decongestant and anti-inflammatory properties. It can help relieve symptoms of colds, flu, and respiratory conditions by loosening mucus and easing breathing. Eucalyptus oil can be inhaled using a steam inhaler or diffuser or applied topically after dilution.

2. **Vitamins and Minerals**: Vitamins and minerals are essential for overall health and well-being. While a balanced diet is the best way to obtain these nutrients, supplements can help fill any gaps in your nutrition.

   - **Vitamin C**: Known for its immune-boosting properties, vitamin C can help reduce the severity and duration of colds and other infections. It also acts as an antioxidant, protecting cells from damage.

   - **Vitamin D**: Vitamin D is important for bone health, immune function, and mood regulation. It can be obtained from sunlight exposure, but supplements may be necessary for individuals with limited sun exposure or dietary intake.

   - **Zinc**: Zinc is crucial for immune function, wound healing, and DNA synthesis. It can help reduce the duration of colds when taken at the onset of symptoms. Zinc supplements are available in various forms, including lozenges, capsules, and tablets.

3. **Probiotics**: Probiotics are beneficial bacteria that support gut health and digestion. They can help balance the gut microbiome, improve digestion, and boost the immune system. Probiotics are available in supplement form or can be obtained from fermented foods like yogurt, kefir, sauerkraut, and kimchi.

4. **Homeopathic Remedies**: Homeopathy is a system of alternative medicine based on the principle of "like cures like," using highly diluted substances to stimulate the body's natural healing processes. While scientific evidence supporting homeopathy is limited, some people find relief from certain symptoms using homeopathic remedies. Common homeopathic remedies include arnica for pain and bruising, and nux vomica for digestive issues.

5. **Acupuncture and Acupressure**: Acupuncture and acupressure are traditional Chinese medicine techniques that involve stimulating specific points on the body to promote healing and relieve pain. While acupuncture requires trained professionals and the use of needles, acupressure can be self-administered using fingers or special tools to apply pressure to the same points.

Incorporating natural remedies and supplements into your home pharmacy can provide a complementary approach to health and wellness, supporting the body's natural healing processes and offering relief from minor ailments. It's important to remember that natural doesn't always mean safe. Some supplements can interact with medications or have side effects, so it's crucial to consult with a healthcare provider before starting any new supplement or remedy, especially if you have underlying health conditions or are pregnant or breastfeeding.

Furthermore, while natural remedies can be effective for minor ailments, they should not replace conventional medical treatment for serious conditions. If you experience severe symptoms or a condition that doesn't improve with self-treatment, seek medical attention promptly.

A well-rounded home pharmacy should include a variety of natural remedies and supplements to address a range of health concerns. By understanding the benefits and limitations of these alternatives, you can make informed decisions about their use, ensuring that you and your family have access to safe and effective treatments for maintaining health and well-being.

Managing Health Conditions Without Outside Help

Recognizing and Treating Common Ailments

In any situation, especially when living off-grid, the ability to recognize and treat common ailments is crucial for maintaining health and preventing minor issues from escalating into serious problems. By understanding the symptoms of these ailments and knowing how to provide first-line treatment, you can manage many health concerns effectively at home. It's also important to recognize when professional medical help is necessary, even in an off-grid situation.

Identifying Symptoms and Providing First-Line Treatment for Common Illnesses

1. **Colds and Flu**:

   o **Symptoms**: Common symptoms include a runny or stuffy nose, sore throat, cough, fatigue, body aches, and fever. The flu generally causes more severe symptoms than the common cold and may include a higher fever, chills, and more intense fatigue.

   o **First-Line Treatment**: Rest is essential. Increase fluid intake to stay hydrated and help thin mucus. Over-the-counter medications like acetaminophen or ibuprofen can reduce fever and relieve aches and pains. For a sore throat, gargling with warm salt water or using throat lozenges can provide relief. Use a humidifier to ease congestion and breathing. If symptoms worsen or persist beyond 7-10 days, or if there is difficulty breathing, chest pain, or a persistent high fever, seek medical attention.

2. **Gastrointestinal Issues (Diarrhea, Constipation, Indigestion)**:

   o **Symptoms**: Diarrhea can lead to dehydration, characterized by loose, watery stools, abdominal cramps, and urgency. Constipation is identified by infrequent, difficult bowel movements, often with straining. Indigestion causes discomfort or pain in the upper abdomen, often accompanied by bloating, nausea, or heartburn.

   o **First-Line Treatment**: For diarrhea, staying hydrated is critical—use oral rehydration solutions to replace lost fluids and electrolytes. Over-the-counter anti-diarrheal medications like loperamide (Imodium) can help, but should not be used if there is a suspicion of a bacterial infection. For constipation, increase fiber intake through diet or supplements, and stay hydrated. Gentle physical activity and the use of stool softeners or laxatives may also help. Indigestion can often be relieved with antacids, while dietary adjustments (avoiding trigger foods) can prevent recurrence. If diarrhea lasts more than two days, is accompanied by severe pain, or there is blood in the stool, seek medical help. Persistent or severe indigestion should also be evaluated by a healthcare provider.

3. **Infections (Skin, Respiratory, Urinary Tract Infections)**:

   o **Symptoms**: Skin infections often present with redness, warmth, swelling, and pain at the site. Respiratory infections can cause coughing, congestion, and fever. Urinary tract infections (UTIs) typically involve burning during urination, frequent urges to urinate, and cloudy or strong-smelling urine.

   o **First-Line Treatment**: For minor skin infections, clean the area with soap and water, apply an antiseptic, and cover it with a sterile bandage. Warm compresses can help reduce pain and swelling. Respiratory infections should be managed with rest, hydration, and over-the-counter medications for symptom relief. UTIs require increased fluid intake to flush out bacteria, and cranberry supplements may help prevent bacterial adhesion. Over-the-counter pain relievers can manage discomfort. Bacterial infections often require antibiotics, so if symptoms of any infection persist or worsen, or if there are signs of systemic infection (like fever, chills, or fatigue), professional medical help is necessary.

4. **Allergic Reactions**:

   o **Symptoms**: Mild allergic reactions may cause itching, hives, and mild swelling. More severe reactions can involve difficulty breathing, swelling of the face or throat, dizziness, or anaphylaxis, a potentially life-threatening condition.

   o **First-Line Treatment**: For mild reactions, antihistamines can relieve symptoms. Applying cool compresses or using calamine lotion can reduce itching and discomfort from hives. For severe reactions, such as anaphylaxis, immediate use of an epinephrine auto-injector (EpiPen) is critical, followed by emergency medical care. Always seek medical help if you suspect anaphylaxis, even if symptoms improve after using epinephrine.

When to Seek Professional Medical Help, Even in an Off-Grid Situation

While being off-grid often requires self-reliance in medical care, certain situations demand professional medical intervention. It's essential to recognize the red flags that indicate a need for help beyond what you can provide at home:

- **Persistent or Severe Symptoms**: If symptoms of a common ailment persist longer than expected or worsen despite treatment, it may indicate a more serious underlying issue that requires medical evaluation. This includes high fevers that don't respond to treatment, severe abdominal pain, prolonged vomiting or diarrhea, or unmanageable pain.

- **Difficulty Breathing**: Any condition that leads to difficulty breathing, such as severe asthma, respiratory infections, or allergic reactions, should be treated as an emergency. Immediate professional medical attention is necessary to prevent life-threatening complications.

- **Uncontrolled Bleeding**: If bleeding cannot be controlled with basic first aid measures, or if a wound is deep, involves a joint, or continues to bleed despite pressure, professional medical care is essential to prevent significant blood loss and infection.

- **Signs of Infection**: Symptoms of a spreading infection, such as increased redness, warmth, swelling, red streaks radiating from the infection site, or systemic symptoms like fever and chills, require antibiotics and medical supervision.

- **Suspected Broken Bones**: While minor fractures can sometimes be managed with splinting and rest, any suspicion of a broken bone, particularly if it involves a major joint, results in significant pain, or causes deformity, should prompt a visit to a medical professional.

Long-Term Management of Chronic Conditions

Managing chronic conditions off-grid requires careful planning, a solid understanding of the condition, and access to necessary supplies. For those with conditions like diabetes, heart disease, or asthma, maintaining health and being prepared for emergencies is a continuous priority.

Strategies for Managing Diabetes, Heart Disease, and Other Chronic Illnesses Off-Grid

1. **Diabetes**:

   o **Blood Sugar Monitoring**: Regular monitoring of blood sugar levels is critical for managing diabetes. Ensure you have an adequate supply of test strips, lancets, and a reliable glucose meter. Consider having backup meters and batteries available.

   o **Insulin Storage**: For those who require insulin, proper storage is vital. Insulin should be kept at a stable temperature, typically between 36°F and 46°F (2°C to 8°C). Off-grid, this might involve using solar-powered coolers or other temperature-controlled storage solutions. Plan for how you will maintain insulin at the correct temperature during extended power outages or when refrigeration isn't available.

- ○ **Diet and Exercise**: Managing diabetes effectively also involves maintaining a balanced diet and regular exercise. Stock up on low-glycemic foods that are shelf-stable, such as beans, lentils, whole grains, and canned vegetables. Regular physical activity helps control blood sugar levels, so consider activities that can be done at home, such as walking or body-weight exercises.

2. **Heart Disease**:

    - ○ **Medication Management**: For those with heart disease, managing medications like statins, beta-blockers, or blood thinners is crucial. Ensure a consistent supply of these medications, and work with your healthcare provider to have an emergency backup supply.

    - ○ **Blood Pressure Monitoring**: Regularly monitoring blood pressure at home can help manage heart disease. A reliable, easy-to-use blood pressure monitor should be part of your home health toolkit. Keep a log of your readings to track any changes that might require medical attention.

    - ○ **Lifestyle Modifications**: Diet and exercise play a significant role in managing heart disease. Stock up on heart-healthy foods, such as nuts, seeds, canned fish, and low-sodium options. Regular physical activity and stress management techniques, such as meditation or deep-breathing exercises, can help maintain heart health.

3. **Asthma and Respiratory Conditions**:

    - ○ **Inhaler Management**: Always have a sufficient supply of both rescue (e.g., albuterol) and maintenance (e.g., corticosteroids) inhalers. Keep backup inhalers in multiple locations, such as at home, in your vehicle, and in emergency kits.

    - ○ **Air Quality Management**: Poor air quality can exacerbate respiratory conditions. Consider investing in a portable air purifier for your home and maintaining good ventilation. If you are in a region prone to wildfires or high pollution, have masks or respirators available to reduce exposure to harmful particles.

    - ○ **Emergency Preparedness**: Know the signs of an asthma attack and have a clear plan for responding quickly. This includes using a rescue inhaler and seeking immediate medical attention if symptoms don't improve.

Maintaining Necessary Supplies and Staying Prepared for Emergencies

1. **Stockpile Essentials**: Ensure that you have a sufficient supply of necessary medications and medical supplies to last at least 30 days, preferably longer. This includes medications, glucose meters, test strips, inhalers, and any other critical items. Rotate your stockpile regularly to ensure nothing expires.

2. **Emergency Kits**: Prepare a dedicated emergency kit for your chronic condition. This should include all necessary medications, medical devices, a list of dosages and medical contacts, and a copy of your medical records. For diabetics, this might also include glucose tablets or gels for low blood sugar, while those with heart disease might need nitroglycerin.

3. **Backup Power Solutions**: If your condition requires the use of electrically powered medical devices, such as a CPAP machine for sleep apnea or a nebulizer for asthma , ensure you have a reliable backup power source. This might include solar panels, a generator, or a battery backup system.

4. **Regular Check-Ins with Healthcare Providers**: Even when living off-grid, maintaining regular communication with your healthcare provider is essential. This can be done through telemedicine if in-person visits are difficult. Regular check-ins allow for monitoring of your condition, adjustment of medications if necessary, and planning for any anticipated changes in your health needs.

Managing common ailments and chronic conditions in an off-grid setting requires careful planning, a well-stocked medical supply, and the knowledge to recognize when to seek professional help. By understanding how to treat minor issues and being prepared for the complexities of chronic illness management, you can maintain your health and well-being even in challenging circumstances. This level of preparedness not only ensures your ability to handle everyday health concerns but also provides peace of mind knowing that you are ready for any medical situation that may arise.

Emergency Medical Procedures

In any survival scenario, knowing how to perform emergency medical procedures can be the difference between life and death. Whether you're dealing with a severe injury, cardiac arrest, or a bone fracture, having the skills and knowledge to act quickly and effectively is crucial. This chapter will guide you through essential emergency procedures, including performing CPR, treating severe wounds, handling fractures, and using advanced medical equipment like defibrillators, oxygen tanks, and emergency splints.

Performing CPR, Treating Severe Wounds, and Handling Fractures

1. **Cardiopulmonary Resuscitation (CPR)**:

   o **CPR Basics**: CPR is a life-saving technique used when someone has stopped breathing or their heart has stopped beating. It involves chest compressions and rescue breaths to manually pump blood through the body and maintain oxygen flow to vital organs until professional help arrives.

   o **How to Perform CPR**: Begin by checking the scene for safety, then check the victim for responsiveness. If they are unresponsive and not breathing, or only gasping, start CPR. Place the heel of one hand on the center of the victim's chest, with the other hand on top. Press down hard and fast, aiming for a depth of about 2 inches and a rate of 100-120 compressions per minute. After 30 compressions, give two rescue breaths by tilting the victim's head back, lifting their chin, and sealing your mouth over theirs. Continue this cycle until help arrives or the person starts breathing on their own.

   o **When to Use an AED (Automated External Defibrillator)**: If available, use an AED as soon as possible. Follow the device's prompts to analyze the heart rhythm and deliver a shock if necessary. The AED will guide you through the process, including continuing CPR after the shock is delivered.

2. **Treating Severe Wounds**:

   o **Controlling Bleeding**: For severe bleeding, immediate action is required to prevent shock. Apply direct pressure to the wound using a clean cloth or bandage. If the bleeding doesn't stop, apply more pressure and consider using a tourniquet above the wound if trained to do so. Keep the injured area elevated above the heart if possible.

   o **Cleaning and Dressing the Wound**: Once bleeding is controlled, clean the wound with sterile saline or clean water to remove debris. Apply an antiseptic, then cover the wound with a sterile dressing or bandage. For large or deep wounds, pack the wound with sterile gauze before bandaging. Monitor for signs of infection, such as redness, swelling, or pus.

   o **Shock Management**: Severe bleeding can lead to shock, a life-threatening condition where the body's organs aren't getting enough blood flow. Symptoms include pale, clammy skin, rapid breathing, and confusion. To treat shock, keep the person lying down with their legs elevated, cover them with a blanket to keep warm, and seek immediate medical attention.

3. **Handling Fractures**:

   o **Identifying a Fracture**: Signs of a fracture include intense pain, swelling, bruising, and an inability to move the affected limb. The limb may appear deformed, or there may be an open wound if the bone has pierced the skin.

   o **Immobilizing the Fracture**: Before moving the injured person, immobilize the fracture to prevent further damage. Use a splint made from rigid materials like wood, plastic, or a rolled-up newspaper, and secure it with bandages or cloth strips. The splint should immobilize the joints above and below the fracture.

- o **Handling Compound Fractures**: For compound fractures where the bone breaks through the skin, control bleeding with sterile dressings before splinting. Avoid trying to realign the bone. Seek professional medical help as soon as possible to prevent complications such as infection.

4. **Using Medical Equipment Like Defibrillators, Oxygen Tanks, and Emergency Splints**

- o **Defibrillators (AEDs)**: As mentioned in the CPR section, AEDs are crucial in treating sudden cardiac arrest. They analyze the heart's rhythm and deliver an electrical shock to help the heart re-establish an effective rhythm. AEDs are designed to be user-friendly, with clear instructions that guide even untrained users through the process. In an emergency, retrieving and using an AED within the first few minutes of cardiac arrest significantly increases the chances of survival.

- o **Oxygen Tanks**: Oxygen therapy may be necessary for individuals experiencing respiratory distress, such as severe asthma attacks, COPD exacerbations, or during recovery from smoke inhalation. Portable oxygen tanks provide a concentrated source of oxygen to help maintain adequate blood oxygen levels. To use an oxygen tank, ensure it is properly set up with a regulator to control the flow rate, typically measured in liters per minute (LPM). The flow rate should be set according to medical advice or the patient's needs, usually between 1-5 LPM for mild to moderate distress. Attach the oxygen mask or nasal cannula and ensure the patient breathes normally. Monitor the patient for improvement or signs of worsening condition, and seek medical attention as necessary.

- o **Emergency Splints**: Emergency splints are used to immobilize fractures or severe sprains until professional medical care can be provided. Prefabricated splints like SAM splints are versatile and can be molded to fit various body parts. In a pinch, makeshift splints can be created from rigid materials like boards, cardboard, or rolled-up magazines. The splint should be padded to avoid pressure sores and secured with bandages or cloth strips. Ensure the splint immobilizes the joints above and below the injury site.

Psychological First Aid

In crisis situations, addressing mental health is just as important as treating physical injuries. Psychological first aid (PFA) involves providing support to individuals who are experiencing emotional distress, anxiety, or trauma. By offering psychological first aid, you can help stabilize individuals, reduce their stress, and promote resilience during and after a crisis.

Addressing Mental Health Issues in a Crisis Situation

1. **Recognizing Psychological Distress**:

- o **Common Signs**: In a crisis, individuals may experience a range of emotional and psychological responses, including anxiety, confusion, anger, fear, and helplessness. Physical symptoms can also manifest, such as headaches, stomachaches, and fatigue. Recognizing these signs is the first step in providing appropriate support.

- o **Risk of Panic**: Panic can spread quickly in a crisis, leading to irrational behavior, which can endanger the individual and others. Recognizing early signs of panic, such as rapid breathing, agitation, and irrational thoughts, is critical for intervening before the situation escalates.

2. **Providing Emotional Support**:

- o **Active Listening**: One of the most effective ways to provide psychological first aid is through active listening. This involves giving the person your full attention, acknowledging their feelings without judgment, and offering reassurance. Allow them to express their fears and concerns without interruption.

- o **Grounding Techniques**: Grounding techniques help individuals stay present and focused during moments of acute stress. Simple exercises like deep breathing, focusing on physical sensations (such as feeling the ground beneath their feet), or describing their environment in detail can help reduce feelings of overwhelm.

- o **Reassurance and Information**: Providing clear, factual information about the situation can help reduce anxiety. Offer reassurance about the steps being taken to manage the crisis and what the person can do to stay safe. Avoid making false promises, and be honest about what is known and unknown.

Techniques for Providing Emotional Support and Managing Stress

1. **Encouraging Healthy Coping Mechanisms**:

   - o **Routine and Normalcy**: Encourage individuals to maintain as much of their normal routine as possible, as this can provide a sense of stability. This might include regular meals, sleep, and even small tasks or hobbies that distract from the crisis.

   - o **Positive Self-Talk**: Help individuals engage in positive self-talk by encouraging them to focus on their strengths and past successes in overcoming challenges. This can help build resilience and reduce feelings of helplessness.

2. **Managing Group Dynamics**:

   - o **Leadership and Communication**: In a group setting, strong leadership and clear communication are vital. A calm, composed leader can help maintain order and reduce panic. Providing clear instructions and regularly updating the group on the situation can help manage stress levels.

   - o **Conflict Resolution**: Stressful situations can lead to conflicts within groups. Address conflicts quickly by encouraging open communication, empathy, and compromise. Ensure that everyone feels heard and validated, and work towards solutions that meet the needs of all parties involved.

3. **Long-Term Psychological Support**:

   - o **Debriefing and Counseling**: After the immediate crisis has passed, ongoing psychological support may be necessary. This can include debriefing sessions where individuals discuss their experiences and emotions, and professional counseling for those who continue to struggle with anxiety, depression, or PTSD.

   - o **Community Support Networks**: Encourage individuals to stay connected with their community, whether through formal support groups or informal networks of friends and family. Social support is one of the strongest predictors of recovery from trauma.

Video BONUS

Chapter 8: Crisis Communication and Networking

Setting Up Emergency Communication Systems

Understanding Communication Needs in a Crisis

Effective communication is a cornerstone of emergency preparedness. In a crisis, having reliable lines of communication can be the difference between safety and danger, confusion and clarity, or even life and death. Understanding your specific communication needs during different types of emergencies is the first step in creating a robust communication strategy.

Assessing Your Communication Requirements During Different Types of Emergencies

The type of emergency you face will largely dictate your communication needs. For instance, a natural disaster like a hurricane or earthquake might disrupt conventional communication infrastructures, requiring you to rely on alternative methods such as radios or satellite phones. In contrast, a pandemic or civil unrest might require discreet, localized communication within a neighborhood or family unit.

1. **Natural Disasters**: In the event of a hurricane, earthquake, or flood, traditional communication networks such as cell towers and internet services may be compromised. Therefore, it's essential to assess how you will maintain contact with emergency services, family members, and neighbors when these systems are down. Consider the following:

   o **Local Communication**: How will you communicate with family members in your home or immediate vicinity? Handheld radios or walkie-talkies can be useful here.

   o **Regional Communication**: For contacting family members or friends who are not in the immediate area, you may need a more powerful solution, such as a HAM radio or a satellite phone.

   o **Emergency Services**: Ensure you have the means to contact local emergency services. This might include a landline phone (if the lines are intact), a radio capable of receiving emergency broadcasts, or a satellite phone.

2. **Civil Unrest or Security Threats**: During civil unrest, the priority is often maintaining communication within a small group while avoiding drawing attention. Your communication needs in such scenarios may include:

   o **Secure Communication**: Consider encrypted communication devices or apps to prevent interception.

   o **Covert Communication**: Low-tech options like signal codes, pre-arranged meeting points, or even written notes may be necessary to avoid detection.

   o **Redundancy**: Have backup methods ready in case primary devices fail or are compromised.

3. **Medical Emergencies**: In a medical emergency, particularly one involving multiple people or requiring rapid response, your communication needs are likely to include:

   o **Direct Communication with Emergency Services**: Ensure that you can quickly and reliably reach emergency medical services. This may involve a reliable cell phone, a landline, or even a dedicated emergency communication device.

   o **Family Coordination**: Communication between family members to coordinate immediate response and care is crucial. Handheld radios, intercom systems, or even a well-established plan for in-person communication can be vital.

o **Remote Assistance**: In some cases, you may need to communicate with medical professionals remotely. A reliable internet connection (if available) or a satellite phone might be necessary for accessing telemedicine services.

Identifying Critical Contacts and Ensuring Reliable Lines of Communication

Once you've assessed your general communication needs, the next step is to identify your critical contacts and ensure that you have reliable ways to communicate with them during a crisis.

1. **Critical Contacts**:

   o **Family Members**: Establish a list of all family members you need to stay in contact with during an emergency. Include their primary and secondary contact methods (e.g., cell phone, email, radio frequency).

   o **Neighbors and Local Community**: Identify key neighbors or community members who will be part of your emergency network. This could include those with specific skills (e.g., medical professionals, emergency responders) or those who have agreed to mutual aid.

   o **Emergency Services**: Ensure you have the correct numbers for local emergency services, such as fire, police, medical, and utility services. Also, include any local emergency broadcast frequencies.

   o **Out-of-Area Contacts**: It can be useful to have a contact outside of your immediate area who can be notified of your situation and assist in coordinating aid if local services are overwhelmed.

2. **Ensuring Reliable Communication**:

   o **Redundancy**: It's crucial to have multiple communication methods in place in case one fails. For example, if cell service is down, you should have access to a radio system or a satellite phone.

   o **Regular Testing**: Communication devices and systems should be tested regularly to ensure they are functional. This includes checking battery levels, signal strength, and familiarity with operation.

   o **Pre-Arranged Signals and Codes**: Establishing pre-arranged signals, codes, or meeting points with your critical contacts can help ensure communication even if traditional methods are compromised.

Choosing the Right Communication Devices

Selecting the right communication devices for your emergency plan is essential. Different devices offer varying benefits depending on the scenario, so it's important to choose tools that align with your assessed needs.

Evaluating Different Devices: Radios (HAM, GMRS, FRS), Satellite Phones, and Mobile Phones

1. **HAM Radios**:

   o **Overview**: HAM radios, or amateur radios, are a popular choice for emergency communication due to their long range and ability to operate independently of existing communication infrastructures.

   o **Pros**: HAM radios offer extensive range, especially with repeaters, and can communicate globally under the right conditions. They are highly reliable and can be used for both local and long-distance communication. HAM radios are supported by a large community of operators who often assist in emergencies.

   o **Cons**: Operating a HAM radio requires a license, which involves passing an exam. The equipment can be complex to set up and use, requiring practice and knowledge. In a crisis, unlicensed use can lead to fines, although there are exceptions during life-threatening emergencies.

2. **GMRS (General Mobile Radio Service) and FRS (Family Radio Service) Radios**:

   o **Overview**: GMRS and FRS radios are commonly used for short to medium-range communication. GMRS requires a license, while FRS does not.

   o **Pros**: These radios are easy to use and widely available. They are ideal for local communication, such as within a neighborhood or small group. GMRS radios typically have a longer range than FRS, especially when used with repeaters.

   o **Cons**: The range of GMRS and FRS radios is limited, especially in urban areas or rugged terrain. FRS radios are limited to lower power, reducing their effectiveness in larger areas. GMRS radios require a license, although the process is simpler than HAM licensing.

3. **Satellite Phones**:

   o **Overview**: Satellite phones connect directly to satellites, allowing for communication in remote areas where other communication infrastructures are unavailable.

   o **Pros**: Satellite phones offer global coverage, making them ideal for remote or isolated locations. They are highly reliable during natural disasters that may destroy terrestrial communication networks.

   o **Cons**: Satellite phones are expensive, both in terms of the device and the cost of airtime. They require a clear line of sight to the sky, which can be problematic in dense urban areas or heavily forested regions. Delays in communication can also occur, depending on satellite positioning.

4. **Mobile Phones**:

   o **Overview**: Mobile phones are the most common communication devices, relying on cellular networks to transmit voice and data.

   o **Pros**: Mobile phones are convenient and familiar, with widespread coverage in most areas. They also offer access to the internet, enabling users to receive real-time information and use apps for emergency alerts and communication.

   o **Cons**: Mobile networks can become overloaded or fail entirely during a disaster, rendering mobile phones useless. Battery life can be limited during extended outages, and reliance on cellular infrastructure makes them vulnerable in widespread crises.

The Pros and Cons of Each Communication Method Based on Range, Reliability, and Accessibility

- **Range**:

  o **HAM Radios**: Excellent for long-distance communication, especially with repeaters.

  o **GMRS/FRS Radios**: Suitable for short to medium-range, ideal for local communication.

  o **Satellite Phones**: Unlimited range, as long as there is a clear line of sight to the sky.

  o **Mobile Phones**: Range is limited to cellular coverage areas; performance can degrade in rural or isolated locations.

- **Reliability**:

  o **HAM Radios**: Highly reliable, especially in scenarios where traditional infrastructure fails.

- o **GMRS/FRS Radios**: Reliable for local communication, but range limitations can be a drawback.

- o **Satellite Phones**: Very reliable in remote areas but can be affected by weather or physical obstructions.

- o **Mobile Phones**: Reliable under normal conditions but prone to failure during disasters or network congestion.

- **Accessibility**:

  - o **HAM Radios**: Requires a license and practice, potentially limiting accessibility for those not familiar with the technology.

  - o **GMRS/FRS Radios**: Widely accessible, with minimal licensing requirements and easy operation.

  - o **Satellite Phones**: Less accessible due to high costs and the need for specialized equipment.

  - o **Mobile Phones**: Highly accessible, with widespread ownership and ease of use, but reliant on infrastructure that may not be resilient in a crisis.

Understanding your communication needs in a crisis and selecting the right devices are critical components of effective emergency preparedness. By carefully evaluating the range, reliability, and accessibility of each communication method, you can ensure that you have the right tools in place to stay connected and informed, no matter the situation.

Setting Up and Maintaining Communication Equipment

In any crisis situation, your ability to communicate effectively depends not only on having the right equipment but also on ensuring that it is properly set up, configured, and maintained. This section will guide you through the essential steps for installing and configuring communication devices, as well as the importance of regular maintenance and testing protocols to ensure they function reliably when needed most.

Installing and Configuring Radios and Other Devices for Optimal Use

1. **Radios (HAM, GMRS, FRS)**:

   - o **Installation**: Begin by selecting an appropriate location for your radio equipment. HAM radios, in particular, may require a more permanent installation with an external antenna for optimal range. Position the antenna as high as possible, ideally on the roof or a dedicated mast, and away from potential sources of interference such as electrical wiring or large metal objects.

   - o **Configuration**: After installation, configuring your radio is crucial. For HAM radios, you'll need to program the frequencies you intend to use, which might include local repeaters, emergency channels, and pre-arranged communication frequencies with your network. GMRS and FRS radios are typically simpler, often requiring only the selection of a channel and privacy code. Ensure that you understand how to switch frequencies quickly and how to adjust the power output to extend or limit your range as needed.

   - o **Testing**: Once installed and configured, perform a range test with another operator to ensure clear communication over the distances you expect to cover. Practice switching channels and using any additional features like encryption or squelch settings.

2. **Satellite Phones**:

   - o **Installation**: Satellite phones require a clear line of sight to the sky, so position yourself in an open area when using the device. Ensure that your satellite phone is fully charged, and if possible, connect it to a reliable power source or keep spare batteries on hand.

- o **Configuration**: Familiarize yourself with the phone's interface, including how to access your contacts, dial emergency numbers, and send text messages. Many satellite phones offer GPS tracking and SOS features—ensure these are properly configured and that you know how to activate them in an emergency.

- o **Testing**: Test your satellite phone periodically by making a call or sending a message to ensure that it connects properly. Practice using any special features, such as the SOS button or location sharing, to ensure you can operate them under stress.

3. **Mobile Phones with Emergency Apps**:

- o **Installation**: Ensure your mobile phone is equipped with essential emergency apps, such as weather alerts, emergency contact lists, and first responder communication tools. Keep your phone charged, and consider investing in a portable power bank or solar charger.

- o **Configuration**: Set up notifications for emergency alerts and ensure they are not silenced during critical periods. Save all essential contacts in your phone with easy access labels like "ICE" (In Case of Emergency).

- o **Testing**: Regularly update and test your apps to ensure they function correctly. Test emergency contact numbers to verify they are current and correct.

Regular Maintenance and Testing Protocols to Ensure Functionality During Emergencies

1. **Battery Maintenance**:

- o **Regular Charging**: Keep all communication devices fully charged. Establish a routine where you check the battery levels of your radios, satellite phones, and mobile phones, and recharge them as necessary. For radios with removable batteries, store extras in a cool, dry place and rotate them periodically to ensure they remain fresh.

- o **Battery Replacement**: Replace rechargeable batteries as they approach the end of their lifespan. For non-rechargeable batteries, keep a stock of spares and check their expiration dates regularly.

2. **Equipment Testing**:

- o **Monthly Drills**: Schedule regular drills to test all communication devices under conditions similar to those you might face in an emergency. This includes testing in different weather conditions, locations, and times of day to account for varying signal strength and reliability.

- o **Signal Clarity**: During each test, assess the clarity of communication. Make adjustments to antenna placement, power settings, or channels as needed to improve performance.

- o **Device Updates**: Regularly check for and install firmware updates for your devices. Updates can improve functionality, security, and compatibility with other equipment.

3. **Physical Maintenance**:

- o **Cleaning and Inspection**: Keep your devices clean and free of dust or debris, which can interfere with operation. Inspect antennas, cables, and connectors for wear and tear, replacing any damaged components immediately.

- o **Storage Conditions**: Store your equipment in a dry, secure place where it won't be exposed to extreme temperatures or moisture, both of which can damage sensitive electronics.

Backup Communication Strategies

Even the best-planned communication system can fail under the strain of a crisis, whether due to equipment malfunction, power outages, or network overload. Having backup communication strategies is essential for maintaining contact with loved ones, neighbors, and emergency services when your primary systems go down.

Planning for Communication Failures: Redundancy, Alternative Methods, and Low-Tech Options

1. **Redundancy**:

   o **Multiple Devices**: Ensure that you have more than one type of communication device. For example, if your primary communication is through a mobile phone, have a radio or satellite phone as a backup. This reduces your dependence on a single network or power source.

   o **Duplicate Equipment**: For critical devices like radios or satellite phones, consider having a second unit in case the primary one fails. This could be as simple as a spare radio or a basic, more rugged satellite phone for extreme conditions.

   o **Separate Power Sources**: Use different power sources for your devices. For instance, if your primary device relies on mains electricity, ensure your backup device runs on batteries or a solar charger. This prevents a single point of failure if the power grid goes down.

2. **Alternative Communication Methods**:

   o **Written Communication**: In the event that all electronic communication fails, written notes can be an effective fallback, especially for leaving messages at designated locations. Pre-print forms for emergency information, such as names, locations, and needs, to speed up communication.

   o **Signal Codes**: Establish simple, universally understood signal codes with your family or community. For example, placing a certain color flag or object outside your home could indicate whether everyone is safe or if assistance is needed.

   o **Physical Delivery**: In extreme cases, you may need to rely on physical delivery of messages, whether by foot, bicycle, or vehicle. Establish a plan for safe routes and couriers within your network who can deliver critical information when other methods fail.

The Importance of Signal Codes, Pre-Arranged Meeting Points, and Written Communication Plans

1. **Signal Codes**:

   o **Visual Signals**: Establish a system of visual signals that can be easily deployed and recognized, such as colored flags, lights, or specific objects placed in windows. These can convey basic messages like "All is well," "Need help," or "Emergency—evacuate." Ensure that everyone in your network understands what these signals mean and when to use them.

   o **Auditory Signals**: If visual signals aren't feasible, consider using sound-based signals like whistles, horns, or bells. Set patterns that correspond to different messages, and practice them regularly to ensure they are recognized and understood.

2. **Pre-Arranged Meeting Points**:

   o **Primary and Secondary Locations**: Designate primary and secondary meeting points for your family or community in case of communication failure. These should be safe, accessible locations known to all members. The primary location might be your home or a central community area, while the secondary could be a nearby landmark or another safe place if the primary is compromised.

   o **Practice Drills**: Regularly practice getting to these meeting points, especially under conditions that might simulate a real emergency, such as nighttime or inclement weather. Ensure that everyone knows the route and understands the importance of arriving at the meeting point promptly.

3. **Written Communication Plans**:

    o **Detailed Instructions**: Develop a written communication plan that outlines what to do if electronic communication fails. Include instructions on how to use alternative communication methods, where to meet, and how to signal for help. This plan should be shared with and understood by all members of your family or network.

    o **Physical Copies**: Keep physical copies of your communication plan in multiple locations, such as in your emergency kit, vehicles, and at work or school. This ensures that the information is accessible even if digital copies are unavailable.

    o **Updates and Revisions**: Regularly review and update your written communication plan as circumstances change, such as new family members, changes in work or school locations, or new technology.

Setting up and maintaining communication equipment is crucial for staying connected during a crisis, but it's equally important to have backup strategies in place for when those systems fail. By planning for redundancy, utilizing alternative methods, and preparing low-tech options like signal codes and written communication plans, you can ensure that you and your network remain informed and coordinated, no matter what challenges arise. This comprehensive approach to communication preparedness helps mitigate the risks of isolation and ensures that help and information can be shared quickly and effectively in any situation.

Establishing a Neighborhood Network

Building Relationships with Neighbors

In a crisis, the strength of your community ties can significantly impact your safety and well-being. Building relationships with your neighbors is not just about creating a friendly atmosphere—it's about fostering a network of mutual support that can be crucial during emergencies. Whether you're facing a natural disaster, civil unrest, or a prolonged power outage, knowing that you can rely on those around you can provide a sense of security and collective resilience.

The Importance of Community Ties in a Crisis

In times of crisis, communities that are well-connected and supportive tend to fare better than those where individuals are isolated. This is because crises often demand resources and skills that no single household can provide on its own. Strong community ties enable the pooling of these resources, the sharing of critical information, and the coordination of efforts to protect everyone's well-being.

1. **Resource Sharing**: During emergencies, certain supplies may become scarce. A connected community can share resources like food, water, medical supplies, and tools, ensuring that everyone has access to the essentials. For example, if one household has a generator, another has a well-stocked first aid kit, and another has extensive food storage, these resources can be shared to benefit the entire community.

2. **Skill Sharing**: Every person in a community has unique skills that can be invaluable in a crisis. Some may have medical training, while others might be skilled in home repairs, cooking, or childcare. When these skills are shared, the community becomes stronger and more self-sufficient. For instance, a neighbor with medical knowledge can help treat injuries, while someone else with experience in logistics can organize supplies and coordinate efforts.

3. **Emotional Support**: Crises are not just physically demanding—they also take an emotional toll. Having a network of neighbors who can provide emotional support, whether through a kind word, a shared meal, or simply the assurance that you are not alone, can make a significant difference in how well individuals cope with stress and fear.

4. **Safety in Numbers**: In scenarios where security is a concern, such as during civil unrest or widespread crime, communities that band together are better able to protect themselves. Neighbors can take turns watching over the area, set up checkpoints, or even create barricades if necessary. A united front can deter potential threats and provide a stronger defense than any single household could manage alone.

Strategies for Fostering Trust and Collaboration Among Neighbors

Building trust and collaboration among neighbors doesn't happen overnight, but with intentional efforts, it can be cultivated over time.

1. **Regular Communication**: Start by establishing regular communication with your neighbors. This could be as simple as greeting each other when you pass by or stopping for a chat. Over time, these small interactions build familiarity and trust. Consider creating a neighborhood contact list that includes phone numbers, email addresses, and any relevant skills or resources that could be useful in a crisis.

2. **Social Events**: Organize social events such as block parties, barbecues, or potluck dinners. These events provide a relaxed environment where neighbors can get to know each other better. The stronger the social bonds, the more likely people will be to help each other in a crisis.

3. **Shared Projects**: Working together on a shared project, such as a community garden, a neighborhood watch, or even a simple maintenance task like painting a fence, can strengthen ties. These projects create opportunities for collaboration and build a sense of collective ownership and responsibility.

4. **Transparency and Honesty**: Be open and honest with your neighbors about your expectations and concerns. If you're forming a group for emergency preparedness, clearly communicate your goals and encourage input from everyone. Transparency builds trust, and when people feel heard and valued, they're more likely to participate actively.

5. **Conflict Resolution**: Inevitably, disagreements will arise. When they do, address them promptly and respectfully. Encouraging open dialogue and working towards fair solutions helps maintain trust and ensures that small issues don't escalate into larger conflicts that could undermine the community's cohesion.

Creating a Neighborhood Watch or Support Group

A neighborhood watch or support group is a formal way to organize your community for mutual aid and protection during emergencies. By establishing clear roles, responsibilities, and communication channels, you can create a structured network that enhances everyone's safety and preparedness.

Steps to Form a Local Watch Group: Roles, Responsibilities, and Regular Meetings

1. **Assess Interest and Recruit Members**: Start by gauging interest among your neighbors. You can do this by hosting an initial meeting to discuss the idea of forming a neighborhood watch or support group. Explain the benefits, such as increased security, better resource management, and enhanced community bonds. Encourage participation by highlighting how each person can contribute, regardless of their skills or resources.

2. **Define Roles and Responsibilities**: Once you have a core group of interested members, define the roles and responsibilities within the group. Common roles might include:

    o **Coordinator**: The person responsible for organizing meetings, maintaining communication, and overseeing the group's activities.

    o **Communications Lead**: The individual who handles communication within the group and with external entities like emergency services.

    o **Resource Manager**: Someone tasked with tracking shared resources, such as emergency supplies, tools, and equipment.

- Security Lead: The person who coordinates safety efforts, including patrolling, setting up security protocols, and liaising with local law enforcement.

- Medical Lead: If someone in the group has medical training, they can take charge of first aid and health-related preparations.

3. **Establish Communication Protocols**: Effective communication is critical for the success of your group. Set up a communication system that works for everyone, such as a group chat on a secure messaging app, a phone tree, or even a dedicated radio frequency. Regularly update contact information and ensure that all members know how to reach each other quickly in an emergency.

4. **Schedule Regular Meetings and Drills**: Regular meetings keep the group engaged and prepared. Use these meetings to review emergency plans, share updates, and practice drills. Drills should simulate various crisis scenarios, such as a natural disaster, home invasion, or medical emergency, to ensure that everyone knows their role and can act quickly under pressure.

5. **Document the Plan**: Create a written plan that outlines the group's structure, roles, responsibilities, and protocols. This document should be accessible to all members and regularly updated to reflect any changes in the group or the broader community context.

Organizing Resources and Skills Within the Neighborhood for Mutual Aid During Emergencies

1. **Inventory Resources**: Conduct an inventory of the resources available within your neighborhood. This might include emergency supplies like food, water, and medical kits, as well as tools, generators, and vehicles. Identify any gaps in resources and work together to fill them, whether by pooling funds to purchase shared equipment or by encouraging individual households to prepare.

2. **Map Skills**: Just as important as physical resources are the skills present in your community. Create a map of skills, noting who has medical training, who can operate heavy machinery, who is skilled in logistics, and so on. This information will be invaluable in assigning roles during an emergency and ensuring that tasks are matched with the right expertise.

3. **Create a Resource-Sharing Agreement**: To facilitate the sharing of resources and skills during a crisis, consider creating a resource-sharing agreement. This document can outline how resources will be distributed, how decisions will be made, and how the group will handle potential conflicts. While formal agreements might not be necessary in all communities, they can help prevent misunderstandings and ensure fair distribution in times of need.

4. **Plan for Vulnerable Members**: Identify neighbors who may be particularly vulnerable during a crisis, such as the elderly, disabled, or those with young children. Ensure that your group has a plan to assist these individuals, whether by checking on them regularly, helping with evacuation, or providing additional resources.

5. **Develop Emergency Response Plans**: Work together to develop detailed emergency response plans that cover various scenarios. These plans should include evacuation routes, communication strategies, and roles for each member during specific types of emergencies. Regularly review and update these plans to ensure they remain relevant and effective.

Building relationships with neighbors and organizing them into a cohesive group is a powerful strategy for enhancing community resilience during a crisis. By fostering trust, clearly defining roles, and pooling resources and skills, you can create a support network that is capable of handling a wide range of challenges. This collaborative approach not only increases the safety and security of your neighborhood but also strengthens the social bonds that will help you all weather difficult times together.

Communication Protocols for Neighborhood Networks

Effective communication is the backbone of any successful neighborhood emergency plan. Developing a shared communication protocol with your neighbors ensures that everyone is on the same page, especially during a crisis when clear, timely communication is critical. Establishing communication hierarchies and decision-making processes further strengthens your neighborhood's ability to respond quickly and effectively to emergencies.

Developing a Shared Communication Plan with Your Neighborhood

1. **Assessing Communication Needs**:

   o The first step in developing a communication plan is to assess the specific needs of your neighborhood. Consider the size of your community, the distance between households, and the types of emergencies you are likely to face. For example, a rural neighborhood might prioritize long-range radio communication, while an urban community might rely more on mobile phones and messaging apps.

2. **Choosing Communication Methods**:

   o Based on the assessment, choose the most reliable and accessible communication methods for your neighborhood. These might include:

      ▪ **Group Messaging Apps**: Platforms like WhatsApp, Signal, or GroupMe can be used for quick, real-time communication. Ensure everyone in the neighborhood has access to the chosen app and is familiar with its basic functions.

      ▪ **Two-Way Radios**: For neighborhoods where cellular service might be unreliable, two-way radios (GMRS or FRS) can be an effective alternative. Assign specific channels for general communication, emergencies, and specific groups (e.g., security, medical).

      ▪ **Phone Trees**: A phone tree can be established for urgent communications. In this system, one person calls a few others, who then call a few more, ensuring that everyone is informed quickly. This method works well for spreading information rapidly when technology might fail.

3. **Establishing Communication Protocols**:

   o Develop clear protocols for when and how to use the chosen communication methods. For example:

      ▪ **Daily Check-Ins**: Establish a routine where neighbors check in with each other at a specific time each day. This ensures that everyone is accounted for and that any emerging issues are identified early.

      ▪ **Emergency Alerts**: Define what constitutes an emergency and how it should be communicated. For instance, a specific word or phrase could be used to indicate an immediate threat, prompting everyone to tune into the designated communication channel.

      ▪ **Information Sharing**: Create guidelines on how to share information during a crisis. Encourage concise, clear communication, avoiding rumors or unverified reports that could cause unnecessary panic.

4. **Accessibility and Inclusivity**:

   o Ensure that your communication plan is accessible to all members of the neighborhood, including those with disabilities, the elderly, and non-English speakers. This might involve using large print for written communication, providing translations, or setting up a buddy system where someone is responsible for checking in on and relaying information to more vulnerable neighbors.

Establishing Communication Hierarchies and Decision-Making Processes During a Crisis

1. **Defining Roles and Responsibilities**:

   o In any crisis, it's essential to have a clear understanding of who is responsible for what. Establish a hierarchy that outlines roles such as:

      ▪ **Communication Coordinator**: The person responsible for overseeing the neighborhood's communication efforts, ensuring that everyone is informed, and relaying information from external sources (e.g., emergency services).

      ▪ **Team Leaders**: Depending on the size of your neighborhood, divide the area into smaller groups, each with a leader who communicates directly with the Coordinator and manages communication within their group.

      ▪ **Specialized Roles**: Assign individuals with specific skills (e.g., medical, security, logistics) to lead efforts in those areas, ensuring that their expertise guides decision-making.

2. **Decision-Making Processes**:

   o During a crisis, decisions need to be made quickly and efficiently. Establishing a decision-making process ahead of time prevents confusion and ensures that everyone knows how to proceed. Consider the following:

      ▪ **Consensus vs. Hierarchical Decision-Making**: Decide whether decisions will be made by group consensus or by designated leaders. In smaller, tightly-knit communities, consensus might work well, while larger neighborhoods might benefit from a more hierarchical approach.

      ▪ **Emergency Decisions**: Define who has the authority to make decisions in an emergency, such as when to evacuate, secure the area, or request external assistance. Ensure that everyone understands and respects this authority to avoid conflicting actions during critical moments.

      ▪ **Information Flow**: Clearly outline how information should flow within the network. For example, critical information should go from the Communication Coordinator to team leaders and then to individual households. This helps maintain order and ensures that decisions are based on accurate, up-to-date information.

Practicing and Drilling with the Neighborhood

Creating a communication plan and establishing roles are crucial steps, but they are only effective if the neighborhood is well-practiced in implementing them. Regular drills and practice sessions are essential for ensuring that everyone knows their role, understands the communication protocols, and can act quickly and effectively when a real crisis occurs.

Conducting Regular Drills to Ensure Preparedness and Coordination

1. **Planning the Drill**:

   o Start by planning a variety of scenarios that your neighborhood might realistically face, such as natural disasters, power outages, or security threats. Each drill should be tailored to test different aspects of your communication and response plans.

   o **Scenario-Based Drills**: For example, a drill could simulate a severe storm that knocks out power and communication. Participants would practice using radios or other backup communication methods, coordinating resource sharing, and checking in on vulnerable neighbors.

- o **Role-Specific Drills**: In some drills, focus on specific roles, such as the medical response team or security leads, to ensure they are fully prepared to carry out their responsibilities under stress.

2. **Executing the Drill**:

   - o On the day of the drill, treat it as though it were a real emergency. Activate your communication plan, initiate the phone tree, or broadcast an emergency message on the designated channel.

   - o Ensure that every participant takes the drill seriously, as the goal is to uncover weaknesses and areas for improvement. Encourage full participation, and make note of any confusion, delays, or communication breakdowns that occur during the drill.

3. **Debriefing After the Drill**:

   - o After the drill, hold a debriefing session with all participants. Discuss what went well and where improvements are needed. Encourage open feedback, as this is an opportunity to refine the plan and ensure everyone feels confident in their role.

   - o Review any issues with communication, such as delays in relaying information or misunderstandings, and work together to find solutions. This might involve tweaking the communication protocols, adjusting the hierarchy, or providing additional training.

Reviewing and Updating the Neighborhood Emergency Plan Based on Drill Outcomes

1. **Updating the Plan**:

   - o Use the feedback from the drill to update your neighborhood's emergency plan. This might include revising roles, adjusting communication methods, or even changing the physical setup of your neighborhood network.

   - o Incorporate new information or resources that may have become available since the last plan was drafted. For example, if a new family with medical expertise has moved into the neighborhood, they might take on a leadership role in medical response.

2. **Revisiting the Communication Hierarchy**:

   - o Based on the drill's outcomes, revisit your communication hierarchy to ensure it is functioning as intended. If certain roles were overwhelmed or certain channels were ineffective, make the necessary adjustments.

   - o Consider adding redundancy to key roles, ensuring that if one person is unavailable or overwhelmed, someone else can step in seamlessly.

3. **Continuous Improvement**:

   - o Emergency preparedness is an ongoing process. Schedule regular reviews of the emergency plan, ideally after each drill or any real-life incident that affects the neighborhood. This continuous improvement approach helps keep the plan relevant and effective, adapting to changes in the community or new threats.

   - o Encourage ongoing training and education for all members of the neighborhood. This might include first aid training, communication skills workshops, or even team-building exercises to strengthen the community bond.

Establishing communication protocols and practicing drills within your neighborhood are critical steps in ensuring a coordinated and effective response during a crisis. By developing a shared communication plan, defining roles and decision-making processes, and regularly practicing these strategies, your community will be better prepared to face any emergency with confidence and resilience. This proactive approach not only enhances safety but also fosters a sense of unity and preparedness that can make all the difference when it matters most.

Staying Informed and Connected During a Crisis

In any crisis, staying informed and maintaining strong communication channels are critical to ensuring safety and maintaining morale. This chapter covers the essentials of monitoring reliable news sources, verifying information, using social media effectively, and supporting personal and group morale through consistent communication.

Monitoring News and Alerts

Staying informed during a crisis requires accessing reliable sources of information. Depend on local news outlets, government alerts, and verified social media accounts to stay updated on developments. Local news channels often provide timely information specific to your area, such as weather conditions, road closures, and emergency services updates. Government alerts, accessible through official apps or SMS services, deliver critical instructions, such as evacuation orders or safety measures.

To ensure you receive these updates promptly, set up emergency alerts on your devices. Most smartphones allow you to enable government alerts under the settings menu, typically labeled as "Emergency Alerts" or "Public Safety Alerts." Apps such as FEMA, Red Cross, or local weather services can provide real-time notifications tailored to your location. Make sure these alerts are not silenced, and consider setting up alternative methods, such as a weather radio, for times when digital devices may fail.

Information Verification and Avoiding Misinformation

In the urgency of a crisis, misinformation can spread quickly, causing unnecessary panic and potentially dangerous situations. Verifying the accuracy of information is crucial before you take action or share it with others. Start by cross-referencing the information with multiple trusted sources. For instance, if you hear about an evacuation order, confirm it by checking the official website of your local government or emergency services.

Recognize the signs of misinformation, which often includes sensational language, lack of sourcing, or content that cannot be confirmed by other reputable outlets. Social media can be a breeding ground for rumors, so be cautious about the information shared on these platforms. Stick to official channels, and when in doubt, refrain from sharing unverified information. Encourage others in your network to do the same, promoting a culture of careful and responsible communication.

Using Social Media for Crisis Communication

Social media plays a significant role in real-time information sharing during crises. Platforms like Twitter, Facebook, and Instagram can be invaluable for staying connected with your community, receiving updates from official sources, and even coordinating with others in your area. Using social media responsibly is crucial to avoid the pitfalls of misinformation and panic.

When using social media during a crisis, prioritize following accounts that provide verified information, such as government agencies, local news stations, and first responders. Use hashtags carefully to track updates related to your specific situation, but be aware that not all information under a hashtag may be accurate.

Best practices for social media during emergencies include:

- **Sharing Information**: Only share information from verified sources. If you come across unverified information that seems important, seek confirmation before passing it along.

- **Community Support**: Use social media to check on neighbors, offer assistance, and organize group efforts. Platforms like Nextdoor can be particularly useful for neighborhood-specific communication.

- **Maintaining Privacy**: Be mindful of what you post, as sharing your location or plans publicly can sometimes attract unwanted attention or create security risks.

Maintaining Personal and Group Morale Through Communication

Staying connected with others during a crisis is not just about exchanging information—it's also about maintaining morale. The psychological benefits of regular communication during stressful times cannot be overstated. Knowing that others are going through the same challenges and having someone to talk to can significantly reduce feelings of isolation and anxiety.

To maintain morale, establish regular check-ins with family members, friends, and neighbors. Even a simple "Are you okay?" text can make a big difference. For groups, consider setting up regular times to meet or talk, whether in person or virtually, to share experiences, offer support, and discuss any new developments.

Emotional support is another key aspect of maintaining morale. Encourage open communication where people feel comfortable expressing their fears and concerns. Offer reassurance, and remind each other of the steps being taken to stay safe. Maintaining a positive outlook, while also being realistic about the situation, can help everyone stay focused and resilient.

In conclusion, staying informed and connected during a crisis involves more than just receiving alerts; it requires a proactive approach to communication. By relying on reliable information sources, verifying what you hear, using social media responsibly, and fostering strong, supportive connections within your community, you can navigate crises more effectively and with greater confidence.

Video BONUS

Chapter 9: Essential Survival Gear and Tools

Navy SEAL Recommended Gear for Home Defense

Firearms and Ammunition

When it comes to home defense, having the right firearms and ammunition can be a crucial part of your overall security plan. It's essential to approach this subject with a deep sense of responsibility, ensuring that any firearms you own are stored safely and maintained properly to be effective in an emergency.

Types of Firearms Recommended for Home Defense

1. **Shotguns**: Shotguns are widely regarded as one of the best options for home defense due to their versatility and stopping power. A 12-gauge pump-action shotgun is particularly popular because of its reliability and the broad pattern of shot it delivers, which increases the likelihood of hitting a target in high-stress situations. The sound of racking a shotgun alone can be a deterrent to intruders.

2. **Handguns**: A handgun, such as a 9mm or .45 caliber pistol, is another effective option for home defense, especially in close quarters. Handguns are compact, easy to maneuver, and can be quickly accessed in an emergency. They allow for one-handed operation, leaving the other hand free to operate a phone, flashlight, or other tools.

3. **Rifles**: While rifles, particularly AR-15 style semi-automatic rifles, are effective for home defense, they are generally more suited to larger properties or rural settings due to their range and potential for over-penetration. For urban or suburban home defense, where engagement distances are shorter, a shotgun or handgun might be preferable.

Safe Storage and Maintenance of Firearms and Ammunition

Owning a firearm for home defense carries with it the immense responsibility of ensuring it is stored securely and kept in optimal working condition. Proper storage not only prevents unauthorized access, especially by children or intruders, but it also ensures that your firearm is ready to function if and when it is needed.

1. **Safe Storage**:

    o **Gun Safes**: The most secure way to store firearms is in a gun safe. Choose a safe that is fireproof and bolted to the floor or wall to prevent theft. Modern safes often come with biometric locks, which allow quick access while preventing unauthorized entry.

    o **Quick-Access Safes**: For firearms intended for immediate home defense, consider a quick-access safe. These safes can be kept in a bedroom or other accessible location and are designed to open quickly using a code, fingerprint, or RFID tag, while still preventing unauthorized access.

    o **Trigger Locks**: If a safe is not available, trigger locks can be used as an additional layer of security. These should only be used when the firearm is not needed for immediate defense, as they slow down the time it takes to ready the weapon.

2. **Ammunition Storage**:

    o **Separate Storage**: Ammunition should be stored separately from firearms in a cool, dry place. This minimizes the risk of accidents and ensures that your ammunition remains in good condition.

- **Ammunition Safes**: Similar to gun safes, there are safes specifically designed for ammunition. These safes protect your ammo from theft, fire, and moisture, ensuring it remains effective over time.

- **Inventory Management**: Keep an inventory of your ammunition, noting the quantities and types you have on hand. Rotate your stock to use older ammo first, ensuring that all rounds are fresh and reliable when needed.

3. **Maintenance**:

- **Regular Cleaning**: Firearms should be cleaned regularly to ensure they function properly. After each use, clean the barrel, chamber, and moving parts to remove any residue or fouling that could impair operation. Even if not used, firearms should be inspected and cleaned every few months to prevent rust and ensure readiness.

- **Function Checks**: Periodically perform function checks to ensure that your firearms operate correctly. This includes checking the safety, trigger, and magazine release, as well as ensuring that the firearm cycles rounds properly.

- **Ammunition Inspection**: Inspect your ammunition regularly for signs of corrosion, dents, or other damage that could affect performance. Discard any compromised rounds safely.

Non-Lethal Defense Options

While firearms are a significant component of home defense, non-lethal options also play a crucial role, especially in situations where the use of lethal force is not warranted or desired. Non-lethal tools such as pepper spray and tasers offer effective ways to deter or disable an intruder without the risk of fatal injury.

Pepper Spray, Tasers, and Other Non-Lethal Self-Defense Tools

1. **Pepper Spray**: Pepper spray is one of the most accessible and effective non-lethal defense tools available. It incapacitates an attacker by causing intense irritation to the eyes, skin, and respiratory system, giving you time to escape or call for help. Pepper spray comes in various forms, including canisters, keychain attachments, and even gels, which are less likely to blow back in windy conditions.

- **Usage**: To use pepper spray effectively, aim for the attacker's face, focusing on the eyes. Maintain a safe distance, typically 6-10 feet, and use short bursts. Be aware of the wind direction to avoid self-contamination.

2. **Tasers and Stun Guns**: Tasers and stun guns are electronic self-defense devices that deliver a high-voltage shock to temporarily incapacitate an attacker. Tasers can be used from a distance, as they shoot out probes attached to wires that deliver the shock. Stun guns, on the other hand, require direct contact with the attacker.

- **Usage**: For tasers, aim for the torso, as this area provides the largest target and is most likely to achieve effective results. Stun guns should be applied to areas with thinner clothing, such as the neck, underarm, or stomach, to maximize the shock's impact.

3. **Other Non-Lethal Options**:

- **Batons**: Expandable or fixed batons offer a physical means of self-defense by delivering blunt force to subdue an attacker. They require some training to use effectively but can be highly effective in close quarters.

- **Personal Alarms**: While not a defensive tool in the traditional sense, personal alarms emit a loud sound when activated, which can disorient an attacker and draw attention from others, potentially deterring further aggression.

When and How to Use Non-Lethal Options Effectively

1. **Situational Awareness**: The key to using non-lethal defense tools effectively is situational awareness. Always be aware of your surroundings and any potential threats. Non-lethal tools are most effective when you have the opportunity to recognize a threat early and deploy your defense before the attacker closes in.

   o **De-Escalation**: Non-lethal tools should ideally be used in situations where de-escalation is possible. If you have the chance to defuse a situation verbally or by showing that you are armed with a non-lethal tool, you may prevent the need to use it entirely.

2. **Distance and Positioning**: Non-lethal tools often require specific distances to be effective. For example, pepper spray is most effective when used at a distance of 6-10 feet, while stun guns require direct contact. Always maintain a safe distance when possible, and position yourself to have a clear escape route after using the tool.

3. **Training and Familiarity**: Just like with firearms, it's essential to be familiar with your non-lethal defense tools. Practice deploying them quickly and accurately, so that in a real emergency, you can use them effectively under stress. Consider taking a self-defense course that includes training with non-lethal tools.

4. **Legal Considerations**: Be aware of the legal implications of using non-lethal tools in your area. Some regions have restrictions on carrying or using certain devices, such as tasers or batons. Understanding the laws in your jurisdiction will help you make informed decisions and avoid legal complications.

Both lethal and non-lethal defense tools play important roles in a comprehensive home defense strategy. By carefully selecting and maintaining your firearms and ammunition, and by incorporating non-lethal options into your defense plan, you can protect yourself and your loved ones effectively while being prepared for a wide range of potential threats.

Home Security Systems

Incorporating a robust home security system is a critical aspect of fortifying your home against potential intruders and threats. While physical defenses like doors and locks are essential, modern technology offers advanced tools that can greatly enhance your home's security. Alarm systems, motion detectors, and surveillance cameras are not just deterrents; they provide real-time monitoring and alerts that can prevent incidents before they escalate.

Recommended Alarm Systems, Motion Detectors, and Surveillance Cameras

1. **Alarm Systems**:

   o **Types of Alarms**: The market offers a wide variety of alarm systems, ranging from basic setups that trigger a loud sound when a door or window is breached, to sophisticated systems that notify law enforcement or private security companies automatically. A recommended option is a smart home security system, which integrates with your smartphone, allowing you to control and monitor the system remotely. These systems often include sensors for doors, windows, and even glass break detectors.

   o **Installation and Coverage**: When selecting an alarm system, ensure it covers all potential entry points, including front and back doors, windows, and any access points to basements or garages. The system should be professionally installed, or if self-installed, thoroughly tested to ensure that all components are functioning correctly.

2. **Motion Detectors**:

   o **Types of Motion Detectors**: Motion detectors are a vital part of any security system. They can be set up to trigger lights, alarms, or cameras when motion is detected in or around your home. Passive infrared (PIR) sensors are the most common, detecting the heat emitted by people or animals. Dual-technology detectors, which combine PIR and microwave sensors, offer enhanced accuracy and fewer false alarms.

- o **Placement**: Strategic placement of motion detectors is key. They should be installed in areas where an intruder would likely pass, such as hallways, staircases, and entry points. Outdoor detectors can be positioned near windows, doors, and in areas where an intruder might approach undetected, such as side yards or dark corners.

3. **Surveillance Cameras**:

- o **Types of Cameras**: Surveillance cameras have become increasingly advanced and accessible. Options include wired and wireless cameras, with features like night vision, high-definition video, and two-way communication. Smart cameras that integrate with home security systems can provide live feeds to your smartphone, record footage, and send alerts when motion is detected.

- o **Placement**: Like motion detectors, the placement of surveillance cameras is crucial. Exterior cameras should cover all entry points, driveways, and perimeters, while interior cameras can be placed in key areas such as living rooms, hallways, and near safes or valuable items. Ensure that cameras are placed out of reach and hidden from obvious view to prevent tampering.

Integrating Technology with Physical Defense Measures

1. **Layered Security Approach**: The most effective home defense strategies combine technology with physical security measures. For example, a reinforced door with a deadbolt is a strong physical defense, but when combined with an alarm system that triggers if the door is breached, it becomes significantly more secure. Similarly, motion detectors paired with exterior lighting can deter intruders before they even reach your home.

2. **Smart Home Integration**: Modern security systems often integrate seamlessly with smart home technologies. This allows for greater control and automation, such as setting lights to turn on and off at specific times to simulate occupancy, or locking doors remotely. These systems can be integrated with voice assistants like Alexa or Google Assistant for hands-free control.

3. **Emergency Response Coordination**: Another benefit of integrating technology with physical defenses is the ability to coordinate a quick response in an emergency. Many advanced systems can automatically contact emergency services or a private security company if a breach is detected, ensuring that help is on the way even if you are unable to call for it yourself.

Tactical Gear

For those who are serious about home defense, particularly in high-risk scenarios, incorporating tactical gear such as body armor and helmets can provide an added layer of protection. While these items are often associated with military or law enforcement, they are increasingly considered by civilians preparing for worst-case scenarios.

Body Armor, Helmets, and Protective Gear Used by Navy SEALs

1. **Body Armor**:

- o **Types of Body Armor**: Body armor is available in various levels of protection, rated by the National Institute of Justice (NIJ). For home defense, NIJ Level IIIA body armor, which protects against most handgun rounds, is often recommended. For higher threats, such as rifle rounds, Level III or IV plates, made from materials like ceramic or polyethylene, provide enhanced protection but are heavier and more expensive.

- o **Vests and Carriers**: The body armor is typically worn in a vest or plate carrier, which distributes the weight across the torso. Tactical vests can also be equipped with pouches for additional gear, such as extra magazines, medical kits, or communication devices.

2. **Helmets**:

- o **Types of Helmets**: Tactical helmets, like those used by Navy SEALs, provide protection against shrapnel, debris, and some ballistic threats. These helmets are often made from advanced materials like Kevlar or high-density polyethylene, offering a balance of protection and weight.

- o **Additional Features**: Modern tactical helmets can be outfitted with accessories such as night vision mounts, communication headsets, and face shields. These features can enhance situational awareness and protection in a defensive scenario.

3. **Other Protective Gear**:

- o **Gloves and Eye Protection**: Tactical gloves protect your hands from cuts, impacts, and burns, while maintaining dexterity for handling weapons or other tools. Ballistic-rated eyewear protects against flying debris and can also reduce glare or enhance vision in low-light conditions.

- o **Knee and Elbow Pads**: In a defensive situation where you might need to move quickly or take cover, knee and elbow pads provide protection and comfort. These are particularly useful if you need to crouch or crawl.

How and When to Use Tactical Gear in a Home Defense Scenario

1. **Assessing the Threat**: Tactical gear should be used when the threat level justifies it. In a typical home invasion scenario, having quick access to body armor and a helmet could be lifesaving, especially if the intruders are armed. Assess the situation carefully—if the threat is high, such as during civil unrest or a severe breakdown in law and order, deploying tactical gear may be necessary.

2. **Training and Familiarity**: As with firearms and non-lethal tools, familiarity and training with tactical gear are crucial. Wearing body armor and a helmet can be cumbersome if you're not used to it, so practice moving, aiming, and responding while wearing the gear. Regular drills in your home can help you become comfortable with the equipment and ensure you can deploy it quickly in an emergency.

3. **Accessibility and Storage**: Tactical gear should be stored in an easily accessible location. If you anticipate needing it, consider keeping your vest, helmet, and other gear near your primary defensive position, such as a safe room or wherever you store your firearms. Quick access is essential—if your gear is locked away or out of reach, it won't be useful when you need it most.

4. **Psychological Preparedness**: Wearing tactical gear can significantly boost your confidence in a high-stress situation, but it also requires mental preparation. Understand that using such gear signals a high level of seriousness and commitment to defending your home. Be mentally prepared for the possibility of confrontation and the consequences that come with it.

A comprehensive home defense strategy incorporates both advanced technology and tactical gear. By integrating alarm systems, motion detectors, and surveillance cameras with physical defenses, and by preparing with tactical gear when necessary, you can create a layered defense system that significantly enhances your ability to protect your home and loved ones in any situation.

Must-Have Tools for Any Crisis Scenario

Cutting Tools

Cutting tools are some of the most versatile and essential pieces of equipment in any survival kit. Whether you're preparing firewood, constructing a shelter, or defending yourself, having the right cutting tool can make all the difference. Selecting the appropriate knife, multi-tool, or axe for various situations and ensuring they are well-maintained is crucial for their effectiveness and longevity.

Knives, Multi-Tools, and Axes: Choosing the Right Cutting Tool for Various Situations

1. **Knives**:

    o **Fixed-Blade Knives**: Fixed-blade knives are a staple in survival situations due to their strength and reliability. They are typically stronger than folding knives, making them ideal for tasks like cutting wood, preparing food, or even self-defense. Look for a knife with a full tang (the metal extends through the handle) for added durability.

    o **Folding Knives**: While not as robust as fixed-blade knives, folding knives are more compact and easier to carry. They are suitable for everyday tasks and can be a valuable backup in survival scenarios. Choose a folding knife with a reliable locking mechanism to ensure safety during use.

    o **Specialty Knives**: Some knives are designed for specific purposes, such as gutting game, filleting fish, or even skinning. If your survival plan includes hunting or fishing, having a specialized knife can greatly enhance your efficiency and success in these tasks.

2. **Multi-Tools**:

    o **Versatility**: Multi-tools combine several functions in one compact device, making them invaluable in a survival situation. Common tools include pliers, wire cutters, screwdrivers, saw blades, and small knives. While they may not be as strong as dedicated tools, their versatility can be a lifesaver when you need to perform a variety of tasks with minimal gear.

    o **Choosing a Multi-Tool**: When selecting a multi-tool, consider the specific tasks you're most likely to encounter. Some multi-tools are geared towards mechanics, with multiple screwdrivers and wrench options, while others are more survival-oriented, featuring saws, blades, and can openers. Ensure the tool is made from durable materials, like stainless steel, and has a reliable locking mechanism for safety.

3. **Axes**:

    o **Hatchets and Small Axes**: Axes and hatchets are indispensable for tasks like chopping wood, clearing brush, and even splitting kindling. A good hatchet or small axe is portable yet powerful, allowing you to handle larger jobs that a knife or multi-tool can't manage. Look for an axe with a sturdy handle, ideally made from hickory or a high-quality composite material, and a sharp, durable blade.

    o **Large Axes**: For those preparing for extended survival situations in the wilderness, a larger axe might be necessary. These are heavier and more challenging to carry but are essential for cutting down trees and splitting large logs. The trade-off in weight and size is often worth it if your survival plan involves setting up long-term shelter or maintaining a steady supply of firewood.

Maintenance and Sharpening Techniques for Longevity and Effectiveness

1. **Cleaning**:

    o **After Use**: After using your cutting tools, clean them promptly to remove any dirt, sap, or other residues. This prevents corrosion and maintains the tool's effectiveness. Use a damp cloth to wipe down the blade, followed by a dry cloth to remove any moisture.

    o **Preventing Rust**: For metal parts, especially blades, apply a light coating of oil (like gun oil or mineral oil) to prevent rust. Ensure that your tools are stored in a dry, cool environment to minimize the risk of corrosion.

2. **Sharpening**:

   o **Knives**: Regular sharpening is essential to keep your knives effective. A dull knife requires more force to use and increases the risk of accidents. Use a sharpening stone or a ceramic rod to hone the blade. Start by holding the blade at the correct angle (typically around 20 degrees) and draw it across the stone, alternating sides to ensure an even edge.

   o **Axes**: Sharpening an axe requires a slightly different approach. Use a file or a dedicated axe sharpener, starting with broad strokes to remove any nicks or damage on the blade. Once the edge is even, switch to a finer grit to hone the edge. Always sharpen away from yourself and use gloves to protect your hands.

   o **Multi-Tools**: Multi-tools often have smaller blades that can be sharpened using a small sharpening stone or a dedicated sharpener designed for serrated edges. For tools like saws or pliers, ensure they are clean and free from burrs or dull spots.

3. **Storage**:

   o **Protective Sheaths**: Always store your knives and axes in protective sheaths to prevent accidental cuts and to protect the blades from damage. For multi-tools, keep them folded and stored in a pouch.

   o **Regular Inspection**: Periodically inspect your cutting tools for signs of wear or damage. Look for cracks in handles, loose components, or chipped blades. Address any issues promptly to ensure your tools remain reliable in an emergency.

Fire-Starting Tools

Fire is one of the most critical elements of survival, providing warmth, a means to cook food, and a way to signal for help. Having reliable fire-starting tools and knowing how to use them in any condition is essential for any survival scenario.

Fire Starters, Lighters, and Matches: Ensuring You Can Start a Fire in Any Condition

1. **Fire Starters**:

   o **Ferro Rods**: Ferrocerium rods (commonly known as ferro rods) are a popular choice for survivalists. When scraped with a metal striker, they produce sparks that can ignite tinder. Ferro rods are highly reliable, even in wet conditions, and can be used thousands of times. They're a must-have for any survival kit.

   o **Magnesium Fire Starters**: Some fire-starting kits include a block of magnesium along with a ferro rod. Shaving off small pieces of magnesium creates a highly flammable material that can be ignited easily, even in damp conditions. Magnesium is a great backup fire starter when your tinder is less than ideal.

2. **Lighters**:

   o **Butane Lighters**: A high-quality butane lighter, such as a windproof model, is an excellent primary fire-starting tool. These lighters are convenient and easy to use, making them ideal for most situations. They can run out of fuel, so it's important to have backups.

   o **Stormproof Lighters**: For more extreme conditions, stormproof lighters are designed to withstand high winds and rain. They are often refillable and come with features like adjustable flames, making them versatile in various environments.

3. **Matches**:

- ○ **Waterproof Matches**: Waterproof matches are a reliable backup for starting a fire, especially if you're caught in wet conditions. These matches are coated to resist moisture and can strike on any rough surface. They should be kept in a waterproof container to ensure they remain usable.

- ○ **Stormproof Matches**: Stormproof matches are even more robust, capable of staying lit even in heavy wind or rain. These matches burn longer and hotter than regular matches, making them ideal for challenging conditions.

Waterproofing and Storing Fire-Starting Tools for Reliability

1. **Waterproofing**:

   - ○ **Storage**: To ensure your fire-starting tools are ready when needed, store them in waterproof containers or pouches. Small, sealable plastic bags work well for matches and lighters, while hard waterproof cases can protect ferro rods and magnesium blocks.

   - ○ **Additional Protection**: Consider applying a thin coat of petroleum jelly to match heads as an extra waterproofing measure. This not only protects the matches but also acts as an accelerant when igniting tinder.

2. **Backup Systems**:

   - ○ **Redundancy**: Always carry multiple fire-starting tools in different parts of your gear, such as a lighter in your pocket, matches in your pack, and a ferro rod on your keychain. This redundancy ensures you're not left without options if one method fails.

   - ○ **Tinder Kits**: In addition to your fire-starting tools, include a small tinder kit in your survival gear. This can include cotton balls soaked in petroleum jelly, char cloth, or commercially available tinder. Store these in a waterproof container for reliability.

3. **Regular Maintenance**:

   - ○ **Inspect Lighters**: Check your lighters regularly to ensure they are full of fuel and functioning correctly. For refillable lighters, carry extra fuel and flints. If you use disposable lighters, replace them periodically to avoid running out of fuel unexpectedly.

   - ○ **Rotate Matches**: While matches have a long shelf life, it's a good idea to rotate them periodically, using older matches for camping or practice and replacing them with fresh ones. This ensures that your matches are always in the best condition.

Having the right cutting tools and fire-starting equipment is fundamental for survival in any situation. By carefully selecting and maintaining knives, multi-tools, and axes, and by ensuring your fire-starting tools are reliable and well-protected, you equip yourself with the means to survive, thrive, and stay safe in the most challenging environments.

Water Filtration and Purification Tools

Access to clean water is vital for survival, especially in emergency situations where your usual supply may be compromised. Having the right tools to filter and purify water ensures that you and your family stay hydrated and safe from waterborne illnesses.

Portable Water Filters, Purification Tablets, and Boiling Kits

1. **Portable Water Filters**:

   - ○ **Types of Filters**: Portable water filters, such as those from brands like LifeStraw or Sawyer, are designed to remove bacteria, protozoa, and some viruses from water sources. These filters are lightweight, easy to use, and can be lifesaving in situations where water quality is uncertain.

- **Usage**: Filters work by passing water through a membrane or other filtration medium that traps contaminants. They are ideal for use in the wilderness or during emergencies where water needs to be consumed immediately without the time to boil or chemically treat it.

2. **Purification Tablets**:

- **Types of Tablets**: Water purification tablets, typically made from iodine or chlorine dioxide, are another essential tool for ensuring safe drinking water. These tablets are compact and easy to carry, making them perfect for bug-out bags or travel.

- **Usage**: Simply drop the tablet into a container of water, wait the recommended amount of time (usually 30 minutes to 4 hours), and the water will be safe to drink. Purification tablets are particularly useful when filtering alone may not be enough to remove all pathogens, such as viruses.

3. **Boiling Kits**:

- **Boiling Water**: Boiling is one of the oldest and most effective methods of water purification, killing bacteria, viruses, and parasites. Boiling kits typically include a lightweight pot or kettle and a portable stove or fire-starting tools.

- **Usage**: Bring the water to a rolling boil for at least one minute (three minutes at higher altitudes) to ensure it is safe to drink. While boiling requires time and fuel, it is a reliable method when you are unsure about the chemical or biological contaminants in the water.

How to Choose the Right Water Purification Method for Different Scenarios

1. **Scenario-Based Selection**:

- **Short-Term Emergencies**: For short-term situations, such as a temporary disruption in water service, purification tablets are often the most convenient and effective solution. They are quick, easy to use, and require minimal equipment.

- **Wilderness Survival**: In the wilderness, where you may have access to streams, lakes, or rivers, a portable water filter is invaluable. It allows you to drink directly from natural sources without the need for fuel or waiting time.

- **Long-Term Preparedness**: For long-term survival situations, such as extended power outages or natural disasters, having a combination of tools is best. A filter for daily use, tablets for backup, and a boiling kit for when you have the time and resources to set up a fire ensure that you are prepared for any water-related challenges.

2. **Considerations**:

- **Water Source**: Consider the quality of the water source. Clear, fast-flowing water may require less filtration and purification than stagnant or murky water. In questionable environments, combining a filter with chemical purification or boiling provides the most comprehensive protection.

- **Portability**: When mobility is a priority, such as in a bug-out scenario, prioritize lightweight and compact tools like portable filters and purification tablets. Boiling kits, while effective, are better suited for situations where you can set up a stable camp.

Shelter and Sleeping Gear

Staying warm, dry, and protected from the elements is crucial in any survival situation. Whether you're caught in a storm, need to set up camp in the wilderness, or are forced to sleep outdoors, having the right shelter and sleeping gear can make all the difference in maintaining your health and morale.

Tents, Tarps, and Sleeping Bags: What You Need to Stay Warm and Protected

1. **Tents**:

   - **Types of Tents**: Tents come in various shapes and sizes, from lightweight one-person bivy sacks to larger family tents. When choosing a tent, consider the environment you'll be using it in—whether you need something weatherproof, lightweight for easy transport, or spacious enough for multiple people.

   - **Usage**: Set up your tent in a location that is sheltered from the wind, away from potential hazards like falling branches or rising water. Ensure that the tent is properly staked down and that the rainfly is securely fastened to protect against moisture.

2. **Tarps**:

   - **Versatility of Tarps**: Tarps are incredibly versatile and can be used as a standalone shelter, a ground cover, or an additional layer of protection over a tent. They are lightweight, packable, and can be set up in various configurations depending on the environment.

   - **Usage**: Use paracord or bungee cords to secure the tarp between trees or poles, creating a lean-to, A-frame, or other shelter shapes. Tarps can also be used to collect rainwater, create windbreaks, or protect gear from the elements.

3. **Sleeping Bags**:

   - **Types of Sleeping Bags**: Sleeping bags are rated for different temperature ranges, from lightweight summer bags to heavy-duty winter models. Down sleeping bags offer excellent warmth-to-weight ratios but require careful maintenance to avoid moisture damage. Synthetic bags are more durable in wet conditions but may be bulkier.

   - **Usage**: Choose a sleeping bag that suits the expected weather conditions. In cold environments, consider using a sleeping pad underneath your bag to insulate against the ground. For added warmth, sleep in layers and use a bivy sack or liner to enhance the bag's temperature rating.

Compact and Lightweight Options for Quick Deployment

1. **Ultralight Tents and Bivy Sacks**: For situations where you need to move quickly and carry minimal gear, ultralight tents or bivy sacks are ideal. These options are designed to be as lightweight as possible while still providing essential protection. Bivy sacks, in particular, are excellent for solo adventurers or as emergency shelters in unexpected conditions.

2. **Compact Tarps**: Compact tarps made from materials like silnylon or Dyneema offer durable protection at a fraction of the weight of traditional tarps. They can be folded down to the size of a water bottle, making them easy to store in your pack. Despite their small size, they can be lifesaving in a pinch, providing shelter from rain, wind, or sun.

3. **Sleeping Mats and Inflatable Pads**: Lightweight sleeping mats and inflatable pads offer comfort and insulation without adding significant weight to your pack. They are particularly important for preventing heat loss to the ground, which can occur even in milder weather. Choose a pad with an appropriate R-value (a measure of insulation) for the conditions you expect.

Communication Tools

In a crisis, effective communication is essential for staying informed, coordinating with others, and ensuring your safety. Having the right communication tools can keep you connected, whether you're in the wilderness, dealing with a power outage, or facing a natural disaster.

Essential Radios, Signal Mirrors, and Whistles

1. **Radios**:

   o **Types of Radios**: Two-way radios (such as GMRS or FRS) are essential for short-range communication, allowing you to stay in touch with family or group members when cell service is unavailable. HAM radios offer longer-range communication and can connect you with emergency services or other radio operators.

   o **Usage**: Keep your radio tuned to an agreed-upon frequency or channel, and ensure that all members of your group are familiar with basic radio operation. For HAM radios, obtaining a license is required, so plan ahead and practice using the equipment before an emergency occurs.

2. **Signal Mirrors**:

   o **Using Signal Mirrors**: Signal mirrors are an effective way to attract attention from a distance, especially in daylight. They can be used to signal aircraft, boats, or people far away. By reflecting sunlight, you can create a bright flash visible over long distances.

   o **Usage**: Hold the mirror in one hand, and use the other to aim the reflected light at your intended target. Many signal mirrors come with a sighting hole to help you aim accurately. Practice using the mirror before you need it, so you can quickly deploy it in an emergency.

3. **Whistles**:

   o **Whistles for Emergencies**: A whistle is a simple but effective tool for signaling your location, especially in low-visibility conditions like fog, dense forest, or at night. A loud whistle can carry farther than your voice, making it easier for rescuers or others to locate you.

   o **Usage**: Attach a whistle to your gear or clothing where it can be easily accessed. In an emergency, use a series of short, sharp blasts (the universal distress signal is three blasts) to attract attention.

Keeping Communication Devices Charged and Ready for Use

1. **Portable Chargers**:

   o **Types of Chargers**: Portable chargers, or power banks, are essential for keeping your communication devices operational when power sources are unavailable. Choose chargers with sufficient capacity to recharge your devices multiple times. Solar-powered chargers are also a good option for extended outings where you may not have access to electrical outlets.

   o **Usage**: Keep your power bank fully charged before heading out and regularly top off your devices. If using a solar charger, position it in direct sunlight and connect your devices during daylight hours.

2. **Battery Management**:

   o **Extra Batteries**: For devices that use replaceable batteries, such as radios or flashlights, carry extra batteries in waterproof containers. Store them separately from the devices to avoid accidental discharge.

   o **Battery Life Conservation**: Conserve battery life by turning off devices when not in use, dimming screens, and using power-saving modes. Regularly check battery levels and recharge or replace batteries as needed.

3. **Emergency Chargers**:

   o **Hand-Crank Chargers**: Hand-crank chargers are a reliable backup option that doesn't rely on stored power or sunlight. By manually generating power, you can charge small devices like radios or phones, ensuring that you can stay connected even in prolonged emergencies.

- Usage: While hand-crank chargers require physical effort, they are invaluable when other charging options are unavailable. Familiarize yourself with the process so you can use it effectively in an emergency.

Selecting the right water filtration and purification tools, shelter and sleeping gear, and communication tools is crucial for survival in a wide range of scenarios. By carefully choosing and maintaining these essential items, you can ensure that you are prepared to stay safe, hydrated, warm, and connected, no matter what challenges arise.

How to Properly Stockpile and Store Survival Gear

Organizing Your Gear

Properly organizing your survival gear is essential to ensure that you can access what you need quickly and efficiently during an emergency. An organized system not only saves time but also reduces the stress of searching for essential items when every second counts.

Categorizing and Labeling Gear for Easy Access During Emergencies

1. **Categorization**:

   - **Functional Grouping**: Start by grouping your gear based on function. For example, place all fire-starting tools in one category, water purification tools in another, and medical supplies in their own section. This method allows you to quickly identify and access specific types of equipment when needed.

   - **Scenario-Based Kits**: Another effective method is to create kits based on different emergency scenarios. For instance, have a dedicated bug-out bag for quick evacuations, a home defense kit for security situations, and a medical kit for health emergencies. Each kit should be self-contained and ready to grab at a moment's notice.

2. **Labeling**:

   - **Clear Labeling**: Label each container, bag, or box with its contents and the category it belongs to. Use large, easy-to-read labels or color-coded tags to help differentiate between categories quickly. For example, red tags could indicate medical supplies, while blue might denote water-related gear.

   - **Multi-Language Labels**: If you live in a household where multiple languages are spoken, consider labeling items in all relevant languages to ensure that everyone can understand and use the gear effectively.

3. **Strategic Placement**:

   - **Accessibility**: Store frequently used items, such as flashlights and basic first aid supplies, in easily accessible locations. Less frequently used items, like long-term food storage or extra ammunition, can be stored in less accessible areas but should still be organized logically.

   - **Redundancy**: Place duplicate items in different locations around your home. For instance, have a flashlight in each major room, so you're never far from a light source during a power outage.

Creating an Inventory System to Track What You Have and What Needs to Be Replenished

1. **Inventory List**:

- **Comprehensive Listing**: Create a detailed inventory of all your survival gear. Include item names, quantities, and locations. This can be done in a notebook or digitally using a spreadsheet or dedicated inventory management app. Make sure to include expiration dates for perishable items like food, batteries, and medical supplies.

- **Regular Updates**: Update your inventory regularly, especially after using items or adding new gear. Keeping an accurate inventory ensures you always know what you have on hand and prevents running out of critical supplies.

2. **Replenishment Schedule**:

- **Tracking Usage**: As you use items, mark them off your inventory and note when replacements are needed. Set reminders to restock essential supplies periodically, particularly those with expiration dates. For instance, check your medical supplies every few months and rotate food storage annually.

- **Automatic Alerts**: If using a digital system, set up automatic alerts to notify you when items are running low or approaching their expiration dates. This proactive approach helps maintain your preparedness without needing to remember every detail manually.

3. **Preparedness Drills**:

- **Regular Drills**: Conduct regular preparedness drills where you simulate an emergency and practice accessing your gear. This not only familiarizes you with where everything is stored but also highlights any gaps or inefficiencies in your organization system.

- **Family Involvement**: Involve all family members in these drills so everyone knows how to find and use the gear. Ensure that children, in particular, are aware of the basics like where to find a flashlight or how to access the first aid kit.

Storage Solutions

Proper storage of your survival gear is crucial to ensure it remains in good working condition and is ready to use when needed. This involves protecting your gear from environmental hazards such as moisture, pests, and temperature fluctuations, as well as regularly inspecting and rotating your equipment.

Best Practices for Storing Gear to Prevent Damage from Moisture, Pests, and Other Hazards

1. **Moisture Control**:

- **Waterproof Containers**: Store gear in waterproof containers or dry bags to protect against moisture damage, especially in damp environments or if there's a risk of flooding. Plastic bins with tight-fitting lids are a good option for indoor storage, while dry bags are ideal for gear that might be exposed to the elements.

- **Desiccants**: Place desiccant packets, such as silica gel, in storage containers to absorb any residual moisture. This is particularly important for items like electronics, metal tools, and ammunition, which are susceptible to rust and corrosion.

2. **Pest Prevention**:

- **Sealed Containers**: Keep food, medical supplies, and clothing in airtight containers to prevent pests from accessing them. Rodents, insects, and other pests can quickly destroy your supplies if not properly protected.

- **Regular Inspections**: Periodically check your storage areas for signs of pests. Look for droppings, chewed packaging, or unusual odors. If you detect any issues, address them immediately by cleaning the area, removing contaminated items, and using pest deterrents like traps or natural repellents.

3. **Temperature and Light Control**:

   o **Climate Control**: Store gear in a climate-controlled environment whenever possible. Extreme temperatures can degrade materials like rubber, plastic, and even some metals over time. Basements, attics, or garages should be avoided if they are prone to temperature fluctuations or high humidity.

   o **UV Protection**: Keep gear out of direct sunlight to prevent UV damage, which can weaken materials like fabrics and plastics. Use opaque containers or cover items with protective sheets if storage in a bright area is unavoidable.

Rotating and Inspecting Gear Regularly to Ensure It Remains in Working Condition

1. **Routine Inspections**:

   o **Monthly Checks**: Set a regular schedule, such as monthly or quarterly, to inspect your gear. Look for any signs of wear, damage, or degradation. Items like flashlights, batteries, and water filters should be tested to ensure they're still functioning properly.

   o **Detailed Reviews**: Perform a more thorough inspection annually, where you examine each piece of gear in detail. This is also a good time to update your inventory list and ensure that everything is accounted for.

2. **Rotating Supplies**:

   o **First-In, First-Out (FIFO)**: Use the FIFO method to rotate consumable items like food, water, and medical supplies. Place newer items behind older ones so that the oldest stock is used first. This method helps ensure that supplies are always fresh and reduces waste.

   o **Seasonal Adjustments**: Rotate gear seasonally to account for changes in weather. For example, ensure that winter clothing and sleeping bags are accessible in the fall, and lighter gear is more readily available in the spring. This practice keeps you prepared for seasonal emergencies and ensures that gear is appropriate for the current climate.

3. **Maintenance and Repairs**:

   o **Proactive Maintenance**: Regularly maintain gear to prevent it from deteriorating. For instance, sharpen knives, oil metal parts, replace flashlight batteries, and clean any fabrics according to manufacturer instructions. Proactive maintenance extends the life of your gear and ensures it's ready to use.

   o **Repair vs. Replace**: During inspections, identify any items that need repairs. Minor issues, like a frayed strap or a loose screw, can often be fixed easily. If gear is beyond repair, replace it promptly to maintain the integrity of your preparedness plan.

Organizing and storing your survival gear effectively is essential for ensuring it remains accessible, functional, and ready to use in any emergency. By categorizing and labeling your gear, maintaining an up-to-date inventory, and following best practices for storage and maintenance, you can significantly enhance your preparedness and peace of mind.

Long-Term Storage Considerations

Storing survival gear for extended periods requires careful planning and the use of specific techniques to ensure that your equipment remains in good condition. Proper long-term storage not only preserves the functionality of your gear but also ensures that it will be ready to use when you need it most.

Protecting Gear That May Not Be Used for Extended Periods

When preparing gear for long-term storage, it's important to consider the environmental factors that could potentially degrade your equipment over time. Factors such as humidity, temperature fluctuations, and exposure to light can all contribute to wear and tear, even if the gear is not being used.

1. **Climate Control**:

   o **Temperature**: Store your gear in a cool, dry place with minimal temperature fluctuations. Extremes in heat or cold can weaken materials like rubber, plastic, and fabrics, leading to cracks, brittleness, or other forms of degradation.

   o **Humidity**: High humidity can cause mold, mildew, and rust, particularly in metal components or fabrics. If possible, store gear in a climate-controlled environment where humidity levels are kept low. Basements and attics, while convenient, may not offer the best conditions for long-term storage unless they are properly sealed and ventilated.

2. **Protection from Light**:

   o **UV Damage**: Continuous exposure to sunlight or UV light can cause colors to fade and materials to weaken. Store gear in opaque containers or cover it with protective sheeting to shield it from light. This is especially important for items like sleeping bags, tents, and clothing.

3. **Regular Inspections**:

   o **Periodic Checks**: Even gear in long-term storage should be inspected periodically, at least once a year. Look for signs of wear, pest infestation, or environmental damage. Regular checks allow you to address issues before they render your gear unusable.

Vacuum Sealing, Desiccants, and Other Methods to Extend the Life of Your Gear

1. **Vacuum Sealing**:

   o **Preserving Gear**: Vacuum sealing is an excellent way to protect gear from moisture, air exposure, and pests. By removing air from the packaging, you reduce the risk of oxidation, which can lead to rust, corrosion, and deterioration of materials. Vacuum sealing is particularly useful for items like clothing, blankets, and small tools.

   o **Space Efficiency**: Besides protecting your gear, vacuum sealing also reduces the amount of space it takes up, making it easier to store more items in a smaller area. This is especially beneficial for those with limited storage space.

2. **Desiccants**:

   o **Moisture Control**: Desiccants, such as silica gel packets, are essential for controlling moisture within storage containers. Place these packets inside sealed containers or bags to absorb any residual moisture, preventing mold, mildew, and rust. Desiccants are particularly useful for metal tools, electronics, and other moisture-sensitive items.

   o **Rechargeable Desiccants**: Some desiccants are reusable and can be recharged by heating them in an oven, which makes them a cost-effective and sustainable option for long-term storage.

3. **Sealed Containers**:

   o **Airtight Storage**: Use airtight, durable containers to store gear, especially items that are prone to moisture damage. Plastic bins with gasketed lids, metal ammo cans, or specialized storage boxes designed for long-term use are ideal. Ensure that the containers are stored off the ground, preferably on shelves, to protect against flooding or other potential water damage.

o **Pest Protection**: Ensure that your storage containers are pest-proof. Mice, insects, and other pests can chew through materials and contaminate your gear. Using sealed containers and adding pest repellents or traps in your storage area can help prevent infestations.

Emergency Kits

Assembling and maintaining emergency kits tailored to different scenarios is a crucial part of preparedness. These kits should be designed to address specific needs, whether for evacuating quickly (go-bags) or sheltering in place (home survival kits). Keeping these kits updated with fresh supplies and rotating perishable items ensures they remain effective and reliable.

Assembling Go-Bags and Home Survival Kits Tailored to Different Scenarios

1. **Go-Bags**:

   o **Purpose**: A go-bag is designed for quick evacuation in an emergency, such as a natural disaster, fire, or civil unrest. It should be lightweight, compact, and include only the essentials you need to survive for 72 hours.

   o **Contents**: Your go-bag should include items like water, non-perishable food, a first aid kit, a flashlight, a multi-tool, personal documents, and basic hygiene products. Consider the specific needs of each family member, including medications, extra clothing, and comfort items for children.

   o **Customization**: Tailor your go-bag to the most likely emergencies in your area. For instance, if you live in a flood-prone region, waterproof gear and additional water purification tablets might be necessary. If you're in an earthquake zone, include sturdy shoes and gloves for navigating debris.

2. **Home Survival Kits**:

   o **Purpose**: Home survival kits are designed to sustain you during a longer-term emergency when sheltering in place is necessary. These kits should be more comprehensive than go-bags, providing enough supplies to last several days or even weeks.

   o **Contents**: A home survival kit should include water storage and purification supplies, a larger food supply, a more extensive first aid kit, tools for home repairs, and equipment for maintaining warmth and light. Also, include items like blankets, a portable stove, and sanitation supplies.

   o **Customization**: Just like with go-bags, customize your home survival kit based on the specific needs of your household. This might include extra supplies for pets, baby care items, or additional security measures.

Keeping Kits Updated with Fresh Supplies and Rotating Perishable Items

1. **Regular Updates**:

   o **Check Expiry Dates**: Every few months, review the contents of your go-bags and home survival kits. Check the expiration dates on food, water, medications, and batteries. Replace any items that are nearing their expiration or have already expired.

   o **Seasonal Adjustments**: Adjust the contents of your kits according to the season. In winter, add extra warm clothing, blankets, and hand warmers. In summer, include sunscreen, insect repellent, and lighter clothing. This ensures that your kits are always suited to the current conditions.

2. **Rotation System**:

- o **First-In, First-Out (FIFO)**: Use the FIFO method to rotate supplies in your emergency kits. When you buy new supplies, place them at the back of your storage area, moving older items to the front. This method ensures that the oldest supplies are used first, minimizing waste.

- o **Routine Replenishment**: Schedule regular times to replenish and rotate the supplies in your kits, such as every six months or annually. This habit helps maintain the readiness of your kits without the risk of finding expired or unusable items during an actual emergency.

3. **Family Involvement**:

- o **Education**: Involve your family in the process of updating and maintaining emergency kits. Teach them where the kits are stored, how to use the contents, and the importance of keeping the kits updated. This not only prepares them for emergencies but also ensures that everyone knows what to do if the need arises.

- o **Practice Drills**: Regularly practice emergency drills with your family, using the go-bags and home survival kits as part of the exercise. This helps identify any gaps in your preparations and ensures that everyone is familiar with the gear and how to use it.

Long-term storage considerations and well-maintained emergency kits are foundational to effective survival planning. By protecting your gear from environmental hazards, using methods like vacuum sealing and desiccants, and regularly updating and rotating your emergency supplies, you can ensure that you are prepared for any situation, with reliable gear and well-stocked kits ready to support you when it matters most.

Video BONUS

Chapter 10: Tactical Self-Defense and Home Defense Strategies

Basic Self-Defense Techniques for Home Protection

Awareness and Situational Preparedness

In the realm of home defense, situational awareness is perhaps one of the most crucial skills you can develop. It is the foundation upon which all other defensive measures are built. Situational awareness involves being constantly alert to your surroundings and recognizing potential threats before they materialize. This proactive mindset not only enhances your ability to protect yourself and your family but also significantly reduces the likelihood of being caught off guard in a dangerous situation.

Understanding the importance of situational awareness begins with recognizing that threats often present subtle signs before escalating into full-blown confrontations. These signs can include unusual noises, unfamiliar vehicles in your neighborhood, or individuals exhibiting suspicious behavior. The key is to train yourself to notice these anomalies and assess them quickly and accurately.

Developing situational awareness requires a combination of mental discipline and practical habits. One effective technique is to conduct regular "environmental scans" of your surroundings, whether you're at home, in your car, or out in public. This means periodically taking a moment to observe and evaluate the environment, noting anything that seems out of place or potentially threatening. At home, this might involve checking that all doors and windows are secure, ensuring that security systems are activated, and being mindful of any changes in the neighborhood, such as new construction or unfamiliar faces.

Another critical aspect of situational preparedness is understanding the layout of your home and identifying potential vulnerabilities. This includes knowing where all entry points are located, as well as having a clear plan for how to respond if one of those entry points is compromised. Familiarize yourself with your home's security systems, including alarm systems, surveillance cameras, and motion detectors. By knowing how these systems work and how to use them effectively, you can greatly enhance your ability to detect and deter intruders before they pose a direct threat.

It's important to train yourself and your family to respond calmly and effectively in high-stress situations. This involves conducting regular drills that simulate different emergency scenarios, such as a home invasion or fire. By practicing these scenarios, you and your family can develop the muscle memory and confidence needed to act quickly and decisively when it matters most.

Physical Defense Techniques

While situational awareness and preparedness are your first lines of defense, knowing how to physically defend yourself if a confrontation occurs is equally important. Basic hand-to-hand combat techniques are invaluable, especially in close-quarters situations where you may not have immediate access to a weapon. The goal of physical defense is not to engage in a prolonged fight but to create an opportunity to escape or neutralize the threat as quickly as possible.

One of the most fundamental principles of self-defense is targeting the most vulnerable areas of an attacker's body. These areas include the eyes, throat, groin, and knees—targets that, when struck, can incapacitate an attacker long enough for you to escape. Simple, effective techniques include palm strikes to the nose, elbows to the throat, and knee strikes to the groin. These moves require minimal strength but can deliver maximum impact, making them ideal for individuals of all sizes and fitness levels.

Along with learning specific strikes, it's important to practice maintaining balance and stability during a physical altercation. A solid stance is the foundation of any effective self-defense technique. Keep your feet shoulder-width apart, with your dominant foot slightly behind the other. This position not only enhances your ability to strike but also helps you absorb and deflect blows without losing your footing.

Another critical aspect of physical defense is learning how to use everyday objects as improvised weapons. In a home defense scenario, you may not always have a firearm or tactical weapon at hand, but almost anything can be used to defend yourself if you understand how to wield it effectively. For example, a kitchen knife, a heavy lamp, or even a sturdy chair can be used to strike an intruder. The key is to recognize the potential of these objects and be prepared to use them without hesitation.

Moreover, it's essential to practice these techniques regularly. Self-defense skills, like any other, deteriorate without consistent practice. Consider enrolling in a self-defense class that focuses on realistic scenarios and teaches techniques that are applicable in a home defense situation. This type of training not only sharpens your skills but also builds confidence, reducing the likelihood that you'll freeze or panic during a real-life encounter.

Lastly, remember that physical defense is always a last resort. Your primary objective should be to avoid physical confrontation whenever possible by using your situational awareness to prevent a threat from escalating. If you do find yourself in a situation where physical defense is necessary, these techniques can give you the upper hand and help you protect yourself and your loved ones effectively.

De-escalation and Conflict Resolution

In any potential confrontation, the best outcome is one where violence is avoided altogether. De-escalation and conflict resolution are critical skills that can prevent situations from becoming dangerous or violent. These techniques are particularly important in home defense, where the stakes are high, and the consequences of a physical altercation can be severe.

De-escalation involves using verbal and non-verbal communication to reduce the intensity of a conflict. The primary goal is to calm the other person and prevent the situation from escalating to violence. This requires a combination of calmness, clear communication, and an understanding of human psychology.

One of the most effective strategies for de-escalation is to maintain a non-threatening posture and tone. When someone feels threatened, their instinct is often to fight or flee. By presenting yourself as non-threatening, you can help defuse the situation. Stand at an angle rather than directly facing the person, keeping your hands visible and open to convey that you are not a threat. This open posture is a powerful tool in calming tensions.

Verbal communication plays a crucial role in de-escalation. The way you speak can either defuse or inflame a situation. It's essential to use a calm, steady voice and to avoid shouting or aggressive language, which can escalate the conflict. Phrases like "Let's talk about this" or "I understand you're upset, how can we resolve this?" can be effective in signaling that you are willing to listen and find a peaceful solution.

Active listening is another key component of de-escalation. Often, people become aggressive or confrontational because they feel unheard or misunderstood. By actively listening—nodding, making eye contact, and occasionally summarizing what the other person has said—you demonstrate that you are taking their concerns seriously. This can help to reduce their anger and make them more open to finding a resolution.

It's also important to acknowledge the other person's feelings without necessarily agreeing with them. Statements like "I can see that you're very frustrated" validate their emotions, which can help to lower their defenses. This must be done sincerely; otherwise, it can come across as condescending, which might escalate the situation further.

Another critical aspect of de-escalation is knowing when to withdraw or disengage. Not every conflict can be resolved through conversation, and there are times when it is safer to remove yourself from the situation. If you sense that the situation is becoming increasingly volatile and that the person is not responding to de-escalation efforts, it may be best to create a safe distance and call for help if necessary.

Along with verbal communication, body language plays a significant role in conflict resolution. Non-verbal cues such as eye contact, facial expressions, and gestures can either escalate or de-escalate a situation. For example, maintaining soft eye contact (as opposed to a hard, confrontational stare) and using slow, deliberate movements can convey calmness and control. Avoid sudden or aggressive gestures, as these can be perceived as threatening.

It's also essential to be aware of the other person's body language. Signs of escalating aggression include clenched fists, a stiff posture, or a raised voice. If you notice these cues, it's a signal that the situation may be deteriorating, and further de-escalation efforts are needed.

Practicing de-escalation techniques can make them more effective in real-life situations. Role-playing scenarios with family members or in a self-defense class can help you develop these skills so that they become second nature. This practice also builds confidence, which is crucial in maintaining control during a potentially volatile situation.

The role of conflict resolution goes beyond just de-escalation. It involves finding a peaceful solution to the problem at hand. This might involve compromise, where both parties agree to make concessions, or it might require more creative problem-solving to find a mutually acceptable solution.

In the context of home defense, conflict resolution might involve offering to call a third party to help mediate, such as law enforcement or a community leader, if the situation warrants it. It could also involve setting clear boundaries and communicating them effectively. For example, if someone is trespassing, calmly but firmly stating that they need to leave your property and that you will call the authorities if they do not comply can often be enough to resolve the situation.

Ultimately, the effectiveness of de-escalation and conflict resolution depends on your ability to remain calm, communicate clearly, and read the situation accurately. These skills not only protect you and your loved ones but also contribute to a more peaceful resolution of conflicts, avoiding unnecessary violence and ensuring that everyone involved can walk away safely.

Utilizing Tactical Tools and Weapons

Selecting the Right Tactical Weapons for Home Defense

Choosing the right tactical weapons for home defense is a critical decision that involves evaluating various factors, including your home environment, legal considerations, and personal comfort level with each type of weapon. The goal is to select tools that you can use effectively to protect yourself and your family in the event of an intrusion or other threat.

Overview of Firearms, Knives, and Non-Lethal Weapons

Firearms are often considered the most powerful and effective tools for home defense, but they come with significant responsibilities. A firearm, when used correctly, can stop an intruder quickly, but it requires a high level of proficiency and a deep understanding of the legal implications of its use. The most common types of firearms for home defense include handguns, shotguns, and rifles.

Handguns are popular for their compact size and ease of storage. They are ideal for close-quarters combat, which is often the scenario in home defense. Shotguns, particularly pump-action models, are highly effective due to their power and the spread of their shot, which can compensate for less precise aiming. Rifles, while powerful, may be less practical in a home setting due to their size and potential for over-penetration, which can pose a risk to others in the home or nearby.

Knives serve as a secondary line of defense when firearms are not accessible or as a backup weapon. Tactical knives are designed for combat and self-defense, featuring durable blades and ergonomic handles that allow for quick, powerful strikes. While knives require close contact with an intruder, they are reliable, do not run out of ammunition, and can be used silently.

Non-lethal weapons, such as pepper spray, tasers, and batons, offer alternatives for those who are uncomfortable with or unable to use lethal force. Pepper spray can incapacitate an attacker temporarily, allowing you time to escape or call for help. Tasers deliver an electric shock that can immobilize an intruder, though their effectiveness depends on the accuracy of the shot. Batons and other blunt instruments can be used to deliver disabling blows to an attacker without the intent to kill.

Criteria for Choosing the Most Effective Tools Based on Your Home Environment

When selecting weapons for home defense, it's essential to consider your specific living situation. For example, if you live in a densely populated area, the risk of a bullet passing through walls and endangering others might make a shotgun or a handgun with hollow-point ammunition a better choice than a high-powered rifle. Hollow-point bullets expand upon impact, reducing the likelihood of over-penetration.

The layout of your home also plays a significant role in your decision. Tight corners, narrow hallways, and multiple rooms may limit the effectiveness of longer firearms like rifles, making a handgun or a short-barrel shotgun more practical. Conversely, if you live in a rural area with larger property, a rifle might be more appropriate, especially for defending against threats at a greater distance.

Ease of access is another critical factor. Your weapon of choice should be stored in a manner that allows you to retrieve it quickly in an emergency but also safely, particularly if there are children in the home. Gun safes with quick-access features or biometric locks can strike a balance between security and accessibility.

Your comfort level and proficiency with the weapon should guide your selection. The most powerful weapon is useless if you're not confident in using it. Consider starting with a weapon that you feel comfortable handling, and then build your skills and expand your arsenal as your proficiency grows.

Training and Proficiency with Tactical Tools

Owning a weapon for home defense is only the first step; regular training and practice are essential to ensure that you can use it effectively under pressure. The stress and adrenaline of a home invasion or emergency can impair your ability to think clearly and act decisively, which is why consistent training is critical.

The Importance of Regular Training with Your Selected Weapons

Training should be an ongoing commitment, not a one-time event. Regular practice builds muscle memory, allowing you to react instinctively in a crisis. This is particularly important with firearms, where accurate aiming and quick decision-making can make the difference between neutralizing a threat and endangering yourself or others.

Firearms training should include not only shooting practice at a range but also drills that simulate home defense scenarios. These might involve moving through your home while maintaining situational awareness, practicing target acquisition in low-light conditions, and reloading under stress. Many ranges offer advanced courses that cover these skills, often taught by instructors with military or law enforcement backgrounds.

For those who choose to rely on knives or non-lethal weapons, the same principles apply. Regular practice with your knife can involve drills that improve your speed and accuracy in striking or blocking. Understanding how to use a knife defensively—such as targeting an assailant's limbs to disable rather than kill—can also be crucial.

Similarly, non-lethal weapons require practice to be effective. For example, using a taser involves more than just pulling the trigger; you need to be close enough for the electrodes to make contact, and you must understand how to aim accurately under pressure. Pepper spray users should practice quick-draw techniques and ensure they can aim effectively while keeping a safe distance from the attacker.

Tips for Improving Accuracy, Speed, and Decision-Making Under Pressure

Improving your skills with tactical weapons requires focused, deliberate practice. Accuracy can be enhanced through consistent range time, using drills that emphasize precision over speed. Start with slow, controlled shots or strikes, gradually increasing your speed as your accuracy improves. Dry-fire practice, which involves simulating shooting with an unloaded firearm, can help you develop your trigger control and aim without the noise and recoil of live ammunition.

Speed is equally important, particularly in high-stress situations where you may only have seconds to react. Speed drills, where you practice drawing your weapon, acquiring a target, and firing as quickly as possible, can help you shave precious seconds off your response time. For non-firearm users, practicing quick deployment of a knife or taser is essential. Speed drills should always balance with accuracy—there's little value in being fast if you miss your target.

Decision-making under pressure is perhaps the most challenging aspect of home defense. Your ability to quickly assess a situation, choose the right response, and execute it effectively is key to surviving an encounter with an intruder. Scenario-based training is one of the best ways to develop these skills. This might involve role-playing exercises where you must decide whether to use force or attempt to de-escalate, or navigating a course that presents you with multiple targets, some of which represent threats and others that do not.

Along with physical training, mental preparedness is crucial. Visualization techniques, where you mentally rehearse different scenarios and how you would respond, can enhance your decision-making capabilities. Combine this with stress inoculation training—practicing under simulated stress conditions—to build resilience and maintain clarity in real-world emergencies.

Selecting the right tactical weapons for home defense and ensuring regular training are foundational to your preparedness strategy. The effectiveness of any weapon ultimately depends on the skill and confidence of the user, which can only be developed through consistent, deliberate practice. By understanding your environment, choosing the right tools, and committing to ongoing training, you can significantly increase your ability to protect yourself and your loved ones in a crisis.

Legal Considerations for Using Weapons in Home Defense

When it comes to home defense, understanding the legal framework surrounding the use of weapons is as important as knowing how to handle the weapons themselves. The laws governing the use of force, particularly deadly force, vary widely across different jurisdictions in the United States. Being informed about these legalities ensures that you can protect yourself and your family without unintentionally violating the law, which could lead to severe legal consequences.

Understanding the Legal Implications of Using Deadly Force

The use of deadly force in self-defense is a highly regulated area. Deadly force generally refers to actions intended to cause, or likely to cause, death or serious bodily harm. In most states, the use of deadly force is justified only under specific circumstances, such as when you believe your life or the lives of others are in imminent danger.

A key concept in the use of deadly force is "reasonableness." This means that your belief in the need to use deadly force must be one that a reasonable person in the same situation would have. The threat must be immediate and unavoidable, with no reasonable alternative to using deadly force. For instance, if an intruder enters your home and you believe they intend to cause serious harm, the use of deadly force might be justified. However, if the intruder is fleeing or poses no immediate danger, using deadly force could be deemed excessive and unjustifiable.

Another important concept is the "duty to retreat," which exists in some states. This rule requires you to retreat from the situation, if possible, before using deadly force. However, many states have adopted "Stand Your Ground" laws, which remove the duty to retreat. These laws allow you to use deadly force if you are lawfully present and under threat, without needing to attempt escape first. Knowing whether your state follows the "Stand Your Ground" principle or requires retreat is crucial in home defense situations.

The "Castle Doctrine" is another key principle, specifically concerning home defense. This doctrine gives individuals the right to use reasonable force, including deadly force, to protect themselves against an intruder in their home. It is based on the idea that one's home is a sanctuary, and individuals should not be required to retreat when threatened inside it. While the Castle Doctrine is widely accepted, its specifics vary by state. Some states require that the intruder be unlawfully and forcibly entering the home, while others provide broader protections.

Additional factors that can influence the use of deadly force include whether the intruder was armed, the intruder's behavior, and whether the homeowner had an opportunity to de-escalate the situation. Outcomes in these cases often depend on the circumstances and how they are interpreted by authorities and the courts.

Along with understanding when deadly force can be used, it is vital to ensure full compliance with local regulations regarding weapon ownership and use. These rules vary not only from state to state but also from city to city, meaning what is allowed in one area may not be in another.

First, it's essential to ensure that you have the necessary permits and licenses for the weapons you intend to use for home defense. Many states require a permit to purchase, own, or carry firearms, with additional restrictions on concealed carry. Some states also have waiting periods, background checks, and restrictions on certain types of firearms or ammunition. Ignoring these regulations can result in severe penalties, including fines, imprisonment, or the loss of firearm ownership rights.

Beyond purchasing, there are also rules governing the storage and handling of firearms at home. Many states have "safe storage" laws, requiring firearms to be locked away or secured with a trigger lock, particularly in homes with children. Failure to comply with these storage rules can result in criminal charges, especially if an unsecured firearm is involved in a crime or accessed by a minor.

It's also important to be aware of any restrictions on non-lethal weapons, such as pepper spray or tasers. While these are typically less regulated than firearms, some states or municipalities have specific rules on the size, strength, or conditions under which non-lethal weapons can be carried. For example, certain types of tasers or stun guns might be banned in some areas, or there may be restrictions on how and where they can be used.

Another critical consideration is understanding the laws regarding the use of weapons against animals. Although home defense usually focuses on human intruders, there may be situations where you need to defend yourself or your property from aggressive animals. The rules governing force against animals often differ from those involving human threats, and improper use of a weapon in such situations can lead to charges of animal cruelty.

It's essential to stay informed about changes in local regulations, as firearm rules and self-defense laws can change frequently in response to political pressure or high-profile incidents. Regularly reviewing your state's laws or consulting with an expert can help ensure that you remain aware of your rights and responsibilities.

Understanding these factors is a crucial part of responsible weapon ownership and preparedness. By staying informed about the rules governing the use of deadly force and complying with local regulations, you can protect yourself and your family while minimizing the risk of serious consequences. This knowledge empowers you to make informed decisions in a crisis and reinforces the ethical responsibility that comes with owning and potentially using a weapon.

Defensive Tactics Against Potential Intruders

Establishing a Defensive Perimeter

Creating a secure home environment begins with establishing a strong defensive perimeter. This involves not only reinforcing the physical barriers of your property but also employing strategies that deter intruders before they even approach your home. A well-planned perimeter defense is your first line of protection, creating layers that make it increasingly difficult for potential threats to breach your sanctuary.

Techniques for Securing Entry Points and Creating Layers of Defense

The most vulnerable points of any home are its entryways: doors, windows, and garages. Securing these points is essential to preventing unauthorized access. Start by reinforcing doors with solid, heavy materials—preferably solid wood or steel—combined with high-quality deadbolt locks. Consider installing door braces or bars that provide additional resistance against forced entry. For windows, invest in shatterproof glass or security film, which makes it much harder for an intruder to break through. Window locks and security bars are also effective in securing these vulnerable points.

Creating layers of defense means not relying solely on your home's immediate barriers. The idea is to establish multiple zones of protection that an intruder would have to bypass, each one designed to slow down or discourage their progress. The outermost layer could be your property line, marked by fences, walls, or natural barriers like thick hedges. A sturdy fence with a locked gate adds an extra level of difficulty for anyone trying to gain entry.

Within your yard, consider installing additional barriers such as thorny bushes or strategically placed obstacles that limit easy access to entry points. Gravel pathways or driveways can also serve as a deterrent, as the noise they create underfoot can alert you to someone's presence. Keep any landscaping well-trimmed to eliminate potential hiding spots for intruders.

How to Use Lighting, Barriers, and Surveillance to Deter Intruders

Lighting is one of the most effective deterrents against intruders. A well-lit property reduces the cover of darkness that criminals rely on to approach unnoticed. Install motion-activated lights around the perimeter of your home, focusing on entry points, pathways, and dark corners. These lights not only startle would-be intruders but also draw attention to their presence. Solar-powered lights can be an energy-efficient solution for areas that are far from electrical outlets.

Barriers such as fences, gates, and walls should be designed not only for security but also for visibility. Solid barriers may provide privacy but can also offer intruders a place to hide. A combination of fencing and see-through elements like wrought iron can provide security without compromising visibility. Gates should be equipped with robust locks and, where possible, an intercom system to screen visitors before allowing them entry.

Surveillance systems are a crucial component of a defensive perimeter. Cameras positioned around your property provide a constant watch, capturing footage that can be used both as a deterrent and as evidence if needed. Modern surveillance systems often include features like night vision, motion detection, and remote viewing via smartphone apps, allowing you to monitor your property even when you're not at home. Place cameras at all entry points, including back doors and side windows, as well as at potential access points like garages or sheds.

Along with cameras, consider integrating alarm systems that are linked to your entry points. These can trigger a loud alarm or silently notify law enforcement if someone attempts to breach your perimeter. Visible signs indicating that your property is under surveillance and protected by an alarm system can also serve as powerful deterrents.

Safe Room Tactics and Emergency Protocols

A safe room is an essential component of any comprehensive home defense plan. It serves as a secure location where you and your family can retreat in the event of a home invasion or other emergencies. The effectiveness of a safe room depends not only on its construction but also on how well it is integrated into your overall emergency plan.

How to Design and Use a Safe Room Effectively During an Intrusion

The location of your safe room is a critical consideration. Ideally, it should be centrally located within your home, away from exterior walls to minimize the risk of forced entry or damage. A basement or an interior room without windows is often the best choice. The door to your safe room should be reinforced with solid construction, equipped with a heavy-duty lock, and designed to withstand forced entry. Consider installing a steel door with multiple locking mechanisms, similar to a bank vault door, which can resist significant pressure.

The interior of the safe room should be outfitted with the essentials needed to sustain your family for several hours or even days if necessary. This includes a communication device, such as a dedicated phone line or a fully charged cell phone, that allows you to call for help. Emergency supplies, such as water, non-perishable food, a first aid kit, flashlights, and batteries, should be stored within the safe room. If possible, equip the room with a surveillance monitor connected to your home's cameras, so you can track the intruder's movements without leaving the secure area.

Using a safe room effectively also requires understanding when and how to retreat to it. Your family should practice drills that simulate a home invasion scenario, ensuring that everyone knows the quickest and safest route to the safe room. Time is of the essence in these situations, so the route should be clear of obstacles, and everyone should be familiar with the process of locking down the room.

Developing a Family Emergency Plan That Includes Evacuation Routes and Communication

A well-developed family emergency plan is essential for ensuring that everyone knows what to do in the event of an intrusion. This plan should cover a range of scenarios, from a full-scale home invasion to more localized threats, such as a fire or natural disaster. The cornerstone of any emergency plan is clear communication and predefined roles for each family member.

Start by establishing a primary and secondary evacuation route for each room in the house. These routes should take into account the most likely points of entry for an intruder and the safest path to either the safe room or an external exit. In multi-story homes, ensure that there are escape ladders accessible from upper floors, and that all family members are trained in their use.

Communication is critical during an emergency. Designate a single family member to contact authorities, while others focus on gathering in the safe room or following the evacuation route. Make sure that everyone knows how to use the communication devices available to them, whether it's a landline, cell phone, or walkie-talkie. Pre-program emergency numbers into phones, and ensure that children understand how and when to call 911.

The emergency plan should also include a rendezvous point outside the home in case the family needs to evacuate. This point should be far enough away to avoid danger but close enough that everyone can reach it quickly. Practice regular drills that incorporate these routes and communication protocols to ensure that everyone remains calm and knows exactly what to do during an emergency.

Establishing a defensive perimeter and integrating safe room tactics with a well-developed emergency plan significantly enhances your home's security. By securing entry points, using lighting and surveillance effectively, and ensuring that all family members are trained in these protocols, you can create a robust defense system that protects your home and loved ones from potential threats.

Responding to a Home Invasion

A home invasion is one of the most terrifying situations a person can face. The sudden, violent breach of your personal space by an intruder requires immediate, decisive action to protect yourself and your loved ones. Knowing exactly what to do in such a scenario can be the difference between life and death. This chapter will outline the critical steps you should take if an intruder breaches your home and how to effectively coordinate with law enforcement under the immense stress of the situation.

Step-by-Step Actions to Take if an Intruder Breaches Your Home

The moment you realize that someone has broken into your home, your priority must shift to ensuring the safety of everyone inside. The first action should be to secure your immediate environment. If you are in a position to do so, gather your family members and retreat to a pre-designated safe room. This space should already be equipped with necessary supplies, including a phone to contact authorities, emergency food and water, and items for self-defense.

Once in the safe room, lock the door securely and remain as quiet as possible. Silence all electronic devices to avoid drawing attention to your location. Your goal is to stay out of sight and avoid confrontation if at all possible. Engaging an intruder directly should be a last resort, only undertaken if there is no other option to protect your life.

If a safe room is not accessible, or if the intruder is already inside the room where you are, quickly assess the situation. If escape is possible—such as through a window or another exit—do so immediately. In such high-stress situations, your instinct might be to confront the intruder, but this should only be considered if there is no safe way to retreat or hide.

Should you be confronted directly by the intruder, remember that your main objective is survival. If the intruder is armed, your options are limited. Attempt to stay calm and comply with their demands if doing so increases your chances of surviving the encounter. If you are armed and have the element of surprise, you may decide to defend yourself, but only after considering all possible outcomes.

Throughout this ordeal, it is crucial to keep a clear head. Adrenaline will surge, and your body's natural fight-or-flight response will take over. Mental preparedness, including having practiced these scenarios beforehand, can help you maintain control. Your ability to think clearly and act decisively is your greatest asset.

Once you have secured yourself and your family, contacting law enforcement is your next critical step. If you are in a safe room, use the phone to dial 911. Speak clearly and calmly, providing the dispatcher with as much information as possible. This includes your name, address, the nature of the emergency, and details about the intruder, such as their location within your home, whether they appear armed, and how many intruders are present.

Keep the phone line open, even if you cannot speak freely. This allows dispatchers to hear what is happening and potentially track your location. Whisper if necessary, but ensure that law enforcement has enough information to respond appropriately. They may ask you to stay on the line until officers arrive, providing real-time updates on the situation.

It's important to prepare for the arrival of law enforcement. When officers arrive, they may not immediately know who is a threat and who is a victim. If possible, communicate your exact location within the home and describe your appearance so that officers can identify you. Avoid making sudden movements or holding objects that could be mistaken for a weapon when officers enter the room.

If you must defend yourself before law enforcement arrives, remember that your actions will be scrutinized after the fact. Use force only when absolutely necessary and in direct response to an immediate threat. The law generally requires that your use of force be proportional to the threat you face. Afterward, when law enforcement arrives, immediately comply with their instructions and explain your actions clearly and calmly.

Stressful situations like a home invasion can impair your ability to communicate effectively, but there are techniques to mitigate this. Before a crisis occurs, it's helpful to practice deep-breathing exercises and mental rehearsal of emergency scenarios, which can help keep you calm under pressure. In the moment, try to focus on your breathing to slow your heart rate and reduce panic. Speak slowly and deliberately, even if it feels unnatural. The clarity of your communication could be vital to the effectiveness of the law enforcement response.

Video BONUS

Chapter 11: Financial and Legal Preparedness

Managing Finances During a Crisis

In the midst of a crisis, whether it's a natural disaster, economic collapse, or a personal emergency, managing your finances effectively becomes crucial for maintaining stability and ensuring that you and your family can weather the storm. Financial preparedness isn't just about having enough money in the bank—it's about understanding how to allocate your resources wisely, protecting what you have, and making strategic decisions under pressure.

The first step in managing finances during a crisis is to reassess your financial priorities. In normal circumstances, your budget might include discretionary spending on entertainment, dining out, or other non-essential items. In a crisis, these luxuries often become unnecessary or even impossible to maintain. Your focus should shift to ensuring that your basic needs—such as food, shelter, utilities, and healthcare—are met. This might require re-allocating funds or dipping into savings earmarked for emergencies.

Having an emergency fund is essential. Ideally, this fund should cover at least three to six months of living expenses. In a prolonged crisis, even a well-prepared individual might need to stretch these resources further. It's important to know exactly how much money you have available, where it's stored, and how accessible it is. If your funds are in a bank, consider keeping a portion of it in cash, as banking systems may become temporarily inaccessible during certain crises. This cash reserve should be kept in a secure, but easily accessible location.

Beyond liquid cash, consider how other assets can be leveraged. If you have investments, such as stocks or bonds, it's important to monitor them closely. In volatile markets, you may need to make quick decisions about selling or holding onto these assets. Avoid panic selling; instead, consider the long-term value and stability of your investments. In some cases, it might be wise to move assets into more stable forms, such as precious metals or other tangible assets that tend to retain value during economic downturns.

Debt management is another critical aspect of financial preparedness. In a crisis, your ability to meet debt obligations might be compromised. Prioritize paying off high-interest debts first, as these can quickly spiral out of control if left unchecked. If you anticipate difficulties in making payments, it's advisable to contact creditors early on to negotiate more favorable terms, such as reduced interest rates or deferred payments. Many lenders offer hardship programs that can provide temporary relief during difficult times.

Budgeting during a crisis also requires a shift in mindset. Instead of planning for the future, you might find yourself focusing on the immediate day-to-day. This means tracking every expense carefully and cutting costs wherever possible. While it's important to maintain some level of normalcy to preserve morale, now is the time to be frugal. Look for ways to reduce utility bills, find cheaper alternatives for necessary purchases, and eliminate non-essential services.

Another key consideration is the diversification of income streams. Relying on a single source of income can be risky, especially in an unstable economic environment. If possible, explore side gigs or freelance opportunities that can supplement your primary income. In some cases, bartering services or goods might become a viable way to meet needs without spending cash. For example, if you have a skill that's in demand—such as carpentry, sewing, or even childcare—you might trade your services for food, supplies, or other essentials.

Maintaining access to digital banking and payment systems is also important. In a crisis where digital infrastructure might be compromised, it's wise to have contingency plans. This could include keeping a small amount of cash on hand, ensuring you have checks or other forms of payment available, or setting up alternative payment methods such as peer-to-peer transfer apps. Make sure that your financial accounts are secure, using strong passwords and enabling two-factor authentication to protect against potential cyber threats.

Emotional and psychological resilience is a crucial component of financial management during a crisis. The stress of financial uncertainty can lead to poor decision-making or a tendency to panic. It's important to stay calm and rational, taking time to evaluate your situation before making significant financial moves. If possible, seek advice from a financial advisor who can provide guidance tailored to your specific circumstances.

In summary, managing finances during a crisis is about being proactive, strategic, and adaptable. By reassessing your priorities, protecting your assets, managing debt, and maintaining emotional resilience, you can navigate the financial challenges of a crisis more effectively. This preparedness not only safeguards your current stability but also positions you to recover and rebuild once the crisis has passed.

Protecting Your Assets: Cash, Digital Currency, and Bartering

In times of crisis, safeguarding your assets becomes a critical priority. The stability of financial systems can quickly become uncertain, making it essential to protect the wealth and resources you have accumulated. Whether through cash reserves, digital currencies, or the age-old practice of bartering, understanding how to secure and utilize these assets effectively can provide a crucial buffer against the unpredictable nature of crises.

Cash: The Cornerstone of Crisis Preparedness

Cash remains one of the most reliable forms of currency during a crisis. When electronic systems fail or banking institutions face disruptions, cash becomes the immediate go-to for transactions. The key to managing cash effectively is ensuring you have enough on hand to cover essential expenses for a set period, typically ranging from a few days to a few weeks, depending on the nature of the crisis.

Storing cash requires a balance between accessibility and security. It's advisable to keep smaller denominations, which are easier to use for everyday transactions, as well as a secure stash in a discreet, yet accessible location within your home. This could be a safe or another secure spot where it can be easily reached in an emergency but remains hidden from potential thieves. Diversifying where you store your cash is also prudent—don't keep all of it in one place. Avoid broadcasting that you have significant cash reserves to minimize the risk of becoming a target.

However, cash has its limitations. Inflation or hyperinflation can rapidly erode its value, making it less effective in long-term crisis scenarios. Therefore, while it is important to maintain a cash reserve, it should be part of a broader strategy that includes other forms of asset protection.

Digital Currency: The Modern Frontier

Digital currency, including cryptocurrencies like Bitcoin, offers an alternative to traditional cash that can be especially useful in a crisis. These digital assets are decentralized, meaning they are not controlled by any single government or financial institution, which can make them less vulnerable to some forms of economic instability. Cryptocurrencies can be transferred quickly and securely across borders, providing a level of flexibility that physical cash does not offer.

The use of digital currency in a crisis comes with its own set of challenges. The value of cryptocurrencies can be highly volatile, and their acceptance as a form of payment is still not universal. It's important to hold digital currencies in secure wallets—preferably hardware wallets that are not connected to the internet, which minimizes the risk of hacking. Regularly back up your digital wallet and keep your recovery keys in a safe place, as losing access to these keys could mean losing your digital assets permanently.

Moreover, access to digital currencies depends on the availability of the internet and functioning digital infrastructure. In scenarios where these are compromised, your ability to use digital currency may be limited. For this reason, digital currency should complement, not replace, your cash reserves and other assets.

Bartering: The Ancient Yet Timeless Practice

When traditional currencies lose value or become inaccessible, bartering can emerge as a practical solution. Bartering involves trading goods or services directly without the use of money. This form of exchange is particularly valuable in local communities where trust and direct interaction are key. It can also be a lifeline in situations where inflation has rendered currency worthless or where official systems of trade and commerce have collapsed.

To prepare for bartering, consider stockpiling items that have intrinsic value in a crisis. These can include non-perishable food, clean water, medical supplies, batteries, fuel, and other essentials that are likely to be in high demand. Skills and services, such as carpentry, medical expertise, or repair work, can also be valuable barter assets.

The key to successful bartering is understanding the needs of your community and building a network of trusted individuals with whom you can trade. This might involve participating in local preparedness groups or simply getting to know your neighbors better. Establishing these relationships before a crisis strikes can give you a significant advantage, as trust and reliability become the cornerstone of barter-based economies.

It's also important to recognize that bartering requires negotiation skills. You'll need to assess the value of your goods and services in relation to what others are offering and be prepared to negotiate fair trades. Being flexible and understanding the fluctuating value of items as the crisis evolves will help you maximize the utility of your assets.

Balancing and Diversifying Your Asset Protection

The most effective approach to asset protection in a crisis is diversification. Relying solely on cash, digital currency, or bartering leaves you vulnerable to the specific risks associated with each. By maintaining a mix of these assets, you can better navigate the complexities of a crisis situation.

For example, having cash on hand provides immediate liquidity, while digital currencies can offer long-term security and mobility. Bartering ensures that you have a fallback option if traditional and digital currencies fail. Together, these strategies create a robust framework that can withstand the various challenges posed by a crisis.

Protecting your assets during a crisis requires a proactive, diversified approach. By strategically managing cash, securing digital currencies, and preparing for the potential need to barter, you can safeguard your financial stability and ensure that you have the resources necessary to navigate any crisis with confidence. This comprehensive strategy not only protects your wealth but also positions you to adapt and thrive, even in the most challenging circumstances.

Legal Considerations in Crisis Situations

When crises occur, whether due to natural disasters, civil unrest, or economic instability, the regulatory environment can shift rapidly. It's essential to understand the implications of your actions during such times to safeguard both your physical safety and your standing within the legal system. In times of crisis, rules governing self-defense, property rights, and financial transactions can become complex and, at times, unclear. Having a solid grasp of these considerations will enable you to navigate these challenges with confidence.

One of the most urgent concerns during a crisis is the use of force in self-defense. Many U.S. states adhere to the "Castle Doctrine," which allows homeowners to use reasonable force, including deadly force, to defend themselves against an intruder. However, what qualifies as "reasonable force" can vary. Knowing the specific self-defense laws in your state and how they apply in different scenarios is essential. For example, some states impose a duty to retreat if possible, while others have "Stand Your Ground" laws that permit the use of force without requiring an attempt to flee.

During a crisis, law enforcement may be delayed or overwhelmed, which increases the likelihood that you may need to defend yourself or your property. Any use of force could be reviewed later, so it's important to document incidents thoroughly, noting the perceived threat and your response. Securing evidence, such as video footage from security cameras, can be crucial if you later need to justify your actions in court.

Property protection is another critical issue. During widespread crises, looting and theft may become common. While it's natural to want to defend your belongings, it's important to understand the limits of property defense. Using excessive force, particularly if it results in serious harm or death, can lead to criminal charges. In many cases, the law places more value on human life than on material possessions. Thus, while taking reasonable steps to secure your property, such as installing security systems and reinforcing entry points, lethal force should only be used as a last resort when life is at risk.

Financial transactions during a crisis also carry certain risks. If traditional banking systems become inaccessible, people might turn to alternative currencies or barter. It's important to understand the rules surrounding such transactions. For instance, trading certain goods might be restricted, especially if they are scarce or classified as essential by the government. Participating in black market activities, even out of necessity, can result in severe consequences.

Bartering services for goods may also come with certain stipulations depending on your location. While bartering is generally permissible, there may be rules regarding the taxation of exchanged goods and services. In some cases, barter may be interpreted as an attempt to bypass price controls or rationing laws, leading to penalties. Keeping transactions transparent and being mindful of local rules is crucial.

Preparing for a crisis also involves ensuring your estate plans and important documents are in order. This includes having a will, power of attorney, and healthcare directives prepared before a crisis strikes. During emergencies, such as those involving widespread illness or natural disasters, accessing legal services may be difficult. Having these documents ready ensures that your wishes are followed and that your family isn't left making decisions on your behalf under stressful conditions.

It's important to consider the potential for martial law during extreme crises. While rare, martial law can be declared, granting military and law enforcement broader powers to maintain order. Under martial law, civil liberties—such as freedom of movement, assembly, and even certain financial transactions—can be significantly restricted. Understanding how martial law works in your area can help you prepare for and adapt to these changes while protecting your rights and assets.

In times of crisis, it's also wise to stay informed about temporary measures that may be enacted. Governments often introduce emergency regulations to manage resources, control prices, or limit certain behaviors. These new rules may affect your ability to purchase certain items, move freely, or conduct business. Staying updated on these changes through reliable sources will help you avoid unintentionally violating any new regulations.

Whenever in doubt, it's crucial to seek expert advice. Making uninformed decisions during a crisis can have serious consequences. Consulting with a professional familiar with crisis management and emergency regulations can provide clarity and help you make decisions that protect both your assets and your rights.

Navigating a crisis requires careful awareness of self-defense, property protection, financial transactions, and emergency rules. By understanding these frameworks, you can safeguard your rights and assets while confidently responding to the challenges that arise during uncertain times.

Video BONUS

Chapter 12: Advanced Fortification and Survival Projects

DIY Projects for Home Fortification

Reinforcing Doors, Windows, and Entry Points

In any home fortification plan, securing the main entry points is crucial. Doors, windows, and other vulnerable areas are often the first targets for intruders. By reinforcing these entry points, you significantly increase the security of your home, making it much more difficult for potential threats to gain access.

Reinforcing Doors with Metal Plates and Upgraded Locks

Doors are the most obvious entry points and often the most vulnerable. Standard residential doors, especially those made of hollow core materials, can be easily breached with force. To enhance the security of your doors, consider upgrading them with solid core or metal doors. If replacing the door isn't feasible, reinforcing the existing door with metal plates can provide added strength. Metal plates, installed on both the interior and exterior sides of the door, help to distribute the force of any attempted breach, making it significantly harder for someone to kick the door in.

Another critical upgrade is the lock system. Standard locks can often be picked or forced open, but installing high-quality deadbolts with at least a one-inch throw bolt offers better resistance to forced entry. Consider adding a reinforced strike plate, which is the metal plate that the bolt extends into when the door is locked. The strike plate should be secured with screws that penetrate deep into the wall studs, providing greater hold and resistance to force. A multi-point locking system, which bolts the door into the frame at multiple points, can further enhance security.

Installing Security Bars and Shatterproof Films on Windows

Windows, while necessary for natural light and ventilation, are a significant security risk if not properly reinforced. To fortify your windows, start by installing security bars. These bars are typically made of metal and are installed over the window frame. While they may seem visually intrusive, modern designs can be quite aesthetic and, most importantly, they serve as a formidable barrier against intruders. Ensure that these bars are securely fastened into the wall structure, not just the window frame, to prevent easy removal.

For those who prefer a less visible security measure, shatterproof films offer an effective alternative. These films are applied directly to the glass and work by holding the shards together if the window is broken, thus preventing an intruder from easily gaining access. Shatterproof films are particularly useful for ground-level windows or those that are hidden from view, where an intruder might feel less exposed while attempting to break in.

Upgrading to impact-resistant windows, which are designed to withstand high-force impacts, can provide an extra layer of security. These windows are typically made with multiple layers of glass and polyvinyl butyral (PVB) interlayers, making them much more difficult to break through.

Strengthening Garage Doors and Other Vulnerable Entry Points

Garage doors are often overlooked in home security plans, yet they can be one of the weakest points of entry. Standard garage doors, especially those made of thin aluminum or fiberglass, can be easily forced open or even cut through. To fortify your garage door, start by installing a garage door reinforcement kit. These kits typically include braces that attach to the door's panels, increasing its resistance to force.

Another critical step is upgrading the garage door's locking mechanism. Many garage doors come with basic locks that are easily bypassed. Installing a heavy-duty slide bolt or a deadbolt lock can prevent the door from being opened without the key. Consider installing a manual lock as a backup in case of a power outage or failure of the electronic system.

Ensure that the entry door from the garage into the house is as secure as your front door. This door should be made of solid wood or metal and equipped with a deadbolt lock. Many homeowners neglect this door, but it can provide easy access to the rest of the house if left unsecured.

Building Defensive Barriers and Perimeter Protection

While securing the entry points of your home is crucial, creating a fortified perimeter around your property adds another layer of defense. By constructing barriers and employing strategic landscaping, you can deter potential intruders before they even reach your doors and windows.

Constructing Fences, Gates, and Barriers to Deter Intruders

A well-constructed fence is the first line of defense in your perimeter security plan. High fences made from sturdy materials like steel, brick, or reinforced wood can significantly slow down or prevent an intruder's access to your property. Fences should be tall enough to prevent easy climbing, typically at least six feet, and topped with anti-climb measures such as spiked railings or even trellises that are difficult to grasp.

Gates are another critical component of perimeter security. A solid, lockable gate that matches the security level of your fence is essential. Gates should be installed with heavy-duty locks, and automatic gates with electronic controls can add an additional layer of security, allowing you to control access remotely. Ensure that the gate's hinges and latches are reinforced and that the gate is positioned in a way that avoids creating a blind spot or easy access point for intruders.

Beyond fences and gates, consider adding physical barriers such as large rocks, boulders, or even strategically placed garden beds, which can obstruct a vehicle's path or discourage foot traffic close to vulnerable areas of your home. Driveway gates or barriers can also prevent unauthorized vehicles from approaching your property.

Using Landscaping Strategically for Security

Landscaping can play a significant role in enhancing the security of your home. Certain plants, such as thorny bushes and dense shrubs, can be planted near windows and other vulnerable areas to create natural barriers. These plants can deter intruders from getting too close to your home while also enhancing the aesthetic appeal of your property.

Along with using plants as barriers, consider the strategic placement of trees and bushes to prevent them from providing cover or hiding spots for intruders. Keep trees and large bushes trimmed back from the house, particularly around windows and doors, to maintain clear sightlines. Low-growing, thorny plants can be placed under windows to deter anyone from attempting to access them.

Pathways and driveways should be designed to be well-lit and visible from the main living areas of the house. This not only deters intruders but also increases the chances of spotting any suspicious activity early.

Setting Up Motion-Activated Lighting and Alarms as Deterrents

Lighting is one of the most effective deterrents against crime. Motion-activated lights can startle and expose would-be intruders, reducing their chances of successfully breaching your perimeter unnoticed. Place these lights around all entry points, including doors, windows, and the garage, as well as along pathways and near any potential blind spots in your yard.

Modern motion-activated lighting systems can be integrated with your home security system, triggering alarms or notifications if movement is detected. This allows you to respond quickly to any potential threat. Along with lighting, consider installing perimeter alarms that trigger if someone attempts to breach your fence or gate. These alarms can be linked to your main security system, providing comprehensive coverage.

In summary, reinforcing your home's doors, windows, and entry points is fundamental to any security plan, but building a robust perimeter defense is equally important. By combining physical reinforcements with strategic landscaping and effective lighting, you create multiple layers of protection that work together to deter and delay any potential intruders. This integrated approach not only secures your home but also gives you the time and information needed to respond effectively in the event of a threat.

Bulletproofing, Blast Protection, and Concealed Safe Spaces

Bulletproofing Walls and Critical Areas

When it comes to fortifying your home against extreme threats, bulletproofing key areas can provide an additional layer of protection, ensuring that you and your loved ones remain safe even in the most dire circumstances. While bulletproofing might seem like an extreme measure, it is increasingly considered by those who prioritize security, especially in high-risk environments or during times of significant unrest.

Materials and Methods for Bulletproofing Key Parts of Your Home

The first step in bulletproofing your home is selecting the right materials. Traditional walls made of drywall, wood, or brick are not sufficient to stop bullets, especially those from high-caliber firearms. To create bulletproof barriers, you will need to reinforce walls with materials specifically designed to absorb and dissipate the energy of a bullet.

Ballistic fiberglass panels are one of the most common materials used for this purpose. These panels are made from woven fiberglass cloth, layered and bonded with resin. They are lightweight, relatively easy to install, and can be placed inside walls during construction or renovation. Ballistic panels come in various thicknesses, with thicker panels offering higher levels of protection. These panels are rated based on their ability to stop different calibers of bullets, so it's important to choose the right level of protection for your needs.

Another material option is steel plating, particularly AR500 steel, which is used for armor applications. While highly effective at stopping bullets, steel is heavy and can be challenging to install. It is often used in combination with other materials, such as concrete or ballistic fiberglass, to create a multi-layered defense system.

For existing structures, retrofitting walls with these materials can be done by removing the drywall, installing the bulletproof material, and then re-covering the wall. This method ensures that your defenses are not immediately visible, maintaining the aesthetic integrity of your home.

Strategic Placement of Bulletproof Materials in Walls, Doors, and Furniture

The strategic placement of bulletproof materials is just as important as the materials themselves. Focus on reinforcing areas where you are most likely to seek shelter during an attack, such as bedrooms, safe rooms, or any central areas where your family might congregate during an emergency.

Start by reinforcing exterior walls, particularly those facing potential points of entry like doors and windows. Next, consider interior walls that protect hallways or rooms where you plan to take cover. Bulletproofing doors, especially those leading to safe rooms or essential escape routes, adds another layer of security. Solid core doors can be upgraded with ballistic panels to resist forced entry and stop bullets.

Along with walls and doors, consider bulletproofing furniture. For example, bookcases, desks, or cabinets can be reinforced with ballistic panels and strategically placed to act as shields in the event of an intrusion. This approach allows for flexible defense options throughout the home, giving you the ability to take cover quickly if necessary.

Integrating Bulletproof Features Without Compromising Aesthetic Appeal

One of the challenges of bulletproofing is integrating these features without sacrificing the aesthetic appeal of your home. Fortunately, modern materials and techniques allow for a seamless blend of security and design.

For example, ballistic panels can be installed behind drywall or other wall coverings, making them invisible to the eye. Doors reinforced with bulletproof materials can be finished with decorative veneers or paints that match the rest of your home's interior. Even furniture can be designed with concealed ballistic protection, ensuring that your home retains its style and comfort while offering enhanced security.

When planning your bulletproofing project, work with professionals who specialize in blending security features with interior design. They can help you choose materials and finishes that complement your home's décor while providing the necessary protection.

Creating Concealed Safe Spaces

Along with bulletproofing, creating concealed safe spaces within your home offers a final line of defense in the event of an intrusion or other emergency. These spaces can serve as a refuge where you and your family can hide safely until help arrives or the threat subsides.

Designing Hidden Rooms and Concealed Compartments for Emergencies

A concealed safe space can range from a small hidden compartment to a fully outfitted panic room. The key to designing these spaces is ensuring they are not easily detectable. This often involves integrating the safe space into the existing structure of your home in a way that blends seamlessly with your surroundings.

For hidden rooms, consider utilizing areas like basements, attics, or even large closets. These rooms can be accessed through disguised doors that might look like ordinary shelving units, mirrors, or wall panels. For example, a bookshelf that swings open to reveal a hidden door is a classic design that combines functionality with concealment. The entrance to your safe space should be easily accessible to you but difficult for intruders to find.

Concealed compartments, on the other hand, are smaller spaces designed to hide valuable items or provide temporary cover. These can be built into floors, behind false walls, or under furniture. These compartments should be large enough to hold essential items like documents, cash, or weapons, and they should be secure enough to resist tampering.

Camouflaging Entry Points and Ensuring Easy Access During a Crisis

The success of a concealed safe space depends largely on its ability to remain undetected. Camouflaging entry points is crucial. This might involve using materials that match the surrounding area or creating distractions that draw attention away from the entrance.

Along with visual camouflage, consider soundproofing your safe space to prevent intruders from hearing any movement inside. This can be achieved by adding sound-dampening materials to the walls and doors, ensuring that even if someone is close by, they won't hear anything that might reveal your location.

While concealment is important, you must also ensure that your safe space is easily accessible during an emergency. Practice accessing the space regularly, and ensure that all family members know how to reach it quickly. The entrance should be easy to open from the inside, with no complicated mechanisms that could fail under pressure.

Stocking and Equipping Concealed Spaces for Long-Term Use

Once your concealed safe space is built, it's essential to equip it with everything you might need if you are forced to stay there for an extended period. Start with basic necessities such as food, water, and medical supplies. Non-perishable food items and bottled water are ideal, along with a first aid kit that includes any necessary medications.

Your safe space should also include means of communication, such as a charged cell phone, two-way radios, or a landline connected to an outside line. This will allow you to call for help or receive updates on the situation outside.

Equip the space with tools that might be necessary for survival, such as flashlights, batteries, fire extinguishers, and basic tools for self-defense. Consider adding a small toilet or waste disposal system if you anticipate the possibility of being in the space for more than a few hours.

Ventilation is another crucial consideration. Ensure that your safe space has a supply of fresh air, either through natural ventilation or a filtered air system. This will prevent suffocation in a sealed environment and protect you from potential threats like smoke or gas.

In conclusion, integrating bulletproofing and creating concealed safe spaces in your home requires careful planning and execution. By strategically reinforcing key areas and designing hidden rooms that offer refuge, you significantly increase your home's security and your ability to protect your family during a crisis. These measures, when done correctly, blend seamlessly with your home's design, ensuring that you remain prepared for any situation without compromising your comfort or style.

Video BONUS

Chapter 13: Adapting to Evolving Crisis Situations

Responding to Different Types of Emergencies

In an unpredictable world, the ability to respond effectively to different types of emergencies is crucial for survival. Each emergency scenario—be it a natural disaster, civil unrest, a pandemic, or a prolonged power outage—presents its own unique challenges. Understanding how to adapt your response to these varying situations is key to protecting your home, your loved ones, and yourself. This chapter will explore how to tailor your actions based on the specific type of crisis you are facing, ensuring that you are prepared for whatever comes your way.

Natural Disasters

Natural disasters, such as hurricanes, earthquakes, floods, and wildfires, often strike with little warning, leaving little time for preparation. The first step in responding to a natural disaster is to have a clear understanding of the risks associated with your geographical location. Knowing whether you live in an area prone to hurricanes or near a fault line can help you prepare in advance, both physically and mentally.

In the event of a hurricane or flood, securing your home against wind and water damage is critical. This may involve boarding up windows, reinforcing doors, and ensuring that your roof is secure. Creating barriers around your property to divert water flow can reduce the risk of flooding. Evacuation might be necessary in some cases, but if you choose to bug in, make sure you have enough supplies to last at least several days without outside help. This includes food, water, medical supplies, and backup power sources.

During an earthquake, the focus shifts to immediate safety within your home. Identify safe spots, such as under sturdy tables or against interior walls, where you can take cover during the shaking. Securing heavy furniture to walls and ensuring that glass or fragile items are stored safely can prevent injuries. After the initial quake, be prepared for aftershocks and ensure that your home is still structurally sound before remaining inside.

Wildfires require quick action and, often, evacuation. If you are unable to evacuate, close all windows, doors, and vents to prevent smoke from entering your home. Create a defensible space around your property by clearing away flammable vegetation and debris, and keep fire extinguishers and hoses accessible.

Civil Unrest

Civil unrest presents a different kind of threat, one that can escalate quickly and become dangerous, especially in urban areas. When responding to civil unrest, situational awareness is paramount. Stay informed about the developments in your area through reliable news sources and social media. If unrest is anticipated, prepare your home by securing entry points and fortifying vulnerable areas. This might include reinforcing doors, adding security bars to windows, and ensuring that your surveillance and alarm systems are fully operational.

If a protest or riot occurs near your home, the safest course of action is usually to remain inside and avoid confrontation. Keep lights off and noise to a minimum to avoid drawing attention. If you need to communicate with law enforcement or emergency services, use discretion and be aware that phone lines and internet connections may be disrupted.

In prolonged periods of civil unrest, it is important to have a plan for securing essential supplies. This might involve coordinating with neighbors for mutual support or identifying alternative routes to reach safe areas or supplies. The ability to adapt your strategy as the situation evolves is critical, as what begins as a peaceful protest can rapidly escalate into something more dangerous.

Pandemics

The global COVID-19 pandemic highlighted the importance of preparedness for biological threats. Unlike natural disasters or civil unrest, pandemics can unfold over extended periods, requiring long-term adaptations to daily life. In a pandemic scenario, the primary concern is limiting exposure to the virus while maintaining access to necessary resources.

During a pandemic, staying informed is crucial. Follow public health guidelines regarding social distancing, mask-wearing, and hygiene practices. Stocking up on essential supplies, including food, water, medications, and personal protective equipment, can help reduce the need for frequent trips to crowded stores. Consider the psychological toll of prolonged isolation and develop strategies to maintain mental health, such as regular communication with loved ones, engaging in hobbies, and staying active.

If someone in your household becomes ill, have a plan for isolation within your home to prevent the spread of the virus. This might involve designating a specific room for the sick individual and ensuring that they have access to a separate bathroom, if possible. Keep disinfectants and cleaning supplies on hand to regularly sanitize shared spaces.

Prolonged Power Outages

Prolonged power outages can occur as a result of natural disasters, infrastructure failures, or cyberattacks. These situations can disrupt not only electricity but also water supply, communication networks, and access to financial services. Preparing for a prolonged power outage involves both short-term responses and long-term strategies.

In the short term, having alternative power sources is essential. This could include generators, solar panels, or battery backups. Ensure that you have enough fuel to keep generators running for an extended period and that you know how to safely operate and maintain them. Solar panels can provide a renewable source of energy, but they may require battery storage systems to supply power when sunlight is not available.

Water is another critical consideration during a power outage. If your home relies on an electric pump for water, have a plan for accessing water, such as storing large quantities in advance or collecting rainwater. Keep a supply of water purification tablets or filters in case you need to use an alternative water source.

Communication can also be challenging during a power outage. Battery-powered radios, satellite phones, and walkie-talkies can provide a way to stay informed and in touch with others. Additionally, keep important documents, such as identification and insurance policies, in a secure, accessible place in case you need to evacuate or access services.

Adapting Your Response

No matter the type of emergency, the ability to adapt your response as conditions change is critical. Each scenario requires a tailored approach, but the underlying principles remain the same: stay informed, prepare in advance, and remain flexible. Crises are inherently unpredictable, and your response plan should be dynamic, allowing you to adjust to new information and evolving threats.

Responding to different types of emergencies requires a combination of preparedness, adaptability, and situational awareness. By understanding the unique challenges posed by natural disasters, civil unrest, pandemics, and prolonged power outages, you can develop strategies that protect you and your loved ones, no matter what crisis you face. This proactive approach not only increases your chances of survival but also empowers you to navigate uncertainty with confidence and resilience.

Learning from Real-World Bug-In Case Studies

Understanding how to effectively bug in during a crisis is more than just theory—it's about learning from real-world scenarios where individuals and communities faced unprecedented challenges. By examining these case studies, we can gain valuable insights into what works, what doesn't, and how to adapt our own preparedness strategies accordingly. These examples, drawn from diverse situations across the globe, highlight the importance of flexibility, resourcefulness, and community support when hunkering down becomes the safest option.

Case Study 1: The Siege of Sarajevo (1992-1996)

One of the most extreme and prolonged bug-in scenarios in modern history was the Siege of Sarajevo during the Bosnian War. For nearly four years, the residents of Sarajevo were trapped in their city, cut off from basic supplies and utilities, and subjected to constant sniper and artillery attacks. The survival strategies developed during this period provide critical lessons for anyone considering a bug-in plan.

The people of Sarajevo relied heavily on community networks to survive. They shared resources such as food, water, and medical supplies, and they supported each other emotionally and psychologically during the darkest times. This case underscores the importance of building strong community ties before a crisis hits. When planning to bug in, consider how you can foster relationships with neighbors and local groups to create a support network that can share information, resources, and protection.

Resourcefulness was another key factor in the survival of Sarajevo's residents. With supplies running scarce, people had to improvise. For example, they converted books and furniture into firewood, made makeshift stoves, and even collected rainwater to drink. This adaptability highlights the need for creativity in a bug-in scenario. It's not just about having a stockpile, but also about knowing how to use what you have in ways you might not have anticipated.

Moreover, the siege demonstrated the importance of mental resilience. With no clear end in sight, maintaining morale was essential. People found solace in routine activities, art, and even humor, which provided a sense of normalcy and helped combat the despair that could easily set in. When bugging in, maintaining mental health should be as much a priority as physical survival, with strategies in place to keep spirits high and prevent psychological breakdown.

Case Study 2: Hurricane Katrina (2005)

Hurricane Katrina is a stark example of how quickly a natural disaster can escalate into a prolonged crisis, leading to widespread chaos and the need for a bug-in strategy. In the immediate aftermath of the hurricane, many residents of New Orleans found themselves trapped in their homes without power, clean water, or access to food and medical care.

One of the critical lessons from Katrina is the importance of preparation before a crisis. Many of the challenges faced by those who stayed behind—such as lack of potable water, food shortages, and power outages—could have been mitigated with proper planning. This case study reinforces the need to have an emergency stockpile that includes not just food and water, but also medical supplies, sanitation items, and backup power sources. It also highlights the necessity of having a plan for how to communicate and signal for help, as traditional lines of communication were quickly overwhelmed.

Katrina also illustrated the dangers of relying solely on external aid. Many residents waited for help that was slow to arrive, and some tragically did not survive the wait. This situation emphasizes the importance of self-reliance and being prepared to fend for yourself and your family for an extended period without outside assistance. It also teaches the value of having multiple backup plans, including knowing the safest routes out of your home and city if evacuation becomes necessary.

The response to Hurricane Katrina shows the importance of flexibility and quick decision-making. Some residents who initially planned to stay were forced to evacuate due to rising floodwaters or other life-threatening conditions. This adaptability is crucial in any crisis scenario, as initial plans might need to be altered as the situation evolves. The ability to assess the situation continuously and make rapid decisions could mean the difference between life and death.

Case Study 3: The COVID-19 Pandemic (2020-Present)

The global COVID-19 pandemic provided a modern, widespread example of bugging in, as billions of people worldwide were forced to stay in their homes to avoid spreading the virus. This case is particularly relevant because it involved a long-term bug-in scenario, affecting not just physical safety but also economic stability and mental health.

The pandemic highlighted the importance of having a well-rounded preparedness plan that includes financial resilience. As jobs were lost and economies shuttered, those with emergency savings, diversified income streams, or a stash of essential supplies fared better than those who were caught unprepared. This case study suggests that bug-in plans should account for financial emergencies, such as loss of income, by including strategies for managing finances, reducing expenses, and possibly even bartering for goods and services.

Another key lesson from the pandemic is the need for digital preparedness. With much of the world moving online for work, education, and social interaction, having a reliable internet connection, digital devices, and the skills to use them became critical. The pandemic teaches us that bug-in plans must now include provisions for staying connected digitally, whether for work, communication with loved ones, or accessing information and services.

The mental health challenges brought on by isolation during the pandemic also cannot be overlooked. Prolonged bug-in situations can lead to feelings of loneliness, anxiety, and depression. Learning from this, it's clear that future bug-in plans should include ways to maintain social connections and mental well-being, whether through virtual gatherings, hobbies, or regular exercise routines.

Applying Lessons from Case Studies to Your Bug-In Plan

The case studies of Sarajevo, Hurricane Katrina, and the COVID-19 pandemic each offer unique insights into effective bug-in strategies. The common thread across all these scenarios is the importance of preparation, adaptability, and resilience. By studying these real-world examples, you can better anticipate the challenges you might face and develop a bug-in plan that is comprehensive, flexible, and tailored to your specific circumstances.

Preparation is more than just stockpiling; it's about understanding the potential risks in your environment and having a plan that covers not only physical needs but also financial stability, mental health, and community support. Adaptability means being ready to change your plans as the situation evolves, whether that's shifting from a bug-in to a bug-out scenario or finding new ways to use the resources you have. Resilience is about maintaining your resolve and staying focused on survival, even when the crisis is prolonged or particularly challenging.

Learning from these real-world bug-in case studies allows you to create a more robust and effective preparedness plan. By incorporating these lessons into your own strategies, you can enhance your ability to protect yourself, your family, and your home in the face of any crisis.

Adjusting Your Plan as Conditions Change

In any crisis, the ability to adapt is crucial. No matter how thorough your initial preparations are, circumstances can shift rapidly, rendering parts of your plan obsolete or insufficient. The key to surviving—and thriving—through such challenges is a mindset that embraces flexibility and a strategy that allows for continuous reassessment and adjustment.

One of the first steps in maintaining an adaptable plan is recognizing the early signs that conditions are changing. Whether you're dealing with a natural disaster, civil unrest, or a prolonged crisis like a pandemic, subtle shifts can signal the need for a new approach. These might include changes in weather patterns, fluctuations in supply availability, new information from trusted sources, or even alterations in the behavior of those around you. Being attuned to these changes requires vigilant monitoring of your environment, staying informed through reliable channels, and maintaining open communication with your network.

As you detect these shifts, the next step is to reassess your current plan. Begin by asking critical questions: Are your resources sufficient for the new circumstances? Do you need to alter your strategy for defense, mobility, or communication? For example, if a natural disaster is more severe than expected, you might need to switch from a bug-in strategy to a bug-out scenario. Alternatively, if civil unrest escalates, you might need to reinforce security measures or relocate to a safer area within your home.

Reassessment also involves reviewing your supply levels. In the initial phase of a crisis, it's easy to rely heavily on your stockpile, but as the situation evolves, you must continuously evaluate your consumption rates and find ways to stretch your resources. This might mean rationing supplies more strictly, finding alternative sources, or bartering with others. Flexibility in managing your resources can make the difference between enduring a crisis and facing critical shortages.

In addition to reassessing your physical supplies, consider the psychological and emotional impact of the evolving situation. Crises that drag on for weeks or months can take a toll on mental health. What may have worked initially—such as maintaining routines or relying on certain stress-relief practices—might need adjustment as fatigue, frustration, and uncertainty grow. Incorporating new coping strategies, whether through developing new hobbies, adjusting daily routines, or increasing virtual social interactions, can help maintain morale and prevent burnout.

Another essential aspect of adjusting your plan is involving your family or household members in the process. Collective decision-making not only distributes the burden of planning but also ensures that everyone is on the same page. Regularly scheduled family meetings to discuss the current situation, reassess roles, and update the plan are crucial. This practice fosters a sense of teamwork and shared responsibility, which can be vital in maintaining cohesion and morale.

Moreover, adaptability involves being prepared for the possibility that you might need to abandon your current location altogether. If the crisis escalates to the point where your home is no longer safe, having a well-thought-out evacuation plan is critical. This plan should include a pre-determined destination, whether it's a relative's home, a community shelter, or a secondary location you've prepared. Ensure that all necessary supplies are packed in easily accessible go-bags and that everyone in the household knows the evacuation procedure.

Evacuation plans should be dynamic, with multiple routes and destinations identified. Road conditions, security checkpoints, and even weather can alter your path, so being flexible in your approach is essential. Furthermore, staying informed about the situation outside your immediate area through reliable news sources or community networks will help you make timely decisions about when and where to evacuate.

As the crisis evolves, keep learning and adapting. Each day of a prolonged crisis offers new lessons about what works and what doesn't. Pay attention to what others in similar situations are doing, and don't hesitate to incorporate successful strategies into your own plan. Continuous learning ensures that your response remains effective and that you are better prepared for any future challenges.

Adjusting your plan as conditions change is not just about reacting to immediate threats but also about proactively managing your resources, maintaining your mental and emotional health, and staying flexible in the face of uncertainty. By embracing adaptability and continuously reassessing your situation, you can navigate even the most challenging crises with resilience and confidence, ensuring the safety and well-being of yourself and your loved ones.

Video BONUS

Chapter 14: Psychological Resilience and Community Support

Coping with Isolation and Prolonged Crisis Situations

Isolation and prolonged crisis situations test the limits of human endurance, both physically and mentally. When a crisis forces you to remain isolated for extended periods, the psychological strain can be as challenging as any physical threat. Coping effectively with these conditions requires a deep understanding of the psychological impacts of isolation, strategies for maintaining mental health, and proactive measures to keep your morale high.

Understanding the Psychological Impact of Isolation

Isolation, especially when imposed rather than chosen, can have profound effects on the mind. Humans are inherently social creatures, and when cut off from regular interactions, feelings of loneliness, anxiety, and depression can quickly set in. The absence of normal routines and the uncertainty of a crisis situation can exacerbate these feelings, leading to a sense of helplessness or despair.

The first step in coping with isolation is recognizing these psychological effects as normal responses to an abnormal situation. Acknowledging that it's okay to feel anxious or down helps to normalize these emotions, making them easier to manage. It's crucial to take proactive steps to prevent these feelings from overwhelming you.

Maintaining a Routine

One of the most effective ways to combat the psychological toll of isolation is to establish and maintain a daily routine. A structured schedule provides a sense of normalcy and control in an otherwise uncertain environment. Even simple routines, such as waking up at the same time each day, planning meals, and setting aside time for exercise or hobbies, can help create a rhythm that keeps your mind focused and engaged.

Within this routine, it's important to include activities that stimulate both the body and mind. Physical exercise, whether through home workouts, yoga, or even simple stretching, not only keeps you physically healthy but also boosts your mood by releasing endorphins. Mental exercises, such as reading, puzzles, or learning a new skill, help keep your mind sharp and distracted from the stress of the situation.

Staying Connected

While physical isolation may be necessary, maintaining social connections is critical to psychological resilience. In the digital age, staying connected with loved ones, friends, and the outside world is easier than ever, even in isolation. Regular communication through phone calls, video chats, or messaging can provide emotional support and reduce feelings of loneliness.

It's also beneficial to participate in online communities or forums where you can share experiences, exchange tips, and offer or receive support from others in similar situations. These interactions remind you that you're not alone and that others are facing and overcoming similar challenges.

Mindfulness and Stress Management

Mindfulness practices, such as meditation or deep breathing exercises, can be powerful tools in managing the stress and anxiety that often accompany isolation. These practices help anchor your thoughts in the present moment, reducing the tendency to ruminate on fears about the future or regrets about the past. Even a few minutes of mindfulness each day can help clear your mind and provide a sense of calm amidst the chaos.

In addition to mindfulness, it's important to actively manage stress by identifying and addressing its sources. If the news cycle is causing anxiety, limit your exposure to it. If a particular task or situation is overwhelming, break it down into smaller, manageable steps. By tackling stress head-on, you prevent it from building up and becoming unmanageable.

Fostering a Positive Mindset

Maintaining a positive mindset during prolonged isolation is challenging but essential. Focus on what you can control rather than what you can't. This might include your daily schedule, the cleanliness of your living space, or the care of your personal health. Setting small, achievable goals each day can provide a sense of accomplishment and purpose, which are vital for maintaining morale.

It's also helpful to find meaning or purpose in the situation. Whether it's using the time to learn a new skill, catching up on reading, or deepening your relationships with those you are isolated with, finding something positive in the experience can shift your mindset from one of survival to one of growth.

The Role of Hope and Optimism

Hope is a powerful antidote to despair. Even in the most challenging circumstances, fostering a sense of hope can sustain you through prolonged isolation. This doesn't mean ignoring the reality of the situation, but rather focusing on the belief that you can and will get through it. Optimism, even cautious optimism, can be a critical factor in resilience.

Create visual reminders of hopeful messages or future goals, such as a photo of a place you'd like to visit once the crisis ends or a list of things you're looking forward to. These reminders can serve as beacons of light, helping you stay focused on the future rather than getting lost in the difficulties of the present.

Engaging in Self-Care

Self-care is more than just a buzzword; it's a necessary practice in maintaining mental and emotional health during isolation. This includes taking care of your physical health through proper nutrition, sleep, and exercise, but it also involves nurturing your emotional well-being.

Allow yourself to experience joy and relaxation, even in small ways. Whether it's enjoying a favorite meal, listening to music, or indulging in a hobby, these moments of pleasure are essential to balance the stress and monotony of prolonged isolation. Don't be afraid to take breaks from the seriousness of the situation to laugh, play, or simply rest.

Preparing for the Long Haul

Prolonged crisis situations often require you to prepare for the long haul. This means not only having enough physical supplies but also cultivating the mental endurance needed to sustain yourself over time. Regularly assess your mental health and make adjustments as needed, whether that's varying your routine, seeking additional social support, or increasing your self-care practices.

Coping with isolation and prolonged crisis situations requires a combination of routine, social connection, mindfulness, and self-care. By understanding the psychological impacts and actively taking steps to mitigate them, you can maintain your resilience and well-being, no matter how long the crisis lasts. The strategies you develop during this time will not only help you survive the current situation but also strengthen your ability to face future challenges with confidence and grace.

Building Mental Toughness and Maintaining Morale

In any prolonged crisis, the importance of mental toughness and maintaining morale cannot be overstated. These qualities are the foundation of resilience, enabling you to not only survive but also thrive under pressure. Building mental toughness and preserving morale are not about ignoring the challenges but about confronting them with a determined and positive mindset. This chapter will explore the strategies necessary to cultivate these essential traits and how to sustain them throughout a crisis.

The Foundations of Mental Toughness

Mental toughness is often misunderstood as simply being "tough" or stoic in the face of adversity. In reality, it is about resilience, adaptability, and the ability to manage stress and discomfort while staying focused on your goals. The first step in developing mental toughness is recognizing that crises are as much about mindset as they are about physical preparedness.

One way to cultivate mental toughness is by setting clear, achievable goals that provide direction and purpose. When faced with uncertainty, having a goal—whether it's as simple as getting through the day or as complex as managing a long-term project—gives you something to work toward and helps to maintain focus. These goals should be realistic and adaptable, allowing you to adjust as circumstances change.

Another key component is learning to embrace discomfort and uncertainty rather than resisting them. This doesn't mean welcoming hardship, but rather understanding that discomfort is often an inevitable part of a crisis. By mentally preparing yourself for challenges and accepting that not everything will go according to plan, you can reduce the shock and stress when difficulties arise.

Training your mind to stay calm under pressure is also crucial. Techniques such as controlled breathing, visualization, and mindfulness can help you manage stress responses and maintain composure during critical moments. Practicing these techniques regularly will make them more effective when you need them most.

Maintaining Morale: The Lifeblood of Resilience

While mental toughness is about inner strength, morale is about the spirit and energy that keep you motivated and positive. High morale can be the difference between feeling overwhelmed and feeling capable, even in the direst circumstances. Maintaining morale starts with a positive outlook, but it also involves practical steps to keep your environment and mindset as uplifting as possible.

Creating a routine that incorporates activities you enjoy is one way to keep morale high. Even in the midst of a crisis, finding time for hobbies, entertainment, or creative pursuits can provide a much-needed mental break. These activities offer a sense of normalcy and can be a powerful antidote to the monotony and stress of a prolonged emergency.

Social connections play a vital role in sustaining morale. Regular communication with loved ones, whether in person or through digital means, provides emotional support and reminds you that you are not alone. Sharing experiences, offering and receiving encouragement, and simply staying connected to others can significantly boost your spirits.

Maintaining a sense of humor is another effective way to keep morale up. Humor helps to diffuse tension, offer perspective, and provide a sense of relief during difficult times. It's important to find moments to laugh, whether through watching a funny movie, sharing jokes with friends, or finding humor in the situation. Laughter can lighten the emotional load and restore a sense of balance.

Resilience Through Adaptation

Resilience is not a static trait but a dynamic process that involves continuously adapting to new challenges. Part of building mental toughness and maintaining morale is being able to adapt your strategies as circumstances evolve. This might mean revising your goals, finding new ways to connect with others, or discovering alternative activities that bring you joy and satisfaction.

Adaptation also involves being kind to yourself. Crises can take a toll on everyone, and it's important to recognize when you need a break or when to adjust your expectations. Allowing yourself time to rest, recover, and recharge is essential to sustaining both mental toughness and morale over the long term.

Reflection is another tool in the adaptation process. Taking time to reflect on what's working and what's not allows you to learn from your experiences and make necessary adjustments. This might involve journaling, discussing your thoughts with someone you trust, or simply taking quiet moments to think about your situation. Reflection helps to reinforce your mental strategies and ensure that your approach remains effective.

Cultivating Hope and Positivity

At the heart of morale is hope. Cultivating a sense of hope, even in small doses, can have a profound impact on your resilience. Hope doesn't mean ignoring reality but rather focusing on what is possible and finding reasons to believe in a better future. This might involve setting future-oriented goals, celebrating small victories, or simply keeping an eye on the positive aspects of your situation.

Positivity, like hope, is a powerful force in maintaining morale. This doesn't mean forcing yourself to be cheerful all the time but rather choosing to focus on positive thoughts and actions. Gratitude practices, where you regularly acknowledge things you're thankful for, can shift your perspective and help maintain a positive outlook.

Positivity and hope are often reinforced through service to others. Helping someone else, even in small ways, can provide a sense of purpose and fulfillment. Whether it's supporting a neighbor, sharing resources, or offering words of encouragement, acts of kindness contribute to your own resilience while also strengthening your community.

Engaging with and Supporting Your Community

In times of crisis, the strength and resilience of a community can be the deciding factor between thriving and merely surviving. Engaging with and supporting your community is not just about mutual aid; it's about creating a network of trust, shared resources, and emotional support that can sustain everyone involved. The power of a well-connected community is immense, offering both practical help and a sense of belonging that can greatly enhance psychological resilience.

The Importance of Community Connections

Humans are inherently social creatures, and in moments of crisis, the need for connection becomes even more pronounced. A strong community provides a safety net, offering support when individual resources run thin and fostering a collective strength that can overcome challenges more effectively than going it alone. Engaging with your community means actively participating in a network where each member contributes to the well-being of others, whether through sharing resources, offering skills, or simply being there to listen.

Building these connections before a crisis occurs is crucial. Knowing your neighbors, understanding their needs, and establishing trust allows for a more coordinated and efficient response when a crisis hits. When people feel connected and cared for, they are more likely to contribute to the community's overall resilience, creating a cycle of support that benefits everyone.

Mutual Aid and Resource Sharing

One of the most practical aspects of community engagement is the sharing of resources. In any prolonged crisis, individual stockpiles may dwindle, but a well-organized community can pool resources to ensure that everyone's basic needs are met. This could include food, water, medical supplies, or even tools and equipment necessary for survival.

Organizing resource-sharing initiatives within your community can be as simple as creating a list of who has what and where it's stored or as complex as setting up a formalized system of distribution. What's important is that everyone understands the shared responsibility and is willing to contribute what they can. This collective approach not only ensures that resources are used efficiently but also strengthens the bonds within the community.

Beyond physical resources, skills and knowledge are invaluable assets that can be shared. In a diverse community, people bring a wide range of expertise—from medical knowledge to mechanical skills to gardening—that can be crucial in a crisis. By identifying these skills ahead of time, you can ensure that they are deployed where they're most needed. This exchange of skills also empowers individuals, giving them a sense of purpose and agency during difficult times.

Emotional Support and Psychological Resilience

The emotional toll of a crisis can be as debilitating as the physical challenges, and this is where community support becomes irreplaceable. Regular check-ins, whether in person, via phone, or online, help to ensure that everyone's emotional needs are being met. Simply knowing that others are going through the same experience can be comforting, reducing feelings of isolation and fear.

Supporting each other emotionally doesn't always require deep conversations; sometimes, it's about shared activities that bring joy and distraction from the crisis. This might involve group meals (while maintaining safety protocols), collective efforts in gardening or repairs, or even virtual events if gathering in person isn't possible. These activities remind everyone that life goes on, even in the midst of a crisis, and that there's still room for joy, laughter, and connection.

A strong community also provides the space for members to express their fears, frustrations, and hopes, offering a kind of collective therapy. By listening and empathizing, community members can help each other process emotions, making the load a little lighter for everyone.

Organizing for Collective Action

In some crisis situations, there may be a need for organized collective action. This could involve coordinated efforts to secure resources, protect the community from external threats, or rebuild after a disaster. Having pre-established leadership or a decision-making process can greatly enhance the efficiency and effectiveness of these efforts.

Leadership within a community doesn't necessarily mean a top-down structure. Often, the most effective leaders in a crisis are those who can facilitate discussion, bring people together, and ensure that everyone's voice is heard. This kind of participatory leadership fosters trust and encourages more people to get involved, knowing that their contributions are valued.

Collective action might also extend beyond the immediate community to neighboring areas, creating a network of support that crosses boundaries. By collaborating with other communities, sharing information, and coordinating efforts, the overall resilience of the region can be significantly strengthened.

Long-Term Community Building

Crisis situations, while challenging, also offer an opportunity to build stronger, more resilient communities for the long term. The relationships and systems established during a crisis can serve as the foundation for ongoing community engagement and support. Even after the immediate danger has passed, maintaining these connections can lead to a more connected, proactive community that is better prepared for future challenges.

Long-term community building involves keeping the lines of communication open, continuing regular meetings or check-ins, and perhaps formalizing some of the systems that were put in place during the crisis. It's also important to reflect on what worked well and what didn't, making adjustments to improve the community's response to any future emergencies.

In conclusion, engaging with and supporting your community during a crisis is about more than just survival; it's about creating a network of care and mutual support that strengthens everyone involved. By sharing resources, offering emotional support, and organizing collective action, you not only enhance your own resilience but also contribute to the well-being of those around you. This sense of solidarity and shared purpose can be a powerful force, turning a crisis into an opportunity for growth, connection, and long-lasting community strength.

Video BONUS

Conclusion

Recap of Key Concepts and Strategies

As we reach the conclusion of this guide, it's essential to revisit the key concepts and strategies that have been explored throughout. Understanding and internalizing these principles will ensure that you are well-prepared to face any crisis with confidence and resilience.

The foundation of any effective preparedness plan begins with a clear understanding of the environment in which you live and the specific risks you might face. Whether dealing with natural disasters, societal unrest, or prolonged emergencies, assessing your situation is the first critical step. This assessment involves not only recognizing potential threats but also understanding your own needs and the resources at your disposal. By conducting a thorough evaluation of your home, community, and personal circumstances, you can create a customized plan that addresses the unique challenges you may encounter.

Mental and physical preparedness are the pillars that support all other aspects of your plan. Building mental toughness is about fostering resilience and the ability to adapt to changing circumstances. This involves developing a mindset that embraces flexibility, maintains morale, and stays focused on long-term goals, even in the face of adversity. Equally important is your physical preparedness, which includes not just stockpiling supplies but also maintaining your health, fitness, and ability to respond effectively to physical challenges.

Your home serves as your fortress during a crisis, and fortifying it is a crucial component of your overall strategy. This involves both physical enhancements—such as reinforcing entry points, setting up defensive barriers, and establishing secure communication systems—and strategic planning, like creating safe rooms and practicing emergency drills with your household. Ensuring that your home is well-protected and that everyone in it knows how to act in an emergency is key to surviving and thriving during a crisis.

Water, food, and energy are the lifeblood of any prolonged survival scenario. Securing reliable sources of these essentials and ensuring their long-term storage and sustainability is vital. This includes setting up water purification systems, creating a diverse and nutritious food stockpile, and establishing off-grid energy solutions. Managing these resources wisely and adapting your consumption based on changing circumstances will help you endure even the most extended emergencies.

In addition to these physical preparations, your ability to stay informed and connected is critical. Effective communication during a crisis ensures that you can receive and share vital information, coordinate with others, and make informed decisions. Establishing robust communication networks, both within your household and with the broader community, is essential for maintaining security and cohesion during turbulent times.

Engaging with your community is another cornerstone of effective crisis management. A strong, well-connected community can provide support, share resources, and offer emotional comfort during challenging periods. By fostering relationships, organizing mutual aid, and participating in collective actions, you contribute to a network of resilience that benefits everyone involved.

Financial and legal preparedness rounds out your strategy. Managing your finances during a crisis, protecting your assets, and understanding the legal implications of your actions are all crucial for long-term stability and security. Being financially prepared means having liquid assets available, understanding how to barter effectively, and ensuring that your legal documents and plans are in order.

In summary, the key to effective preparedness lies in a holistic approach that combines physical security, mental resilience, resource management, and community engagement. Each of these elements supports the others, creating a comprehensive plan that equips you to face any crisis with confidence and strength. As you move forward, continue to refine and adapt your strategies, always learning from new experiences and information. By doing so, you ensure that you and your loved ones are not only prepared for the next crisis but are also empowered to live with greater peace of mind, knowing that you can handle whatever comes your way.

Final Thoughts on Preparedness and Resilience

As we conclude this guide, it's important to reflect on the journey you've embarked upon in strengthening your preparedness and resilience. Preparing for crises, whether natural disasters, societal upheavals, or unforeseen emergencies, is not merely about stockpiling resources or fortifying your home. At its core, preparedness is about adopting a mindset that prioritizes adaptability, resourcefulness, and a proactive approach to life's uncertainties.

Resilience, in its truest sense, is the ability to bounce back from adversity—not just to survive, but to thrive in the face of challenges. It's about developing the mental toughness to handle stress and unpredictability with grace, the physical readiness to endure hardships, and the emotional stability to maintain a positive outlook, even when circumstances are difficult. Resilience also involves a willingness to continuously learn and adapt, recognizing that no plan is perfect and that the ability to pivot and adjust is key to long-term success.

Preparedness is not a one-time effort; it's an ongoing process that requires regular reassessment and adjustment. As the world changes, so too should your strategies and plans. The tools and techniques you've learned throughout this guide provide a solid foundation, but it's essential to stay informed about new developments, innovations, and potential threats. By staying engaged with the latest information and continuously refining your approach, you ensure that your preparedness remains effective, no matter what challenges arise.

Moreover, true preparedness goes beyond the individual. It encompasses the well-being of your family, your community, and even the broader society in which you live. By fostering strong connections, sharing knowledge, and participating in mutual aid efforts, you contribute to a network of resilience that supports not just your own survival but the survival and thriving of others. This collective strength is a powerful force, amplifying the impact of individual efforts and creating a community that is capable of withstanding even the most severe crises.

As you reflect on the concepts and strategies covered in this guide, consider how they apply to your unique situation. Think about the specific risks you face, the resources you have available, and the people who depend on you. Use this knowledge to craft a preparedness plan that is both comprehensive and flexible, one that can evolve as your circumstances do.

In the end, the goal of preparedness and resilience is not to live in fear of what might happen, but to live confidently, knowing that you are equipped to handle whatever comes your way. It's about taking control of your circumstances and ensuring that you and your loved ones are as safe and secure as possible, no matter what the future holds.

This journey of preparedness is one that never truly ends. It's a continuous cycle of learning, adapting, and growing. By committing to this path, you empower yourself to face the uncertainties of life with courage and clarity. You build a legacy of resilience that will serve you and those around you for years to come.

As you move forward, keep in mind that every step you take toward preparedness strengthens your ability to protect and provide for yourself and your loved ones. Stay vigilant, stay informed, and most importantly, stay resilient. The strength you cultivate now will carry you through any challenge and enable you to emerge from any crisis not just intact, but stronger than before.

Next Steps: Continuing Your Preparedness Journey

As you reach the end of this guide, it's important to recognize that the journey toward preparedness and resilience is not a finite process but a continuous one. The knowledge and strategies you've acquired are the foundation upon which you will build and refine your ability to navigate crises, protect your loved ones, and sustain yourself through challenging times. Now, it's time to consider the next steps in your preparedness journey.

First, take a moment to assess where you currently stand. Reflect on what you've learned and how you've implemented these strategies in your life. Are there areas where you feel confident? Are there aspects of your plan that still need work? Being honest with yourself about your strengths and weaknesses is crucial as you move forward.

One of the most important next steps is to make preparedness a regular part of your routine. This doesn't mean living in constant fear or anxiety, but rather integrating preparedness into your daily life in a way that feels natural and sustainable. Regularly review your supplies, update your plans, and stay informed about any new developments that might affect your situation. Consider setting aside time each month to revisit your preparedness efforts—this could involve checking your stockpiles, reviewing your emergency plans with your family, or practicing drills to ensure everyone knows what to do in a crisis.

Continued education is another critical component of your preparedness journey. The world is constantly changing, and so too are the challenges we face. Stay curious and open to learning new techniques, whether it's through reading, attending workshops, or engaging with online communities of like-minded individuals. The more you learn, the more adaptable and resourceful you will become, enhancing your ability to respond effectively to any situation.

Engaging with your community should also be a priority as you continue your preparedness journey. Building and maintaining strong relationships with your neighbors, local organizations, and even online networks can provide invaluable support during a crisis. These connections can offer not only practical assistance but also emotional resilience, helping you to feel less isolated and more empowered in difficult times. Consider organizing community preparedness events, sharing your knowledge with others, or simply staying connected with those around you.

It's also essential to remember that preparedness is not just about survival; it's about thriving. As you continue on this journey, think about how you can maintain a quality of life that is both meaningful and fulfilling, even in the face of adversity. This might involve developing new skills, cultivating hobbies that bring you joy, or finding ways to contribute positively to the world around you. By focusing on personal growth and well-being, you can ensure that your preparedness efforts enrich your life rather than dominate it.

Approach your preparedness journey with a mindset of flexibility and adaptability. Crises are unpredictable, and even the best-laid plans can require adjustments. Be willing to pivot, learn from your experiences, and continuously refine your strategies. This mindset will not only help you in emergencies but also in everyday life, as you become more resilient, resourceful, and capable of handling whatever comes your way.

As you move forward, keep in mind that every step you take toward preparedness is a step toward greater security, confidence, and peace of mind. This journey is ongoing, but it's also empowering. By committing to continuous improvement, staying informed, and remaining engaged with your community, you are not just preparing for potential crises—you are building a life of resilience and strength that will serve you well in all circumstances.

Checklists: Emergency Supplies, Gear, and Food

Creating comprehensive checklists for emergency supplies, gear, and food is essential to ensure you are fully prepared for any crisis situation. These checklists serve as both a guide and a reminder, helping you to systematically organize and verify that you have everything you need to survive and thrive in challenging circumstances. Below is a detailed, exhaustive list of items to include in your emergency preparedness kit.

1. Emergency Supplies Checklist

Water Supply:

- **Water Storage Containers:** Ensure you have containers for storing water, including large barrels, jugs, and portable bottles. Aim for at least one gallon per person per day for drinking and sanitation, with a minimum supply for two weeks.

- **Water Filtration Systems:** Include portable water filters, purification tablets, and a boiling kit. Consider investing in a high-quality home filtration system for long-term use.

- **Rainwater Collection System:** If possible, set up a rainwater harvesting system with appropriate containers and filters.

Medical and First Aid Supplies:

- **Comprehensive First Aid Kit:** Stock with bandages, gauze, antiseptics, adhesive tape, scissors, tweezers, and disposable gloves.

- **Advanced Medical Supplies:** Include suture kits, splints, emergency tourniquets, burn treatments, and eye wash solutions.

- **Prescription Medications:** Ensure you have a supply of necessary prescription medications for each family member, along with a list of dosages and expiration dates.

- **Over-the-Counter Medications:** Pain relievers, fever reducers, antihistamines, cold remedies, and digestive aids.

- **Natural Remedies and Supplements:** Herbal supplements, vitamins, essential oils, and other natural treatments that you regularly use.

Sanitation and Hygiene:

- **Personal Hygiene Items:** Soap, toothpaste, toothbrushes, deodorant, razors, and feminine hygiene products.

- **Sanitation Supplies:** Portable toilet, waste bags, disinfectants, bleach, hand sanitizer, and paper towels.

- **Cleaning Supplies:** Multi-purpose cleaners, scrub brushes, sponges, and disposable gloves.

Lighting and Power:

- **Flashlights and Lanterns:** Battery-operated, solar-powered, and hand-crank options, along with extra batteries.

- **Candles and Matches:** Long-lasting candles, waterproof matches, and lighters.

- **Portable Generator:** Ensure you have fuel and a plan for safe operation. Consider solar-powered generators for long-term use.

Communication Devices:

- **Two-Way Radios:** HAM, GMRS, or FRS radios for communication within your group or neighborhood.

- **Emergency Weather Radio:** A battery-operated or hand-crank radio that receives NOAA alerts.

- **Satellite Phone:** Consider for remote communication when traditional cell service is unavailable.

- **Signal Devices:** Whistles, signal mirrors, and emergency flares for attracting attention.

Shelter and Clothing:

- **Emergency Shelter:** Tents, tarps, and plastic sheeting for temporary shelter. Consider thermal blankets and sleeping bags rated for cold weather.

- **Weather-Appropriate Clothing:** Sturdy boots, thermal underwear, rain gear, and layered clothing for varying conditions.

- **Protective Gear:** Dust masks, work gloves, hard hats, and eye protection.

2. Survival Gear Checklist

Firearms and Ammunition:

- **Home Defense Firearms:** Consider shotguns, rifles, and handguns. Ensure you have sufficient ammunition and secure storage.

- **Non-Lethal Defense Options:** Pepper spray, tasers, and stun guns.

- **Tactical Gear:** Body armor, helmets, and protective vests.

Cutting Tools:

- **Knives:** Survival knives, folding knives, and multi-tools with sharp blades.

- **Axes and Hatchets:** For chopping wood, shelter building, and defense.

- **Sharpening Tools:** Whetstones or sharpening kits to maintain cutting edges.

Fire-Starting Tools:

- **Fire Starters:** Waterproof matches, lighters, ferro rods, and magnesium fire starters.

- **Tinder and Kindling:** Cotton balls soaked in petroleum jelly, dryer lint, and dry wood chips.

- **Fireproof Storage:** Keep fire-starting tools in waterproof and fireproof containers.

Water Filtration and Purification Tools:

- **Portable Water Filters:** High-quality filters for removing bacteria and parasites.

- **Purification Tablets:** Chlorine dioxide or iodine tablets for water purification.

- **Boiling Kit:** Portable stove or fire setup to boil water for purification.

Shelter and Sleeping Gear:

- **Tents and Tarps:** Lightweight, durable tents and tarps for quick deployment.
- **Sleeping Bags:** Rated for cold weather, compact, and easy to carry.
- **Ground Pads:** Insulated pads for warmth and comfort.

Communication Tools:

- **Radios:** Emergency two-way radios with a reliable range.
- **Chargers:** Solar-powered or hand-crank chargers for all devices.
- **Emergency Whistles:** Loud whistles for signaling and communication.

3. Food Storage Checklist

Staple Foods:

- **Grains:** Rice, oats, quinoa, and flour stored in airtight containers.
- **Legumes:** Dried beans, lentils, and peas for protein and fiber.
- **Pasta:** Long shelf-life varieties stored in cool, dry places.

Canned and Jarred Foods:

- **Vegetables and Fruits:** Canned beans, tomatoes, corn, and a variety of fruits.
- **Meats and Fish:** Canned tuna, chicken, spam, and other preserved meats.
- **Soups and Stews:** Ready-to-eat canned soups and stews for quick meals.

Dehydrated and Freeze-Dried Foods:

- **Vegetables and Fruits:** Freeze-dried peas, carrots, apples, and berries.
- **Full Meals:** Pre-packaged freeze-dried meals with a long shelf life.
- **Powdered Milk and Eggs:** For protein and essential nutrients.

Nutrient-Dense Foods:

- **Nuts and Seeds:** Long-lasting sources of healthy fats and protein.
- **Peanut Butter and Nut Butters:** High-energy spreads with a long shelf life.
- **Energy Bars and Protein Bars:** Compact and calorie-dense for on-the-go nutrition.

Cooking Essentials:

- **Cooking Oil:** Olive oil, coconut oil, and other shelf-stable oils.
- **Spices and Seasonings:** Salt, pepper, herbs, and spices for flavor.

- **Baking Supplies:** Baking powder, yeast, and sugar for preparing baked goods.

Food Storage Solutions:

- **Vacuum-Sealed Bags:** For preserving the freshness of dried foods.

- **Mylar Bags and Oxygen Absorbers:** For long-term storage of grains and legumes.

- **Mason Jars:** Airtight jars for preserving and storing foods.

Rotating and Managing Your Stockpile:

- **Inventory System:** Keep a detailed inventory of your food supplies, including expiration dates and quantities.

- **Rotation Schedule:** Implement a first-in, first-out (FIFO) system to ensure older items are used before newer ones.

- **Regular Inspections:** Periodically check your stockpile for signs of spoilage or damage and replace items as needed.

Made in the USA
Columbia, SC
23 October 2024

44648202R00096